Pictured Rocks Gal

A Photographic Tour of Pictured Rocks National Lakeshore & Surrounding Area

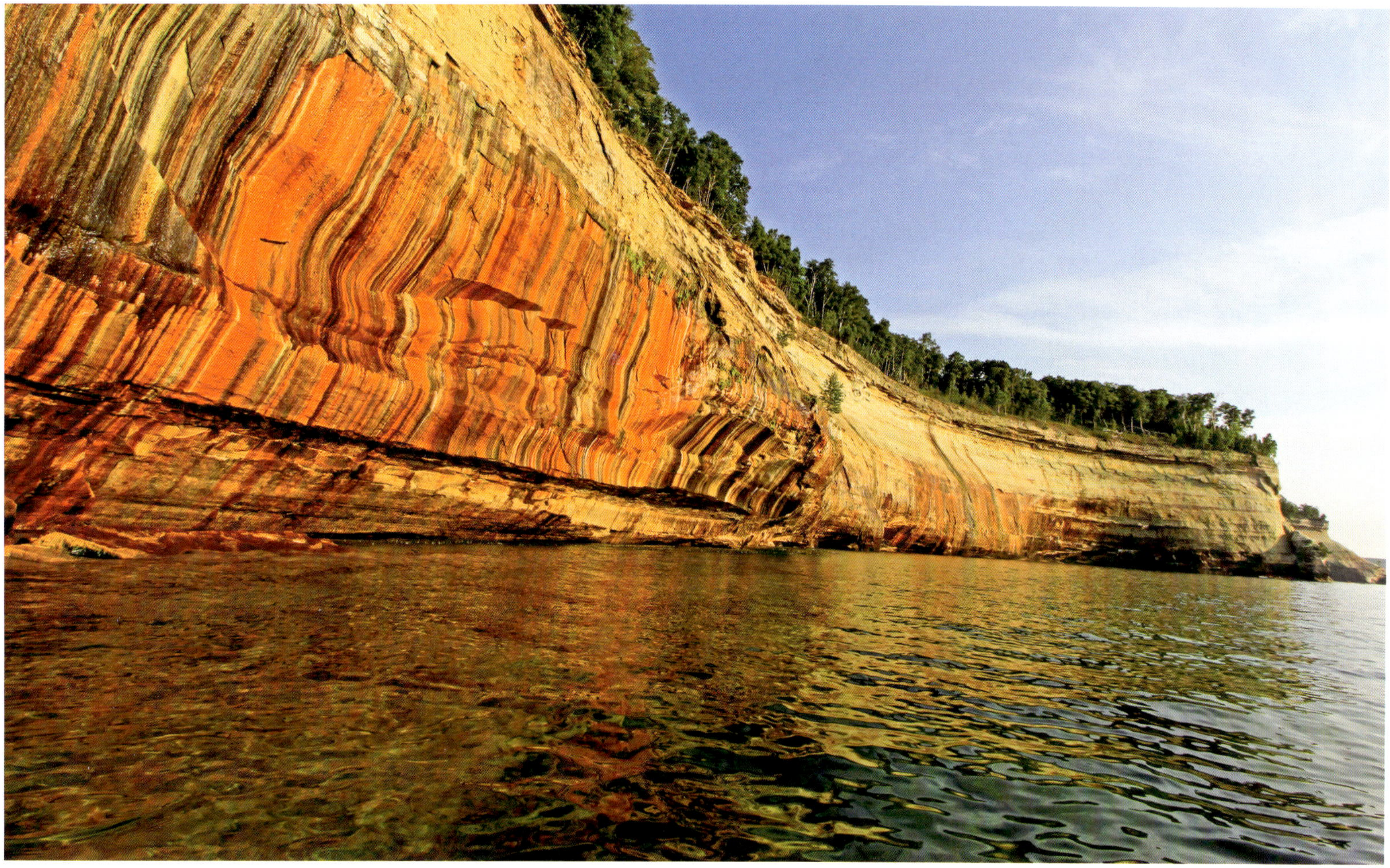

By Local Photographer Shelly Dinsmoore

What a Wonderful World! Shelly Dinsmoore

ISBN 978-0-692-75701-7

Printed in Canada by Friesens

Cover Design by Shawn Curtin

Layout and Design by Melissa VanBrocklin

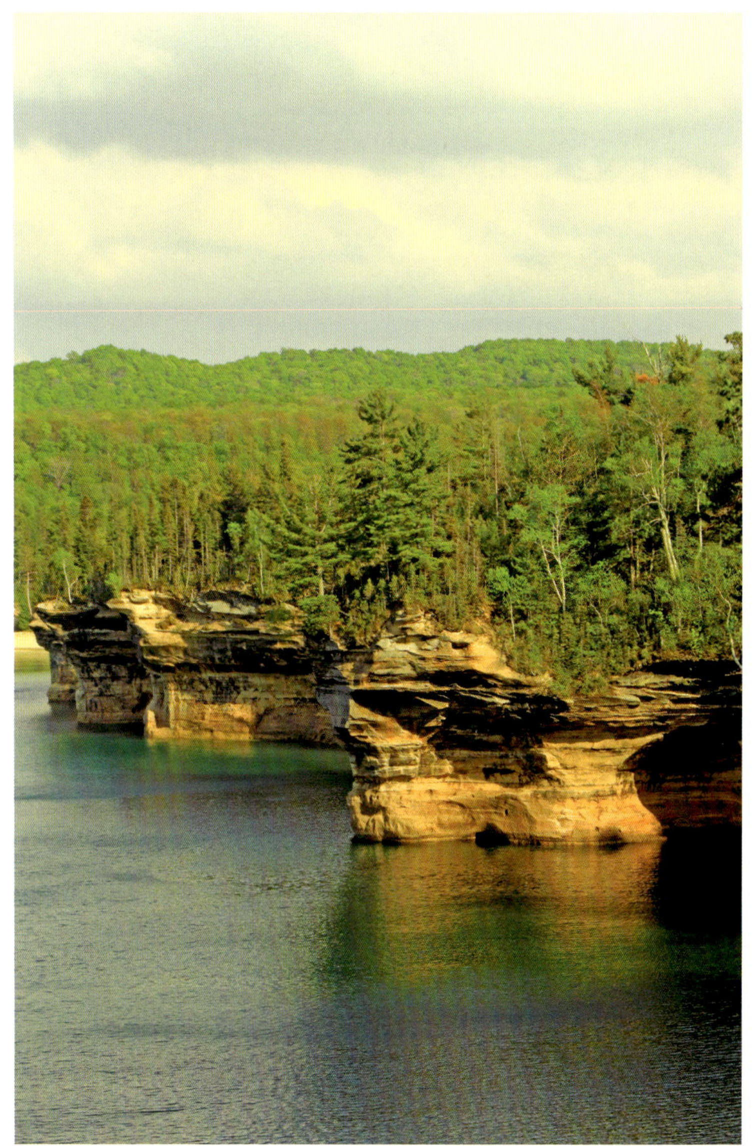

Thank you for purchasing this book and allowing me to share my world with you. Thanks to my hiking buddies; Becky (RIP), Mary, Susan, Betty, Abby, Devin and Paul. Thanks to Derek for giving me security and freedom at the same time. Thanks to my Mom, Patricia Hoffmeyer, for assisting with this project. Some people make your life easier, Karen is one of them and so was my Grandmother. Thanks to Cassie for making me a Grandma. Thanks to Jim and the gang at BenFranklins Marquette, Michigan for excellent advice and photo enlargements.

Note: A couple of these pictures were taken in areas prior to the Park Service and Michigan Nature Association (MNA) fencing them off. The recent influx of Park visitors has forced certain measures. I realize that one person's footprint is insignificant; a million footprints can be devastating. Please respect boundaries.

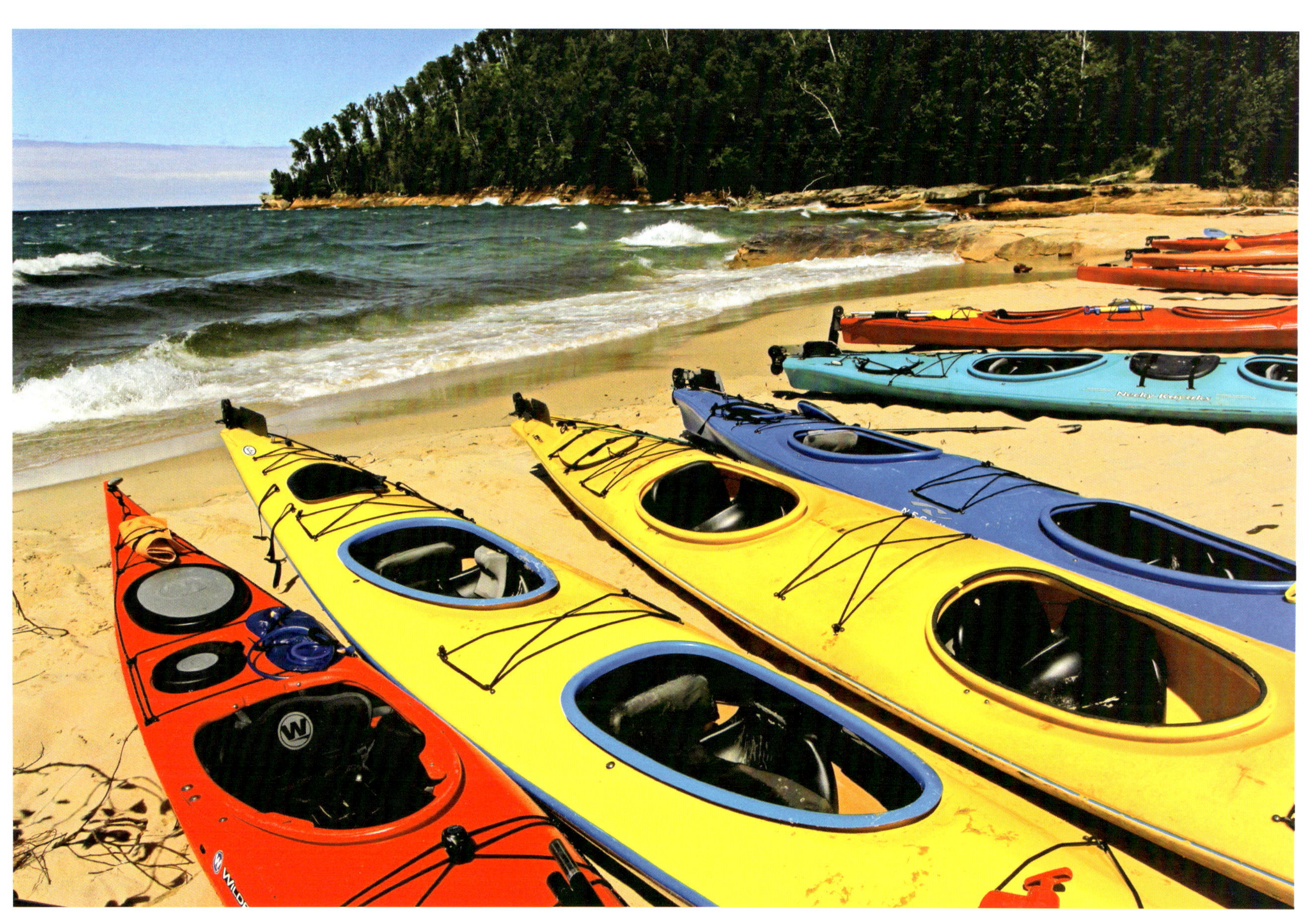

A Great Place to Start

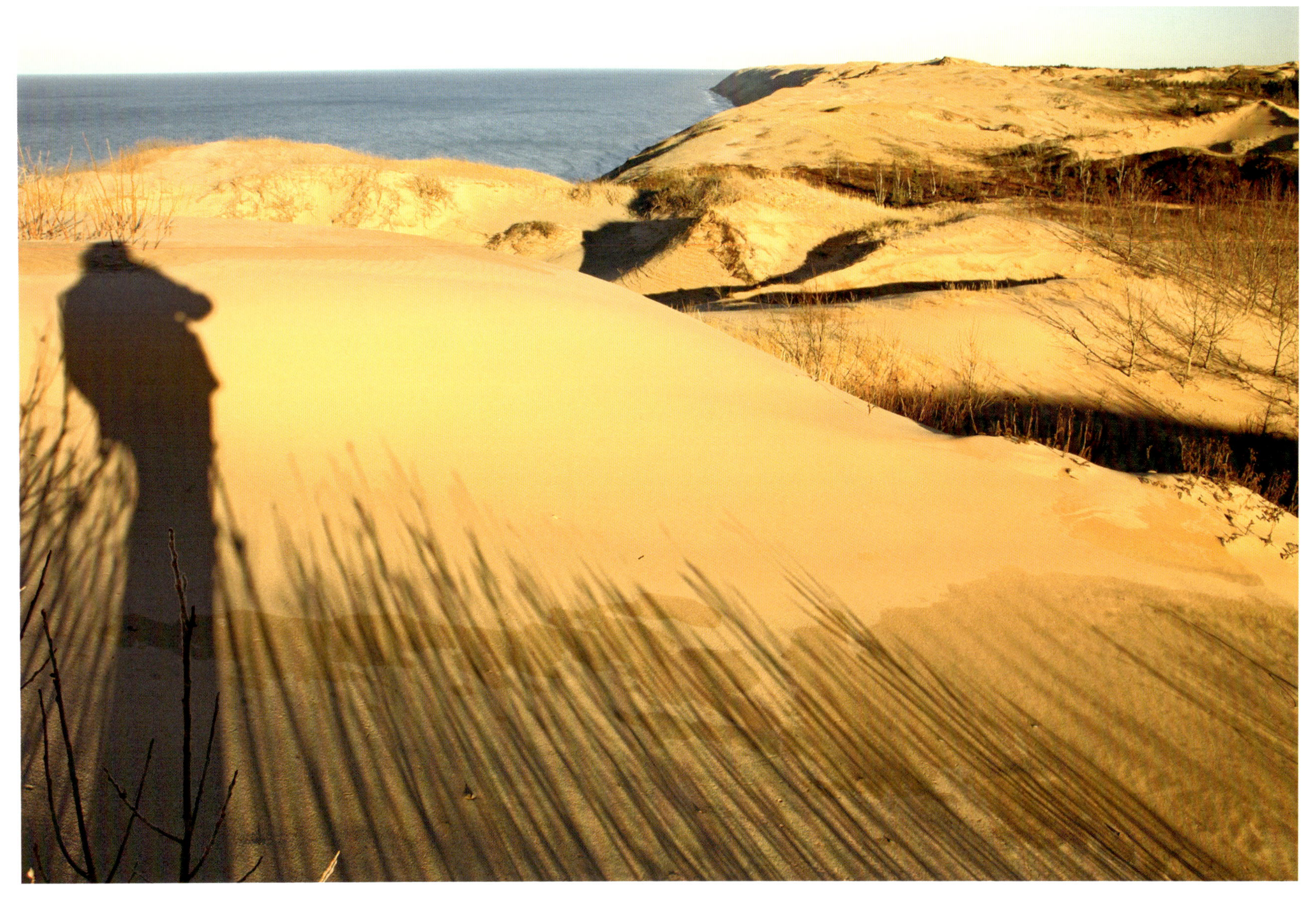

Shadow Dance

About the Author

Pictured Rocks National Lakeshore is my favorite place. Since moving to Munising 25 years ago, I would like to think that I have spent more time at this magnificent place than anyone. Virtually every day that I am not working, you can find me somewhere in the Park. It has filled my life with joy, beauty, and an endless supply of adventure and exploration. I know it like an old friend that I visit again and again, ever changing, always something new. I have stood in some of the most majestic places and witnessed some of the most incredible sites imaginable. Places that left me so awestruck that all I could do is stand there and say "WOW".

I took up photography in an attempt to capture some of these glorious sites. Whether hiking the beautiful trails, or kayaking along its shores, Pictured Rocks is the place I long to be. I love extremes. I love a long cool rainy spring. The kind that makes everything saturated with the greenest green. A spring that makes the wildflowers so full and lush that they fill the entire forest floor like a dense carpet. Waterfalls raging in golden cascades racing to Lake Superior. A still misty spring day, I love that.

I love weather extremes, especially in winter. Rare but intense are the winters that beat all of the old records, like the most consecutive days below zero degrees. It makes it safe to ski 20 miles out along the cliff line. It's like an adventure into a frozen wonderland of orange, yellow, and blue ice clinging to the color streaked sandstone walls. Just amazing. The special days, like the first hard freeze that puts the streams into a short lived transitional state, not quite sure if it is fall or winter. I love the snowfall that dumps 18" into a fluffy white blanket that coats every branch, twig, and weed. It is good to be the first one to set foot in this virgin ground cover. Intense blizzards and gale force winds that blow freezing spray transforming the world into a temporary sparkling crystal paradise. These are the days I get excited about. And the summer, moss and mushrooms in old growth hemlock stands so magical that I am sure that there are gnomes watching me. Summers, when the colors on the cliffs build up deeper and more vibrant than I have ever seen. I paddle by slow oozing pigment in topaz, tangerine, and cobalt, and then the sun begins to set, throwing an orange cast onto everything. That is what I live for. And fall, trees in all their glory. Like a competition for the best dressed on the red carpet, throwing confetti. They are not in the least concerned about the coming winter. Sure, this obsession with photography has gotten me into trouble. Like observing swans on a fifteen below zero degree day, not noticing that all of my fingers were frostbitten. They are okay now, after they became numb and the flesh peeled off. Not to mention, the thousands of mosquito bites in bogs, tumbling down icy slopes, collapsing on the beach after pushing the envelope of "safe kayaking", and encounters with wild animals, all in the name of photography. But, I can't seem to help it. I don't have a choice. P.S. I also like a good cup of coffee and chocolate. These too are good things.

Whether you are looking at this book to remember where you have been, or just taking a trip and never leaving the farm, so to speak, I hope you enjoy. - Shelly

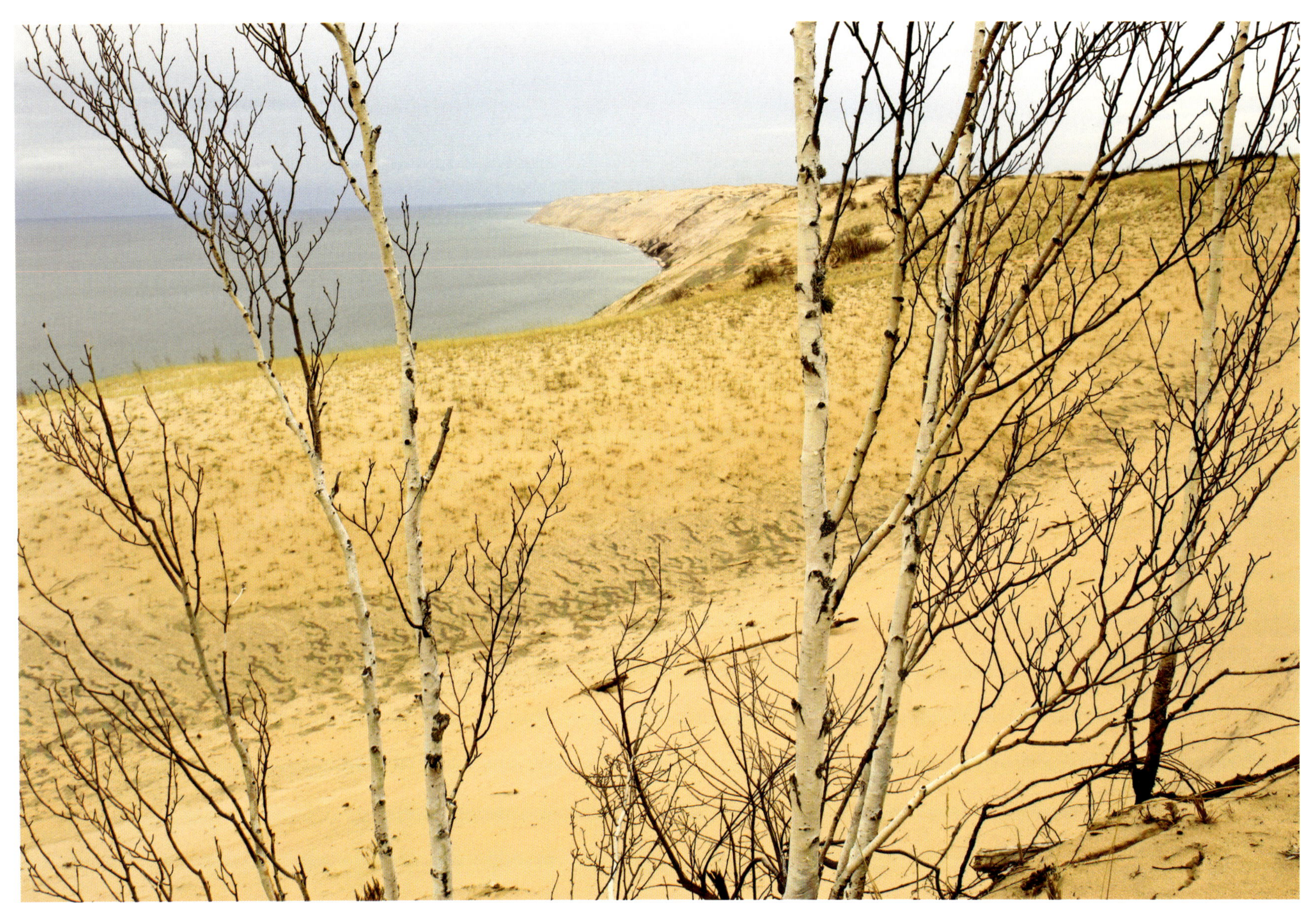

Sandman: Grand Sable Dunes

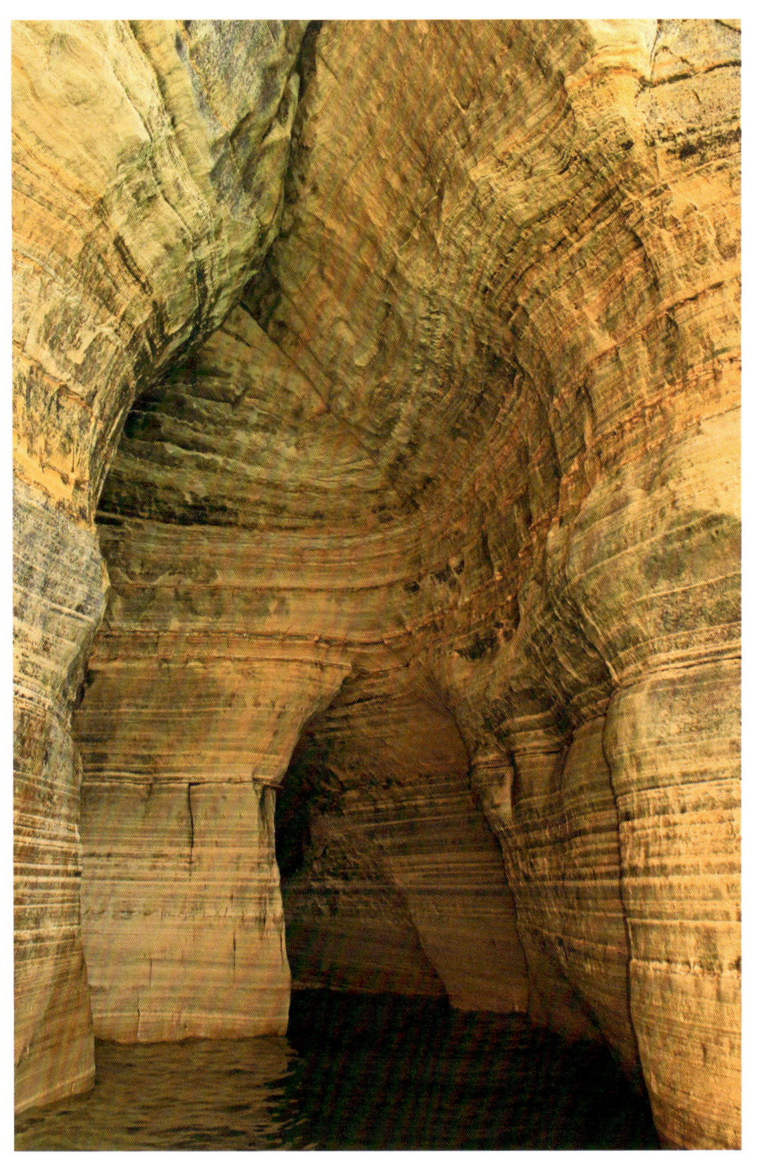

Miner's Grotto

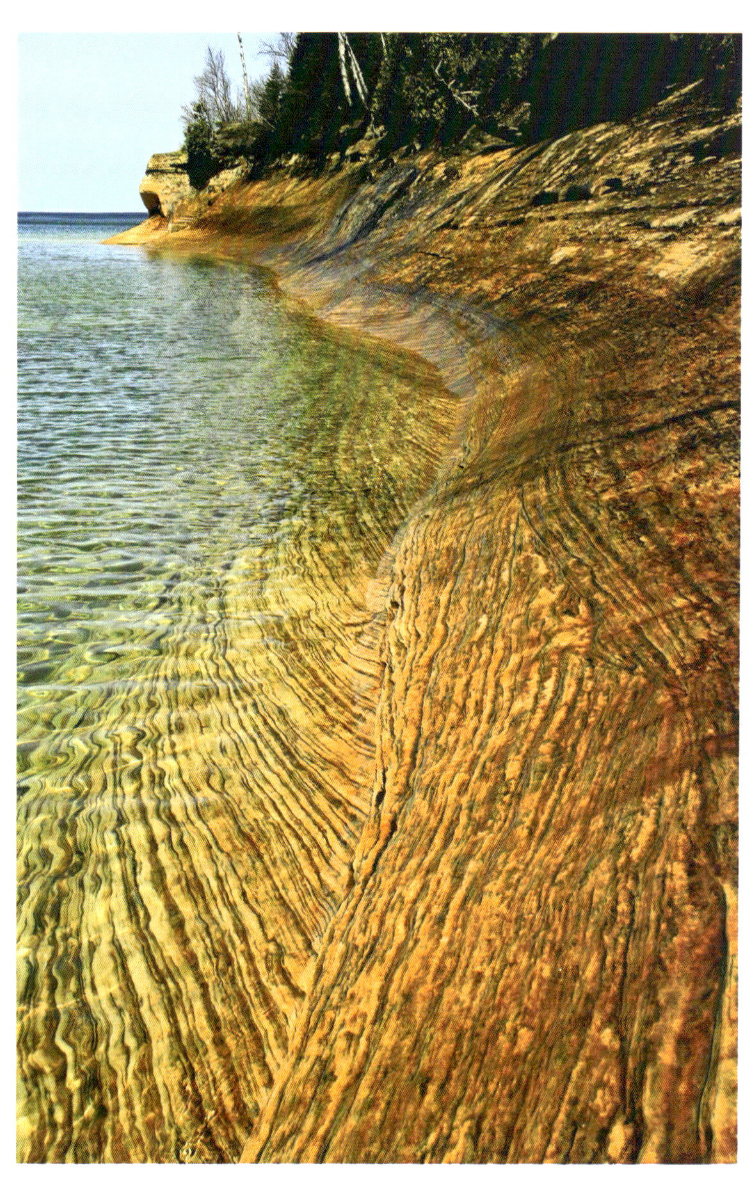

Braided Rock

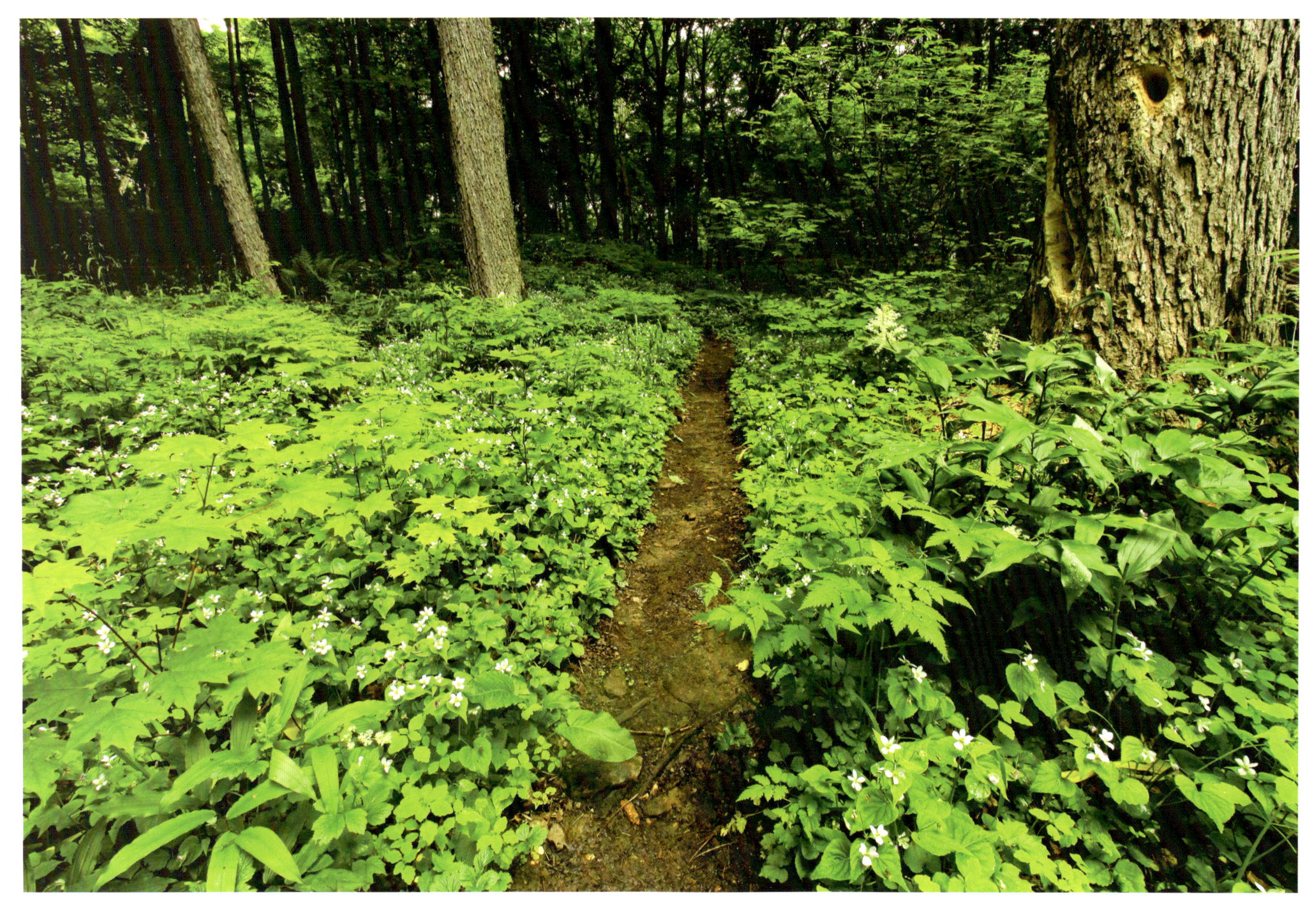

The Scenic Route: Walking to Mosquito Beach

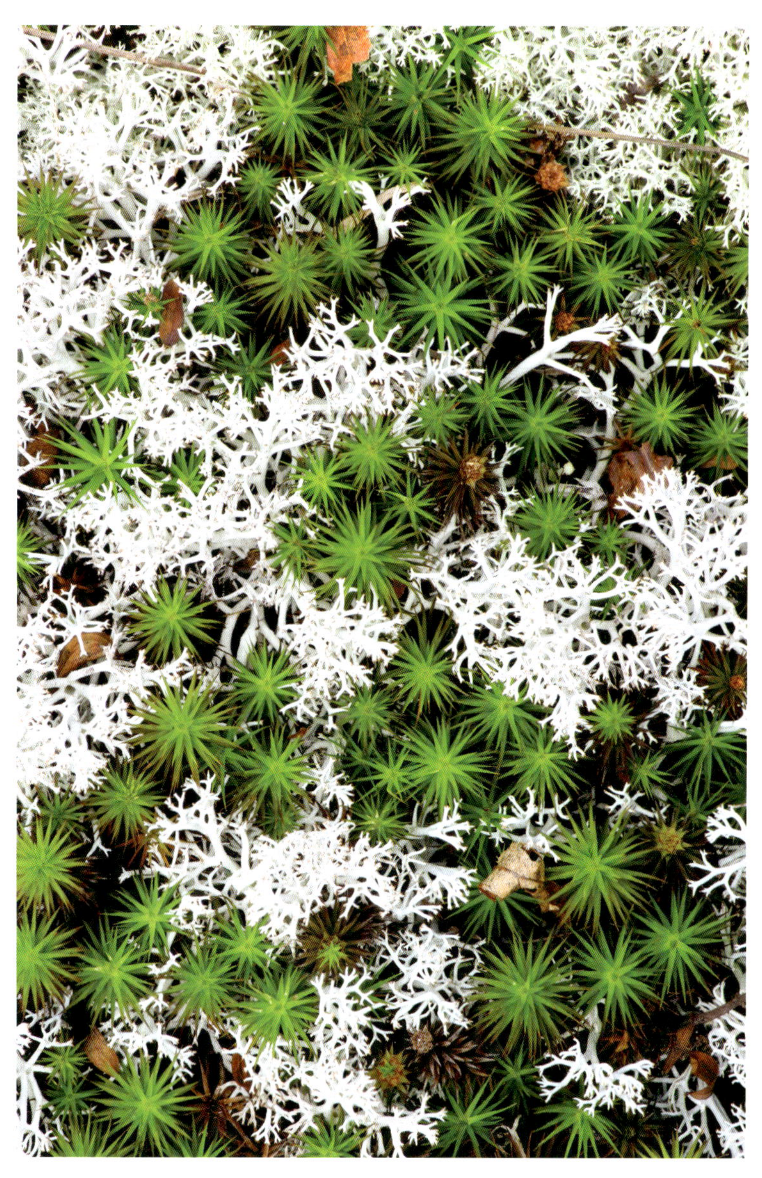

White Matter

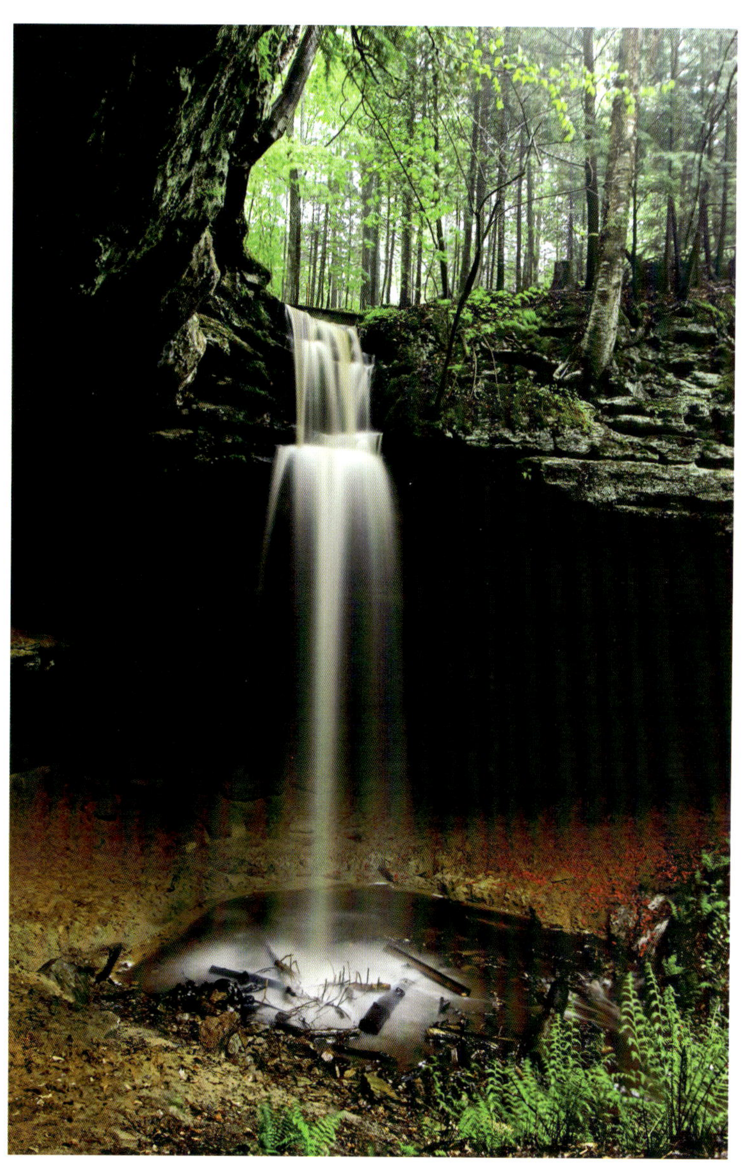

Rose Colored Glasses: Upper Twin Falls

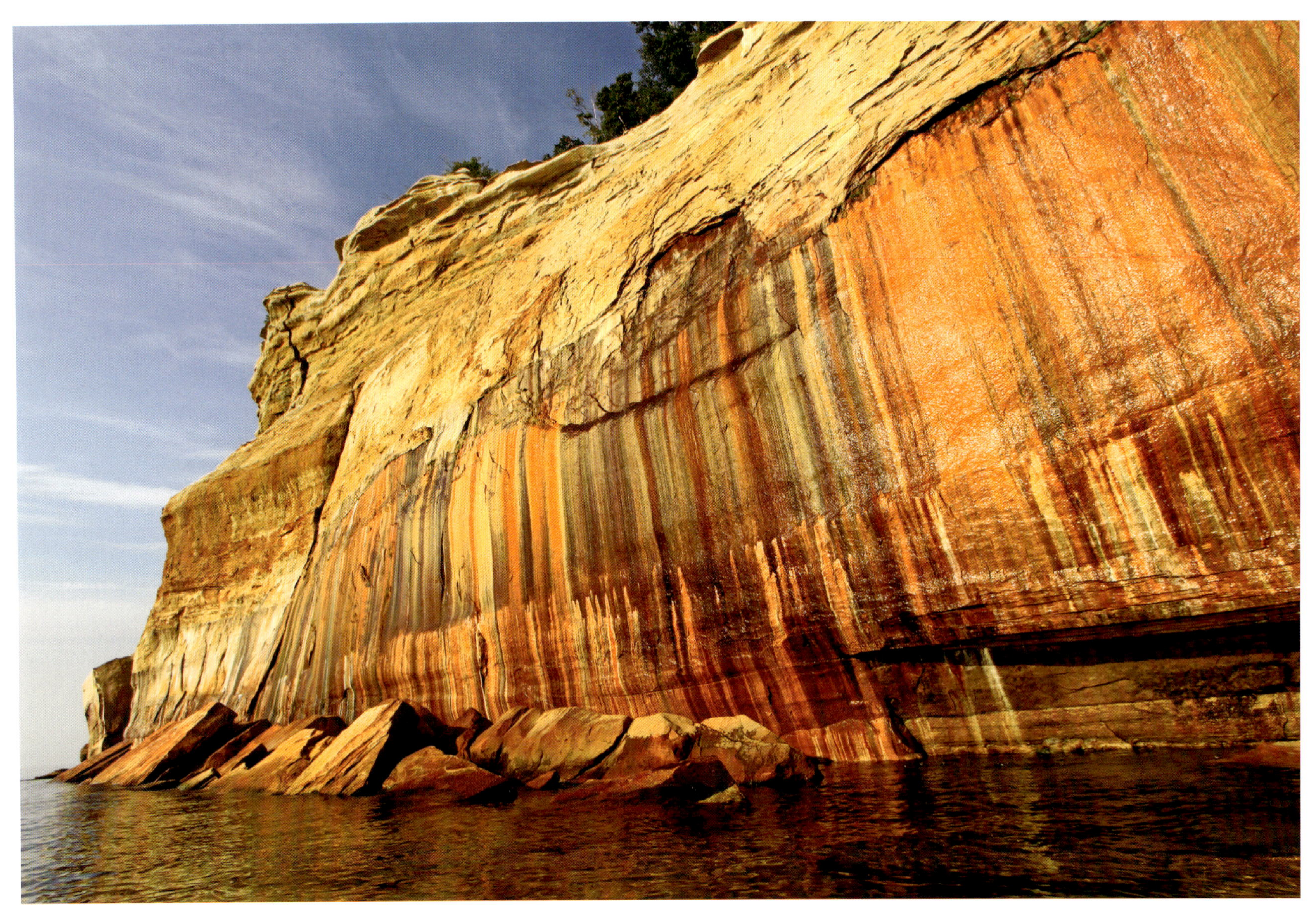

Coat of Many Colors

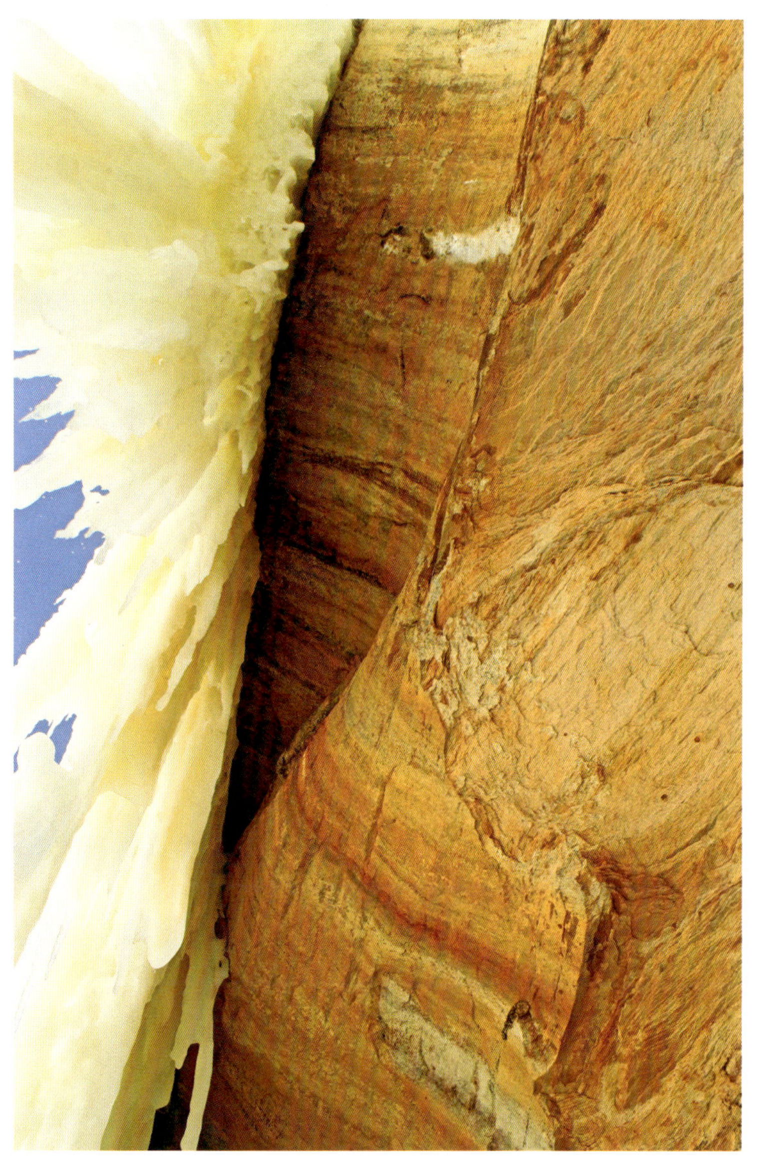

Lemon Ice

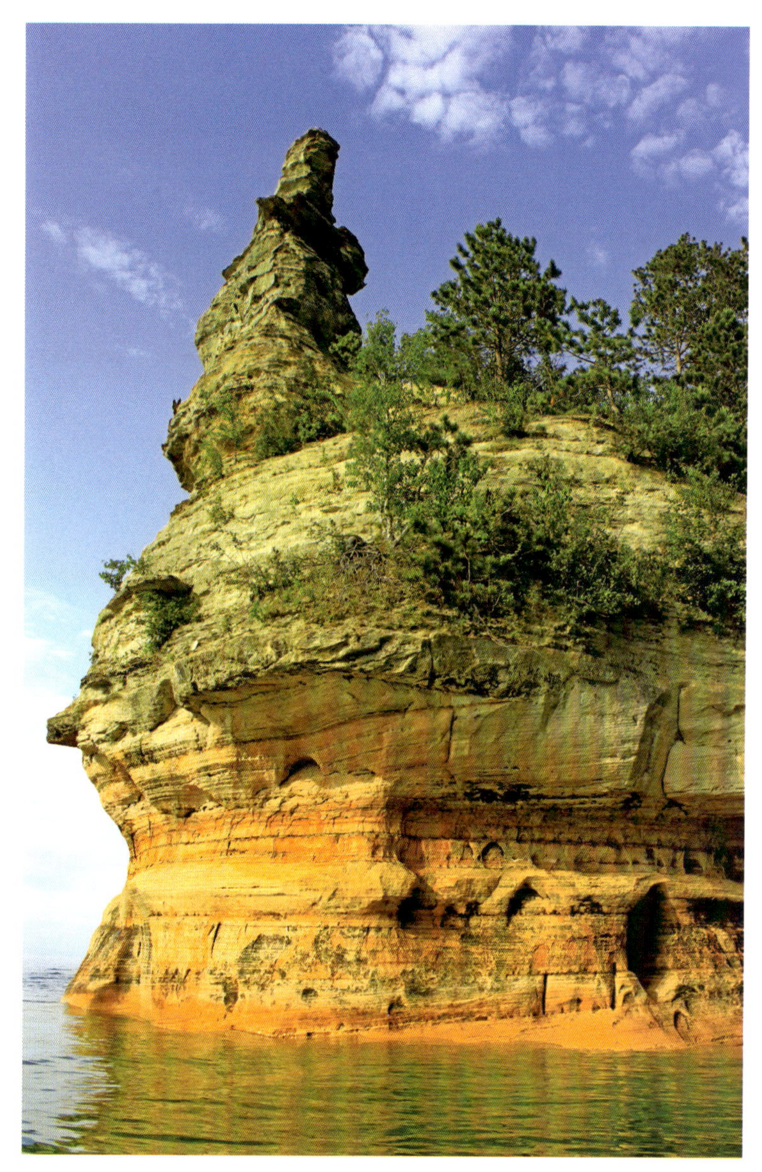

Majesty: Miners Castle

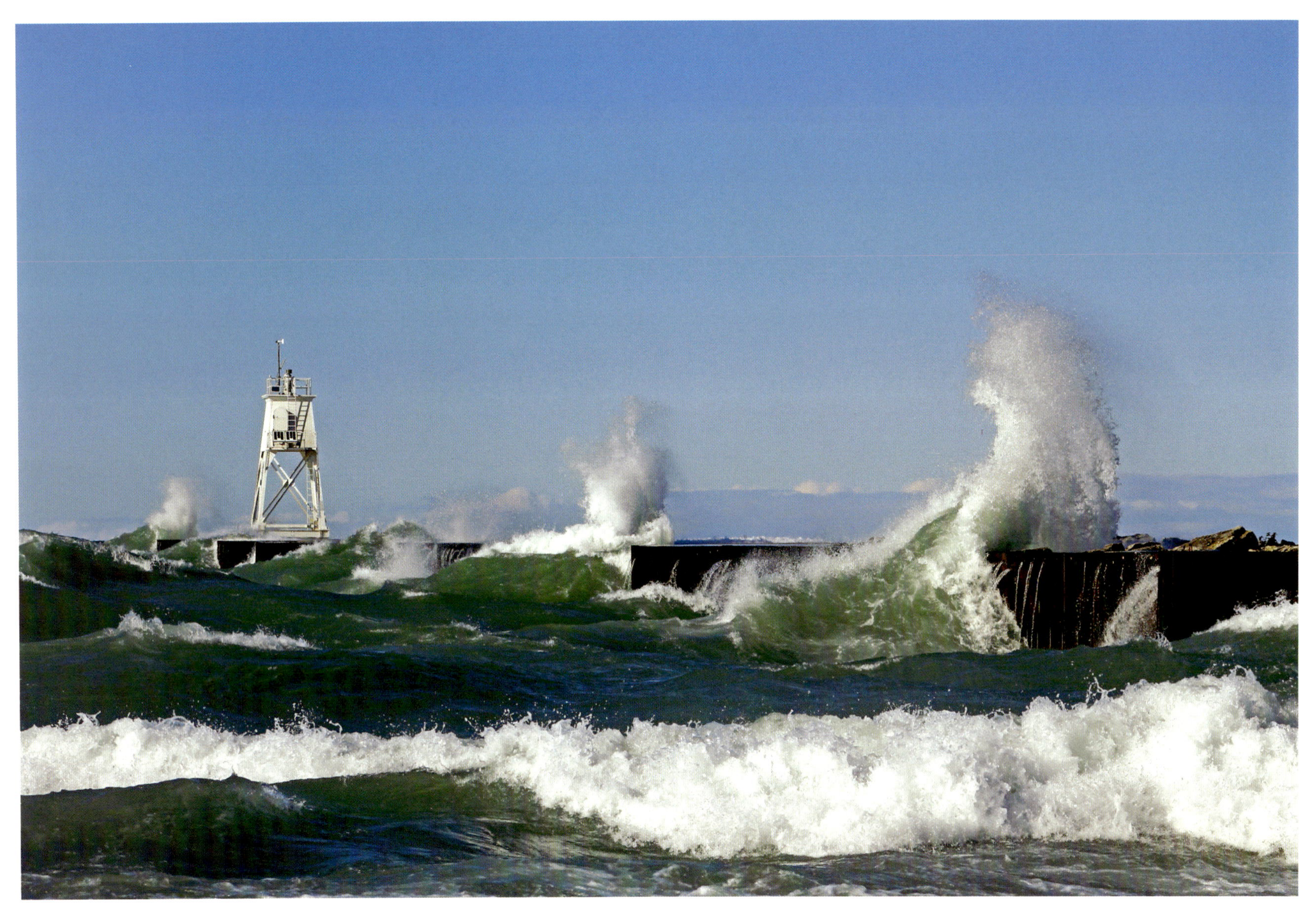

Making a Splash: Grand Marais Lighthouse

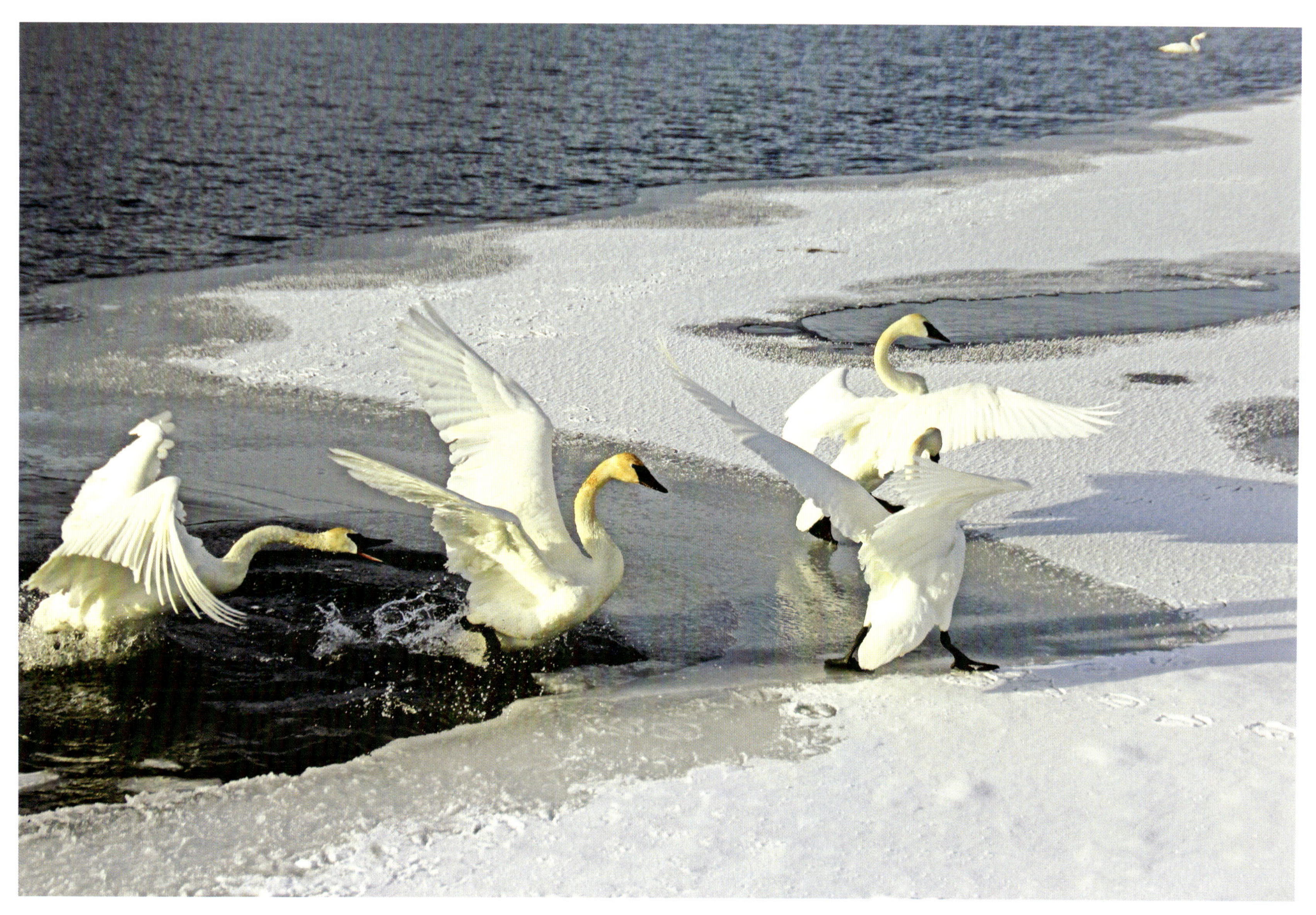

Slip and Slide

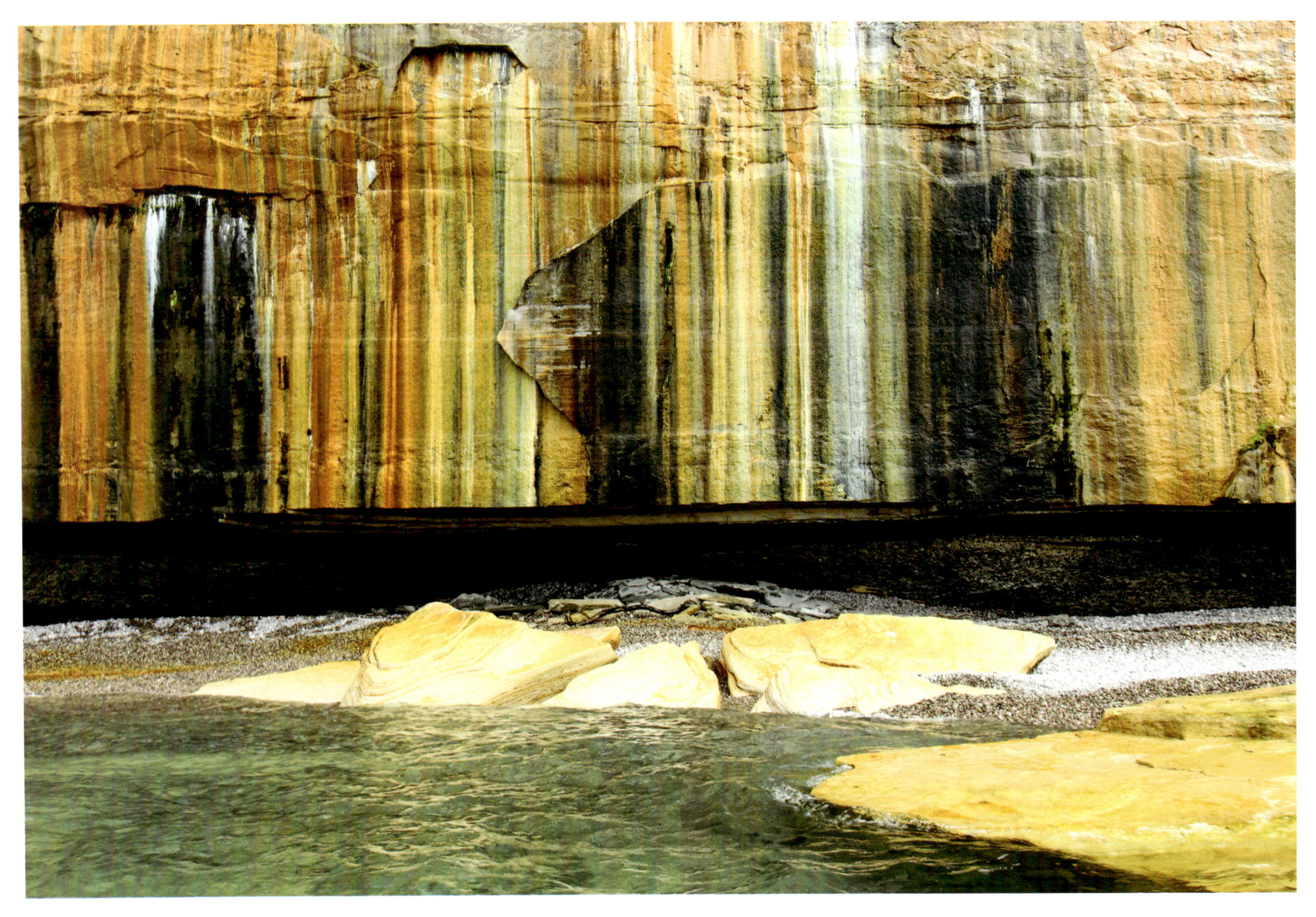

Runs in Streaks

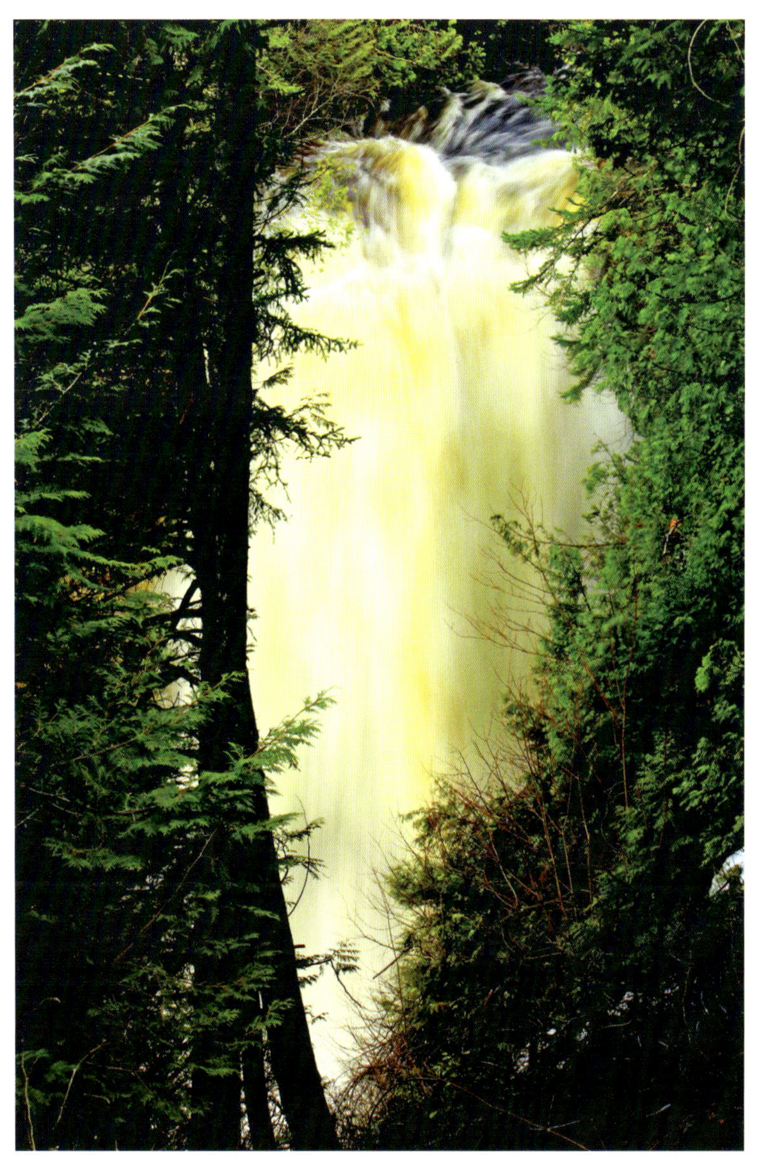

The Harder They Fall:
Miners Falls

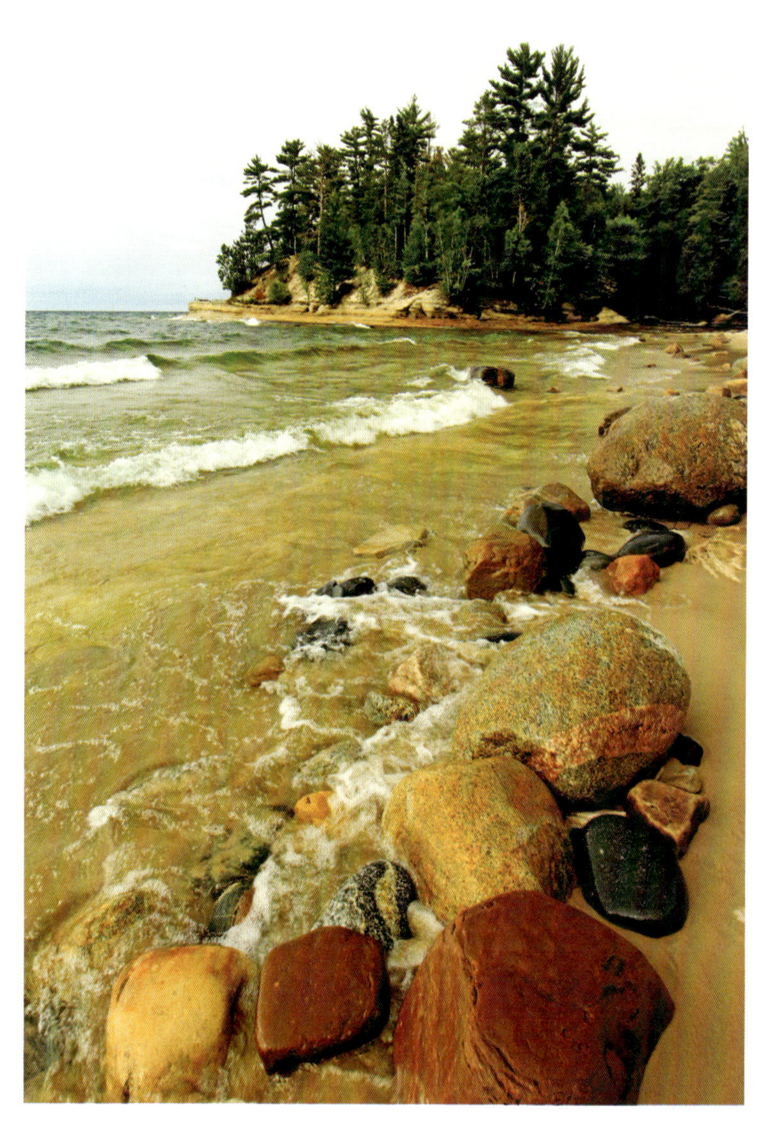

No Stone Unturned
Mosquito Beach

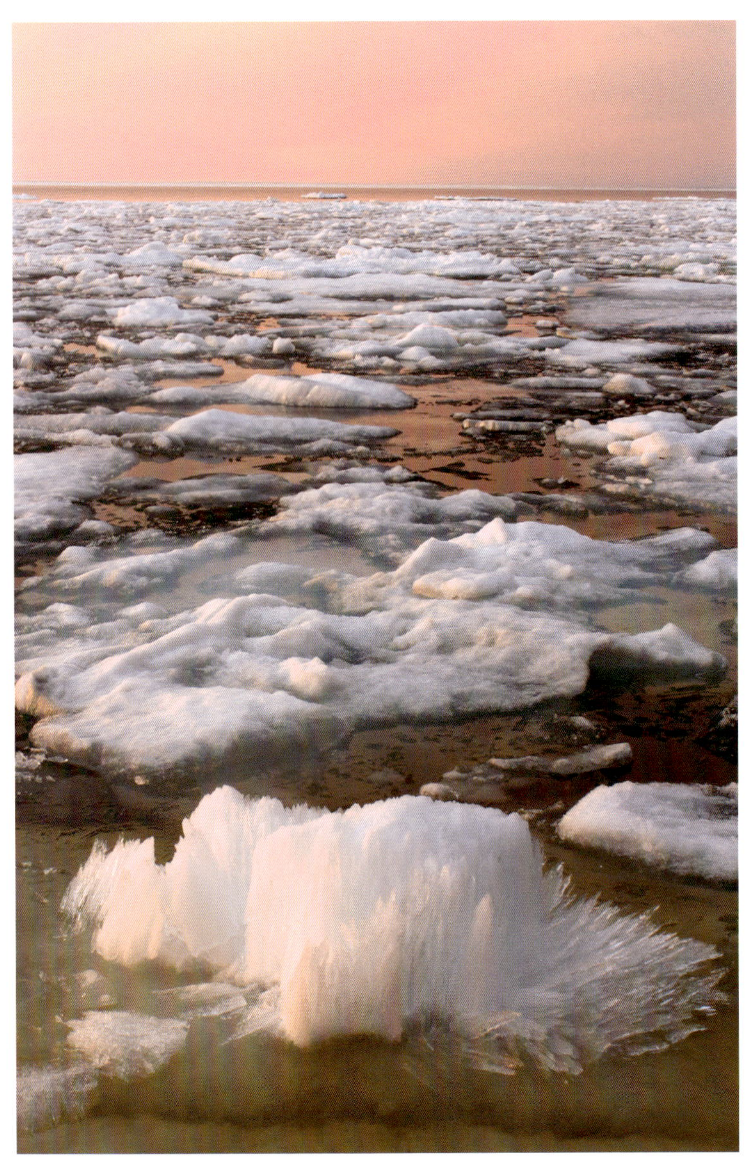

Strawberry Daiquiri

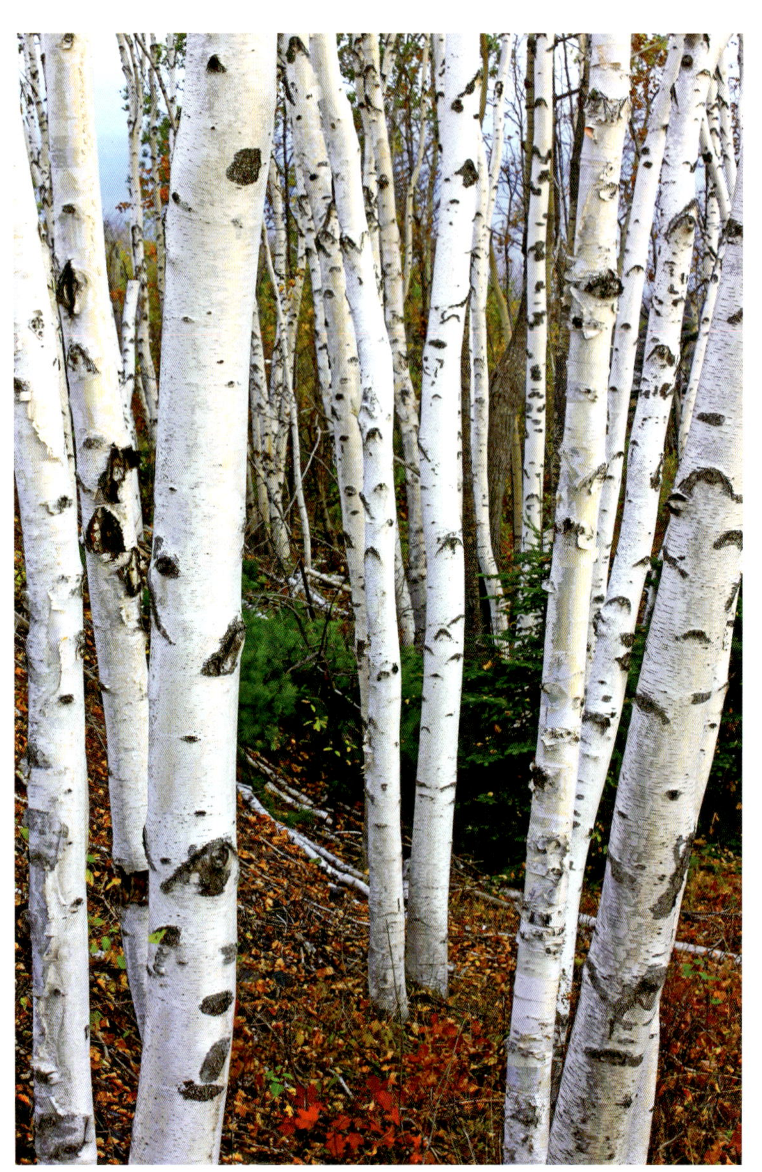

Ink Blots

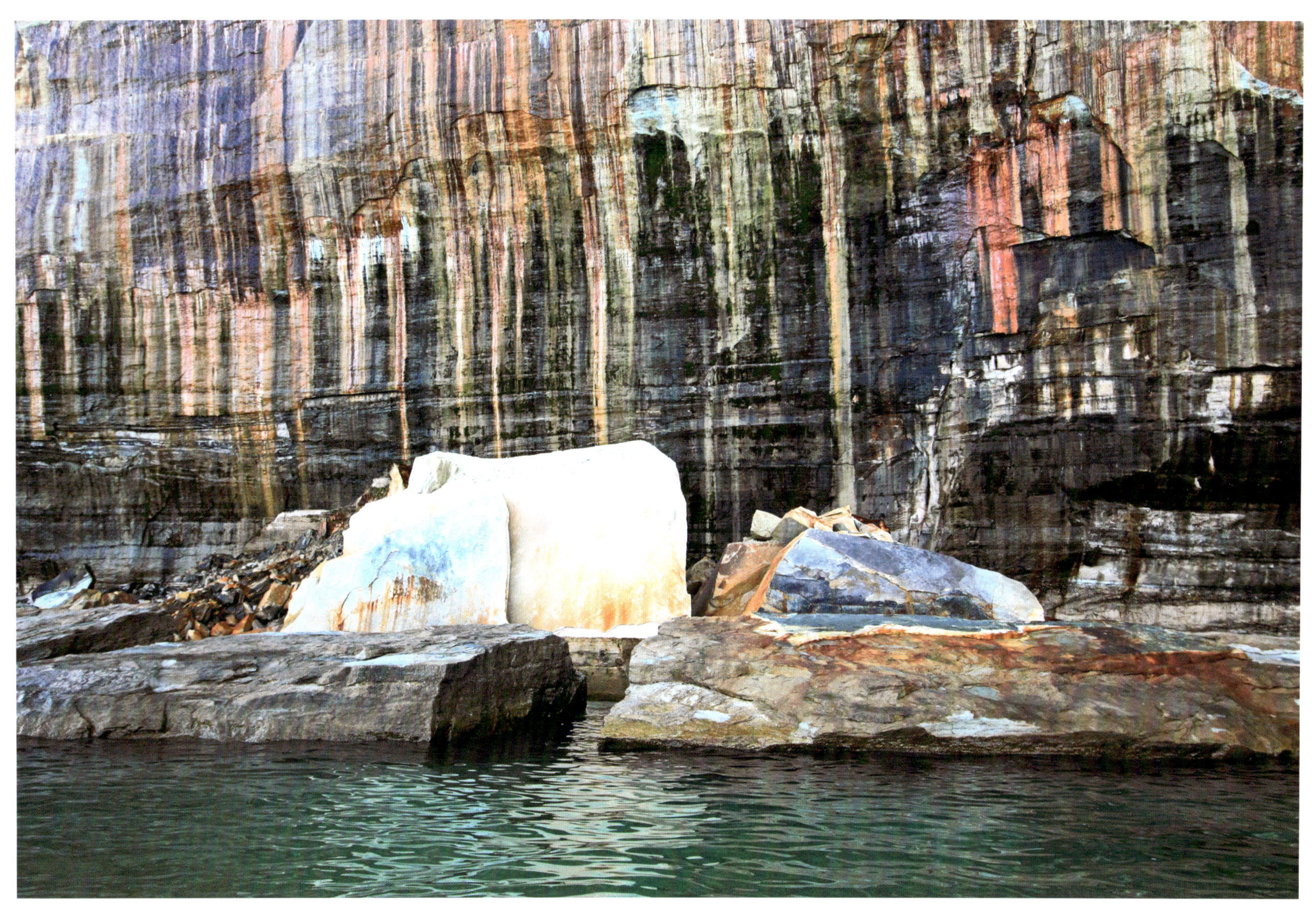

Mineral Spirits

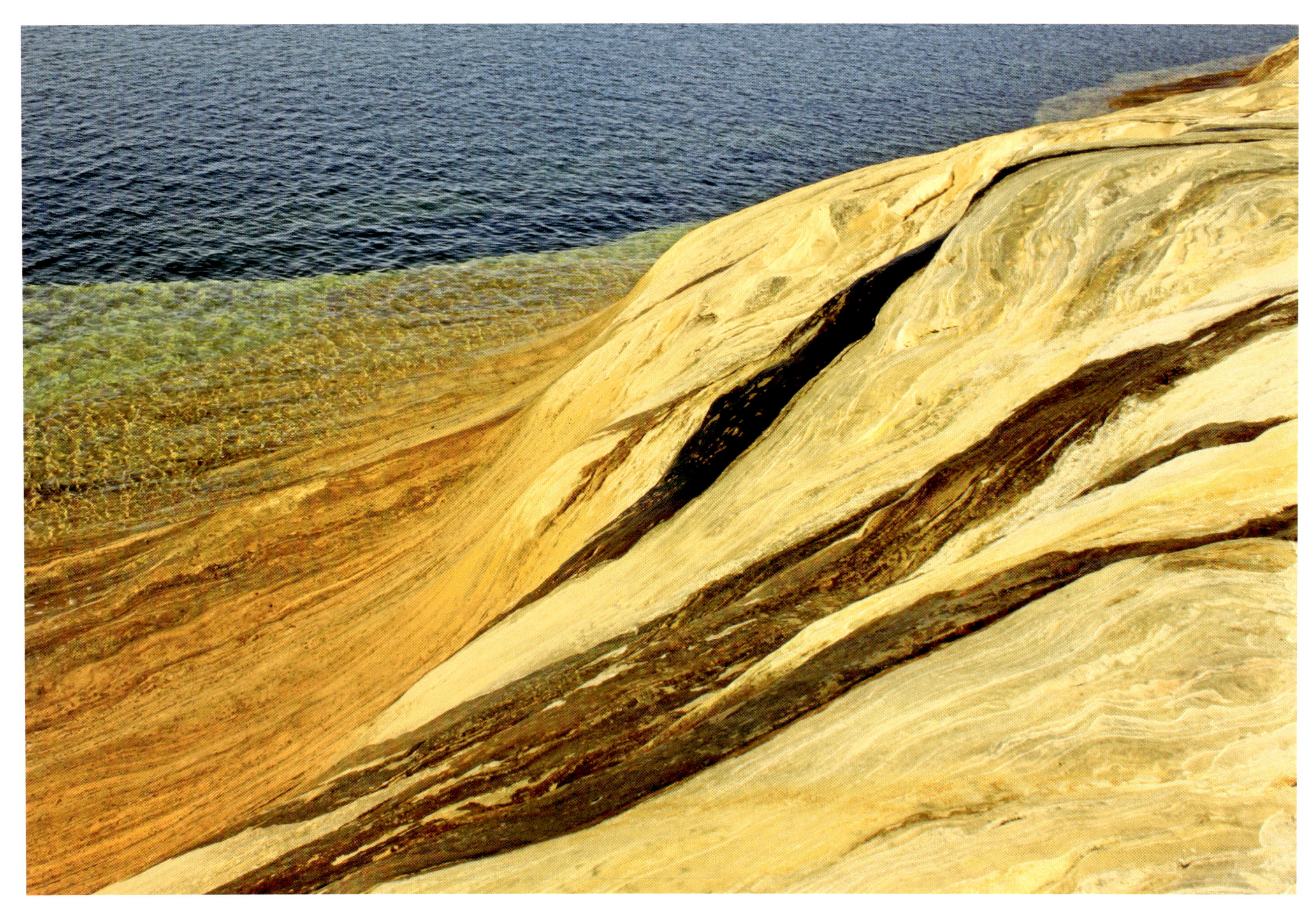

Getting into Deep Water

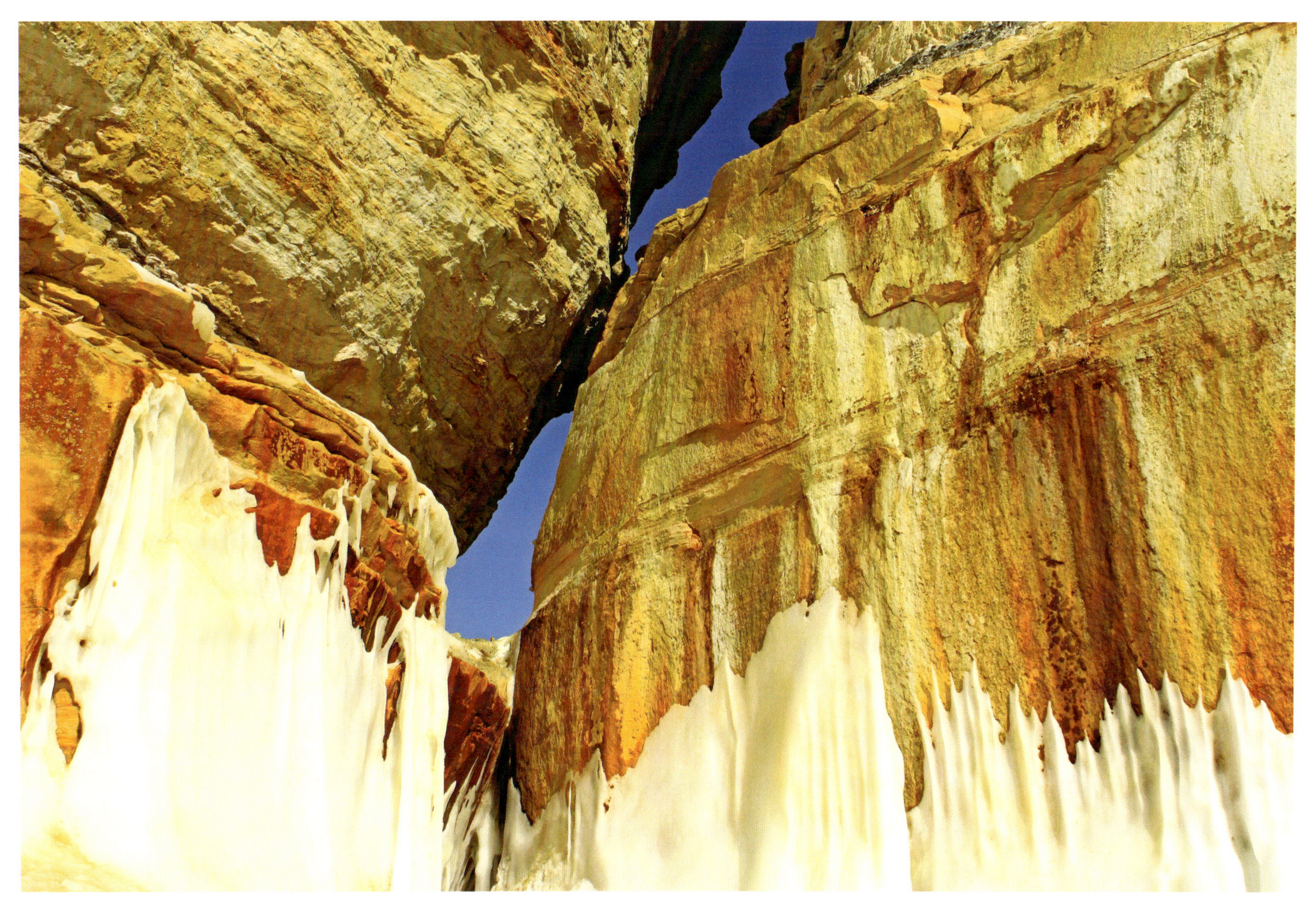

Lean on Me: Skiing to Mosquito Beach

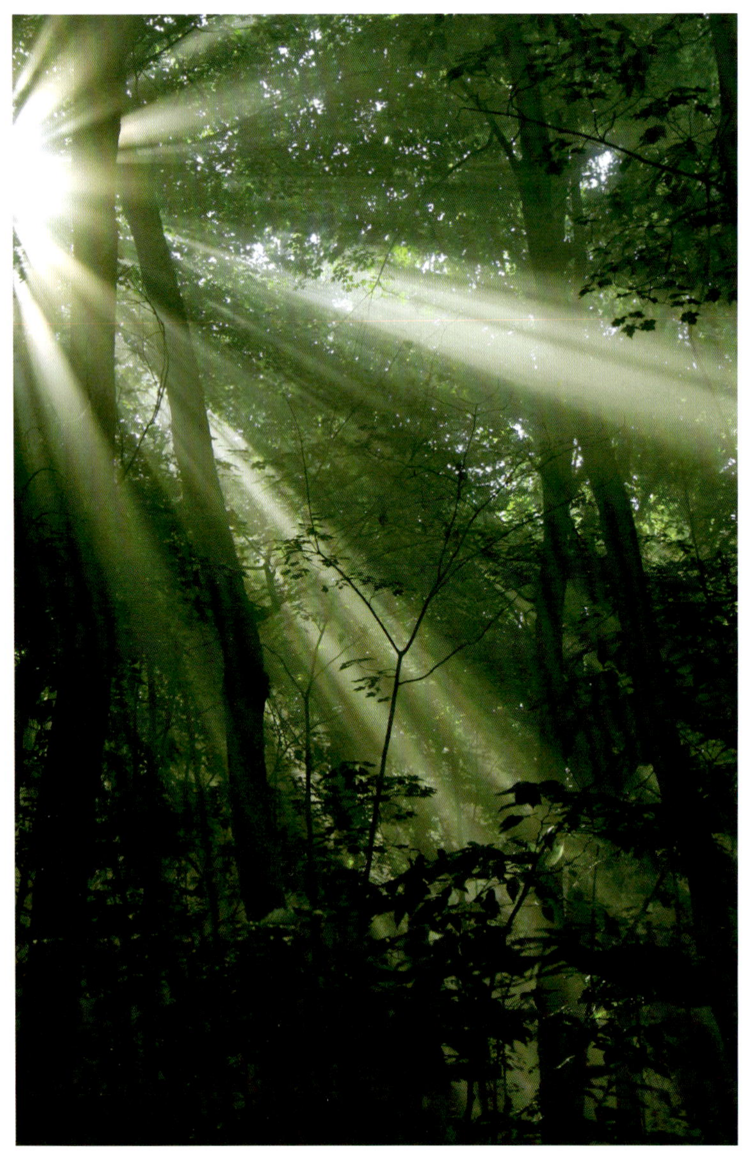

Let There Be Light

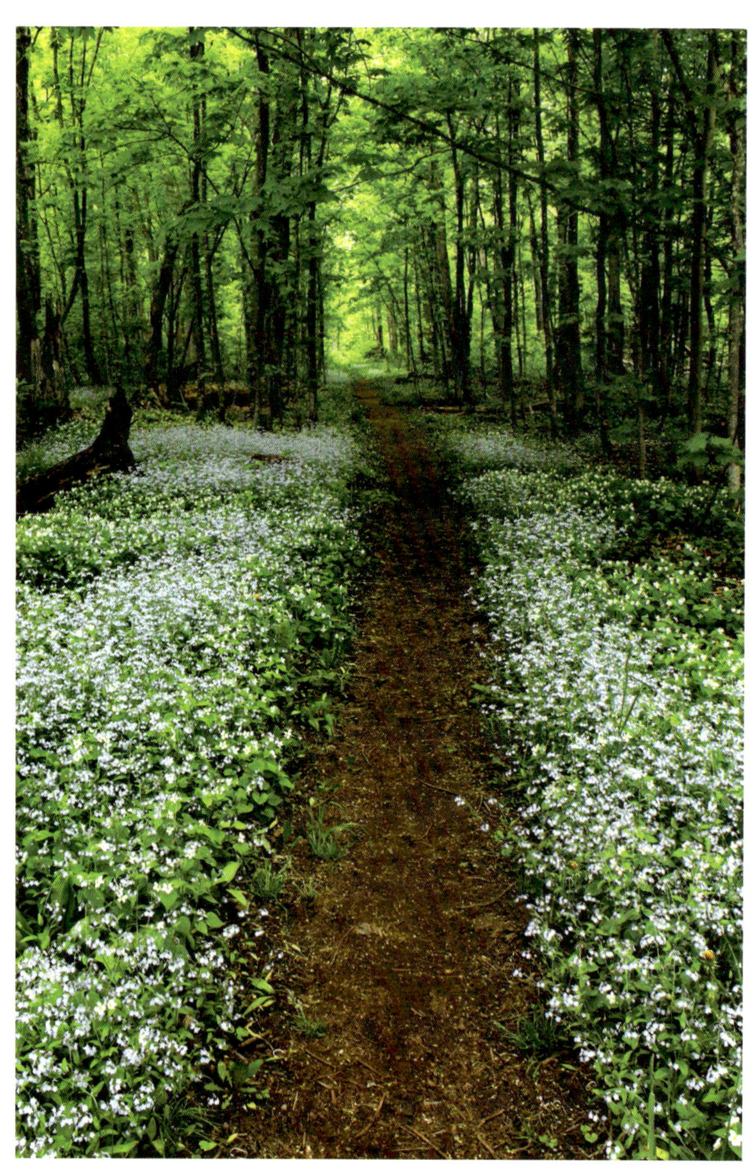

Forget Me Not

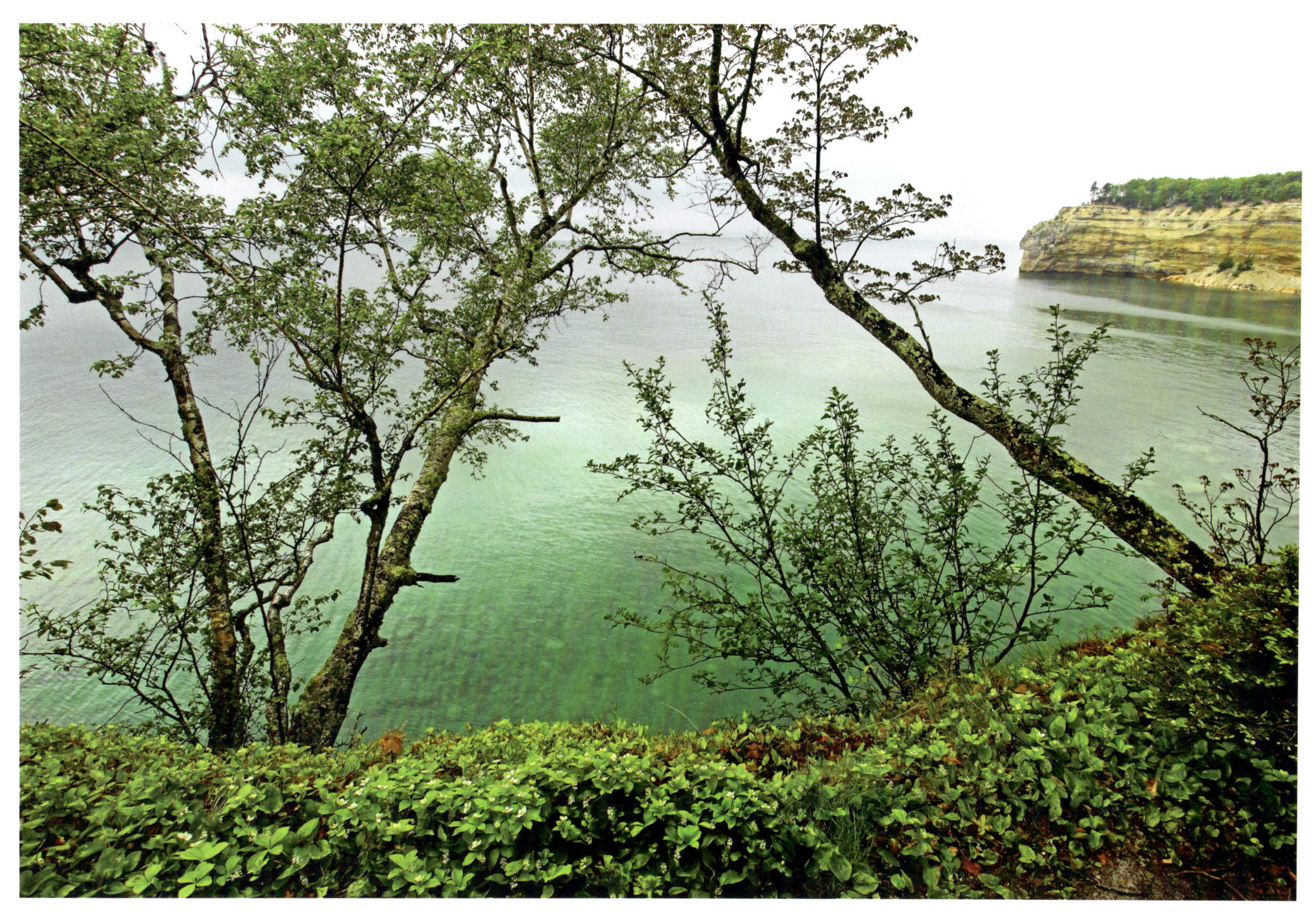

Rain Dance: Chapel Loop

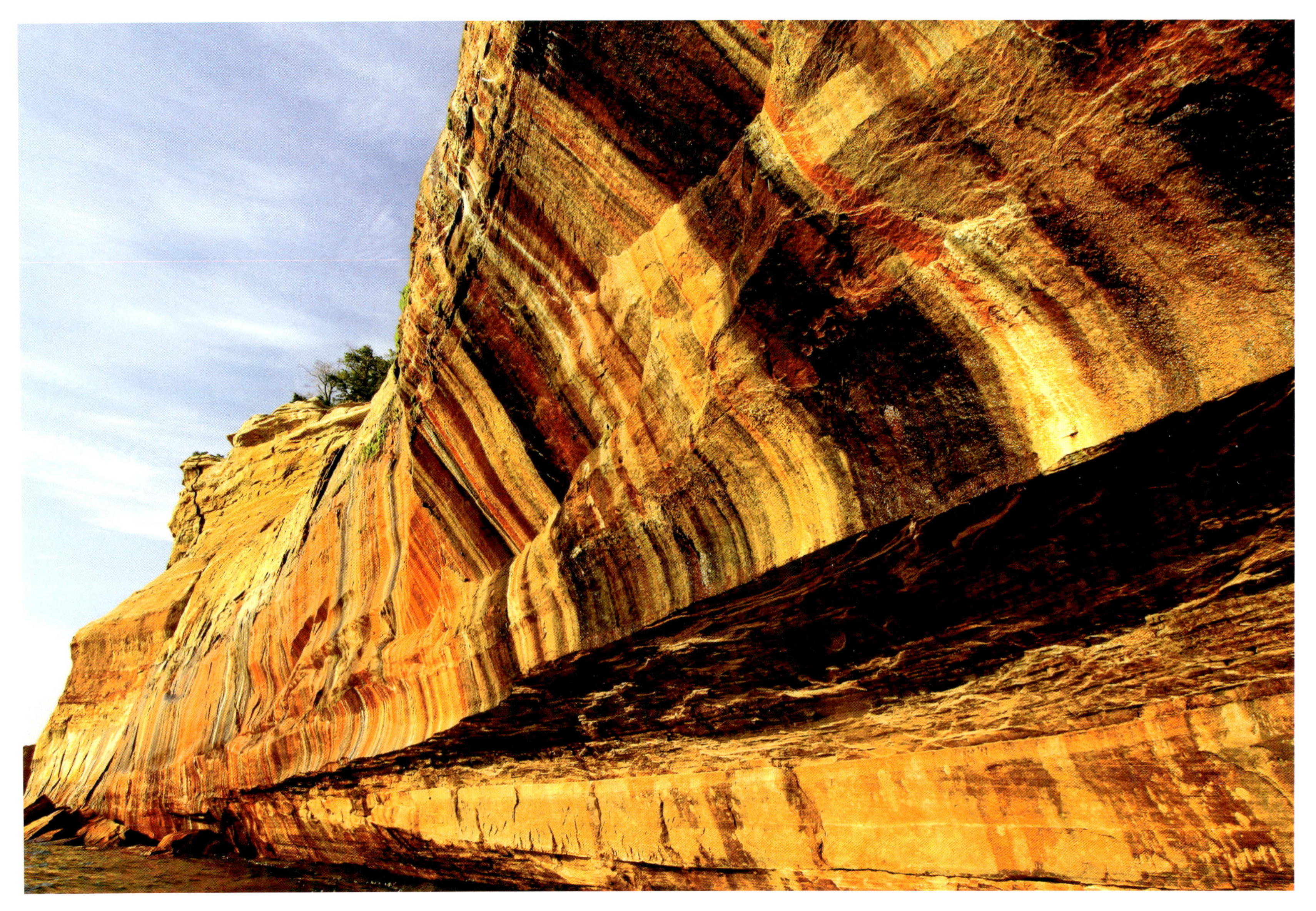

Hot Streak

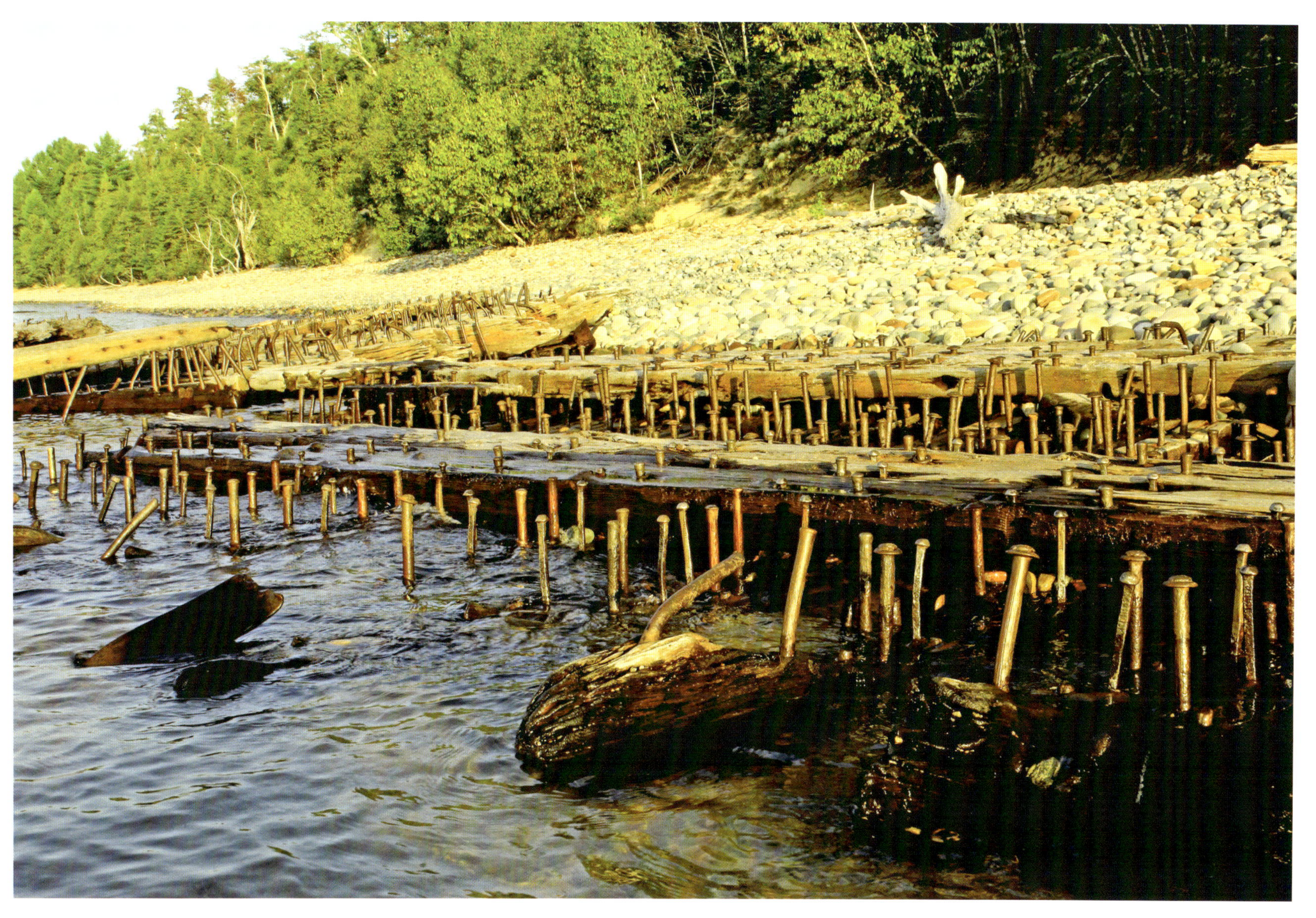

Skeletal Remains: Shipwreck Between
Hurricane River and AuSable Lighthouse

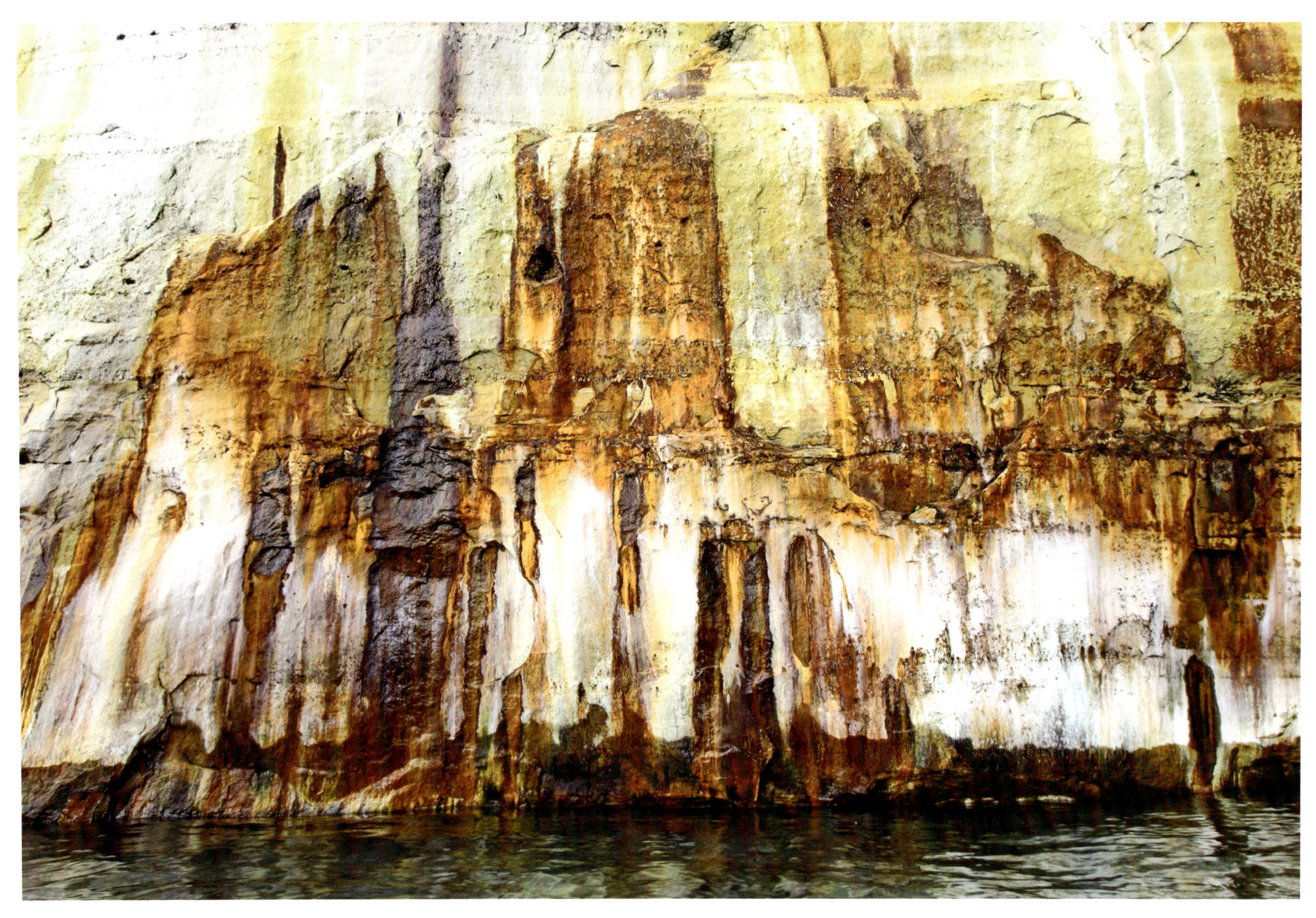

Lake Superior Tapestry

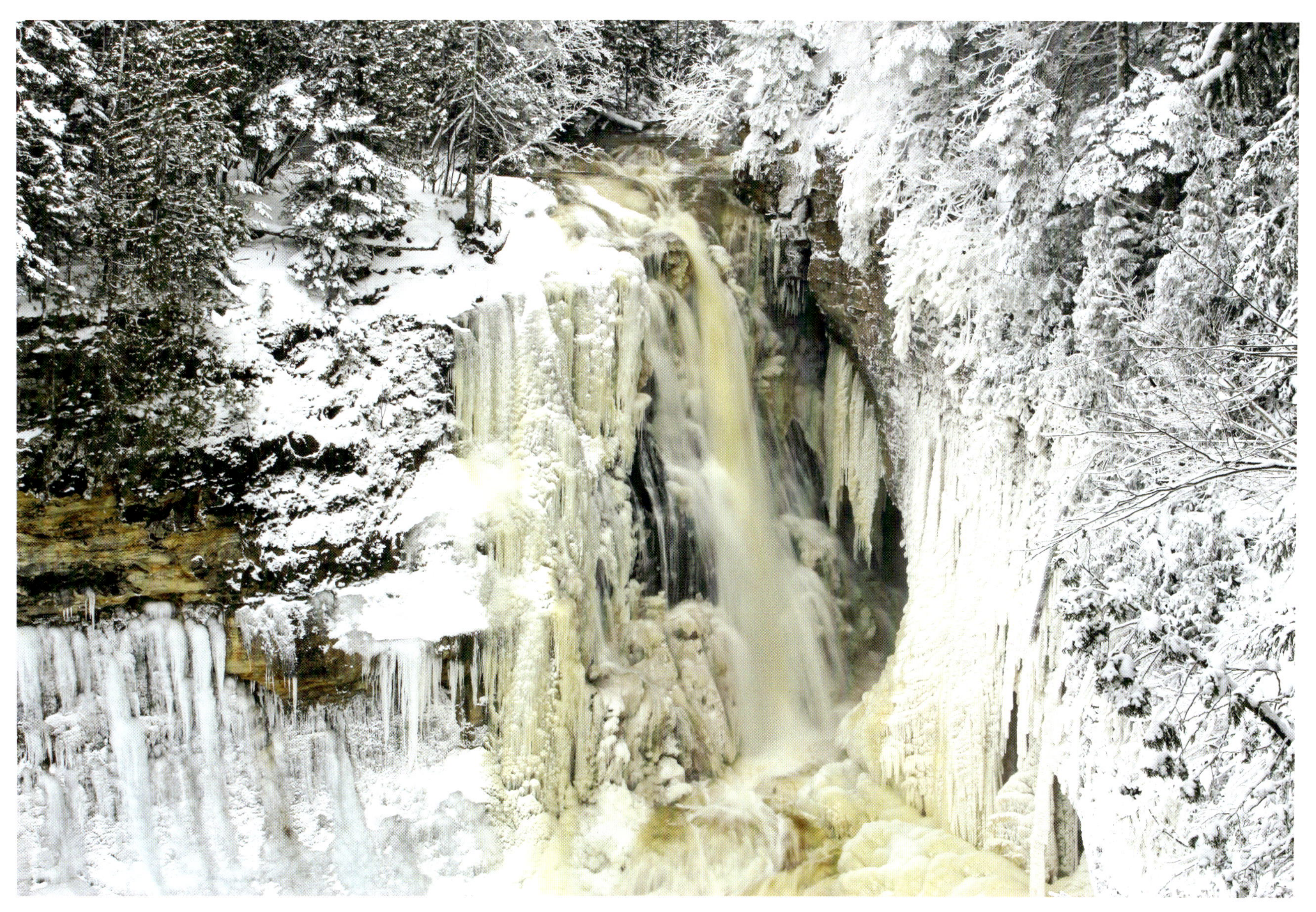

Freeze Frame: Miners Falls

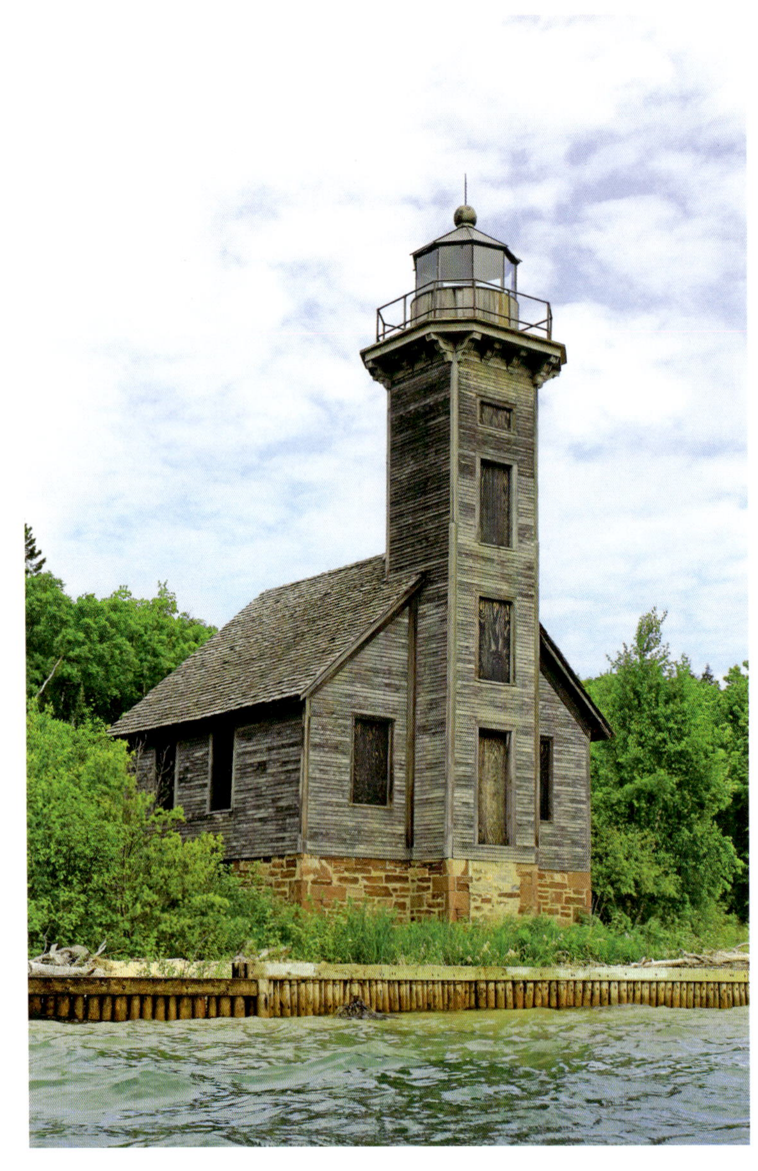

Guiding Light: East Channel Lighthouse, Grand Island

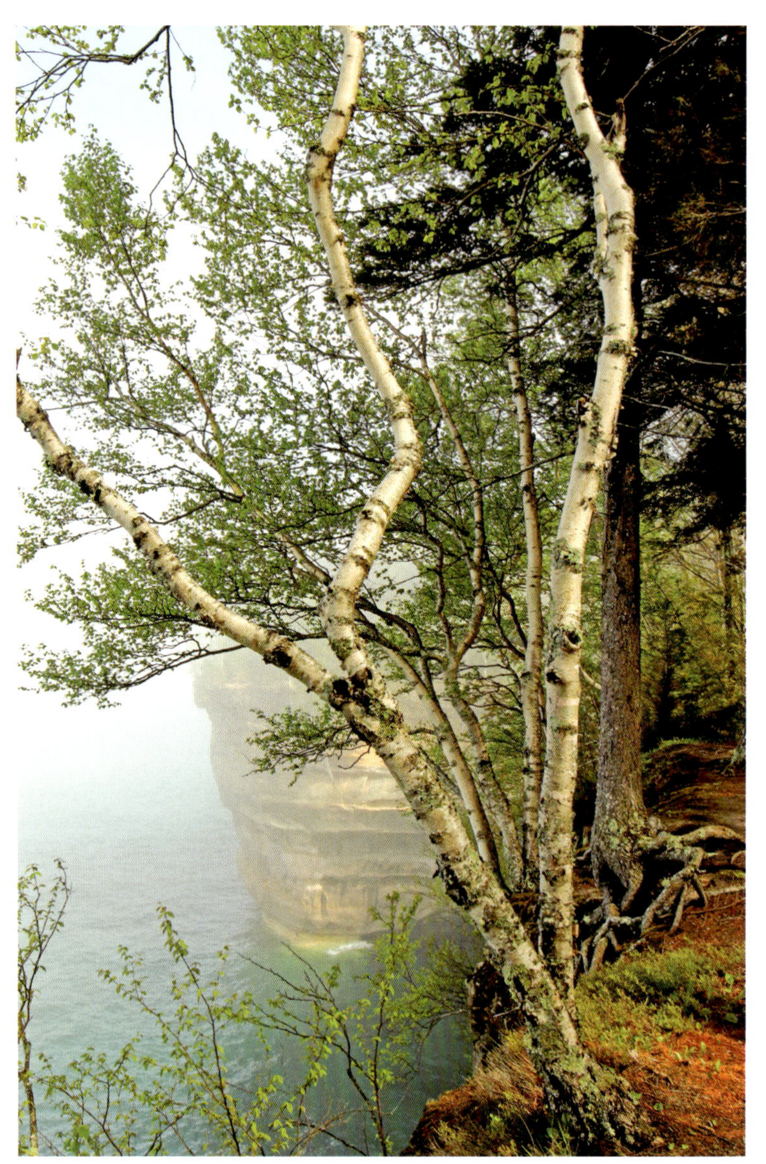

Hazy Daze

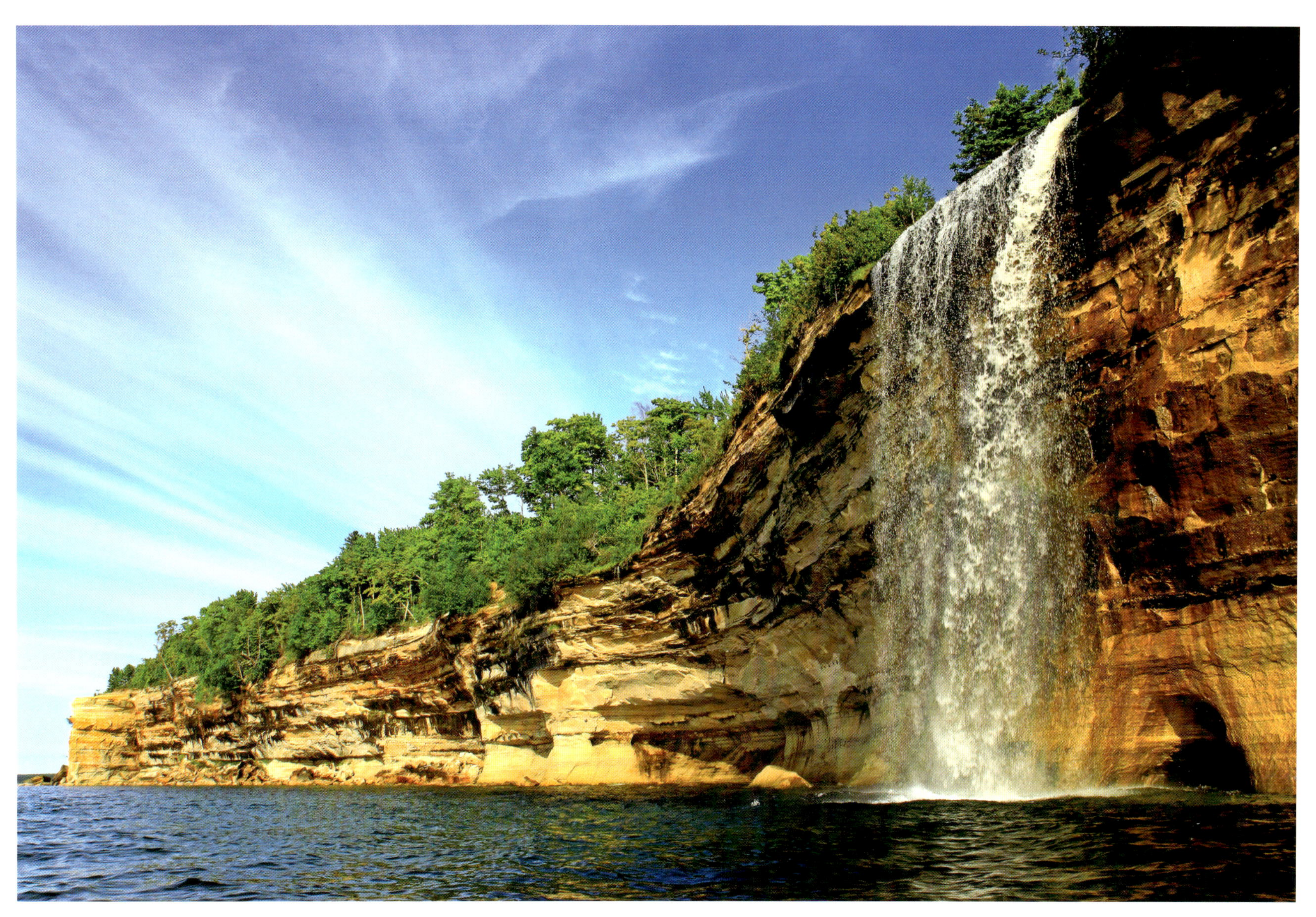

Over the Top: Spray Falls

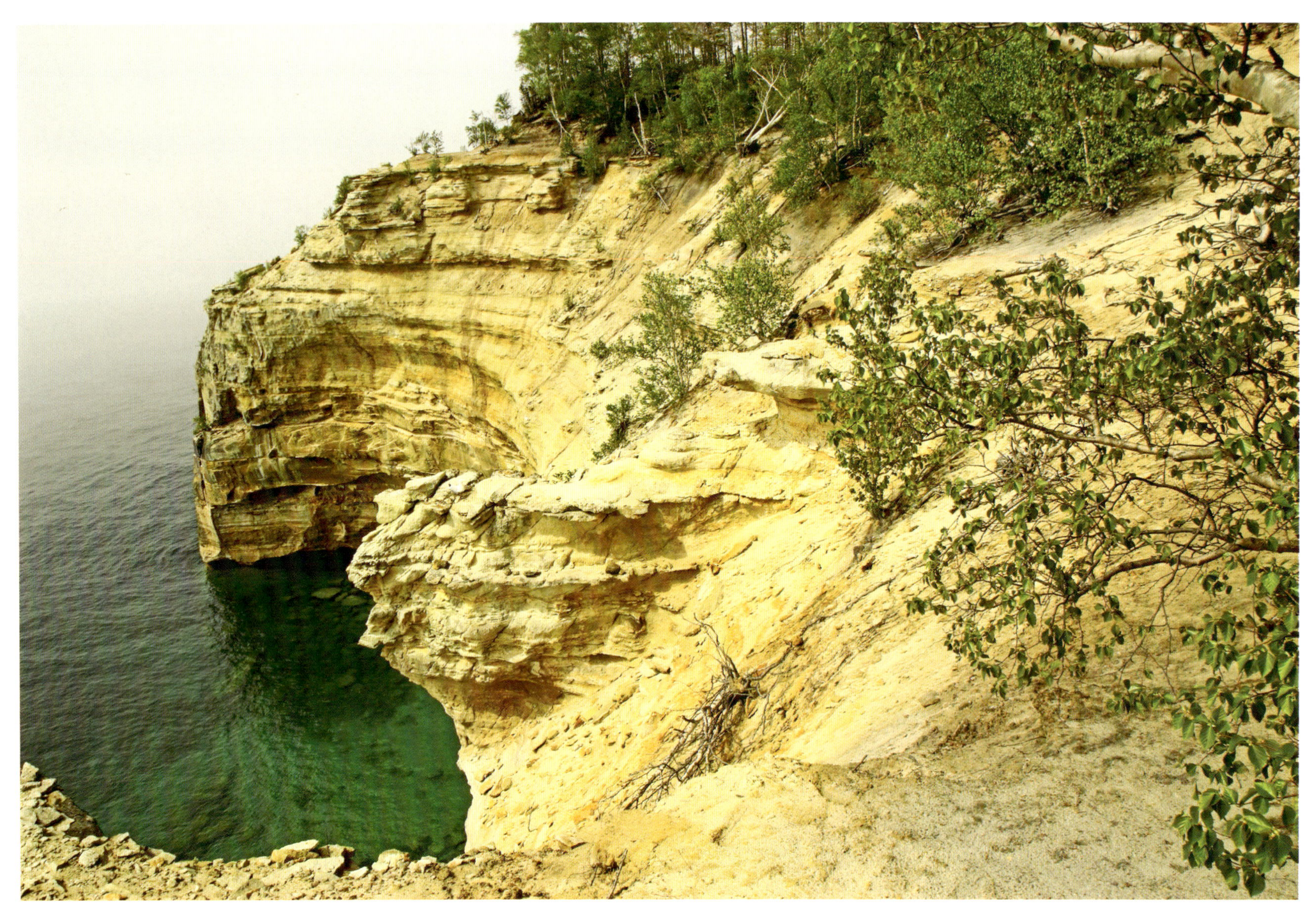

Birds Eye View

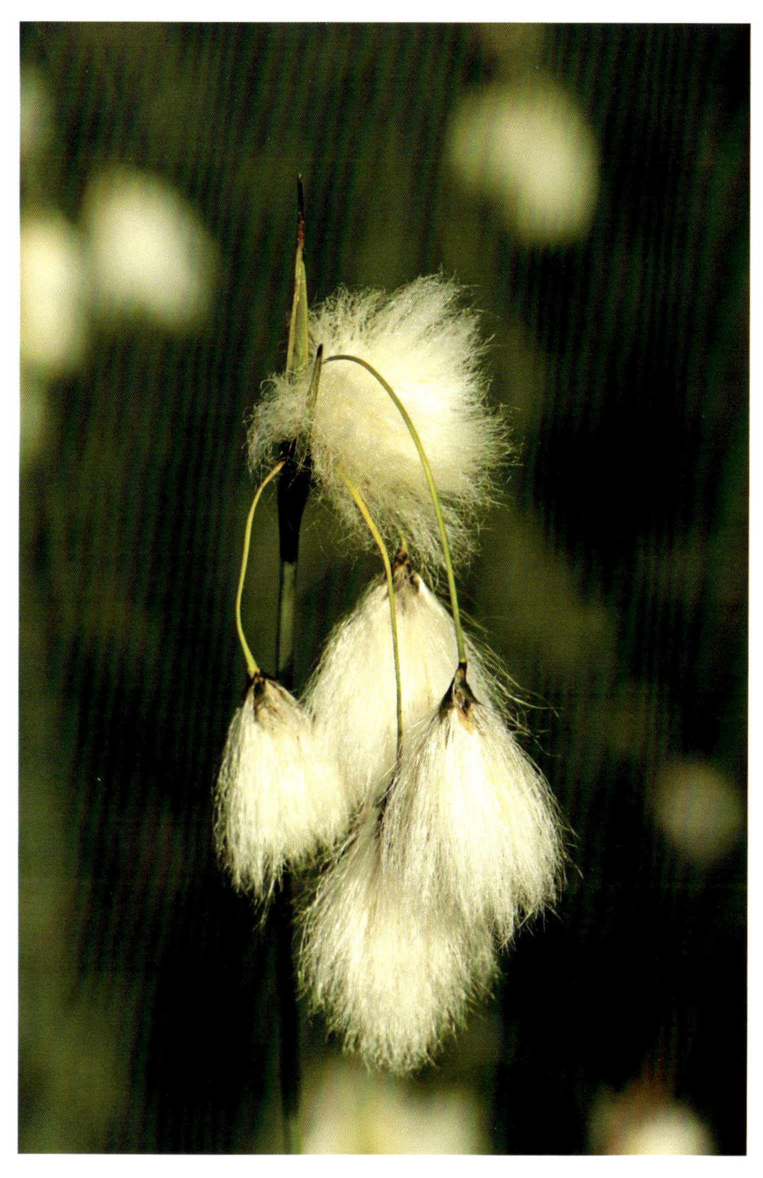

Headdress

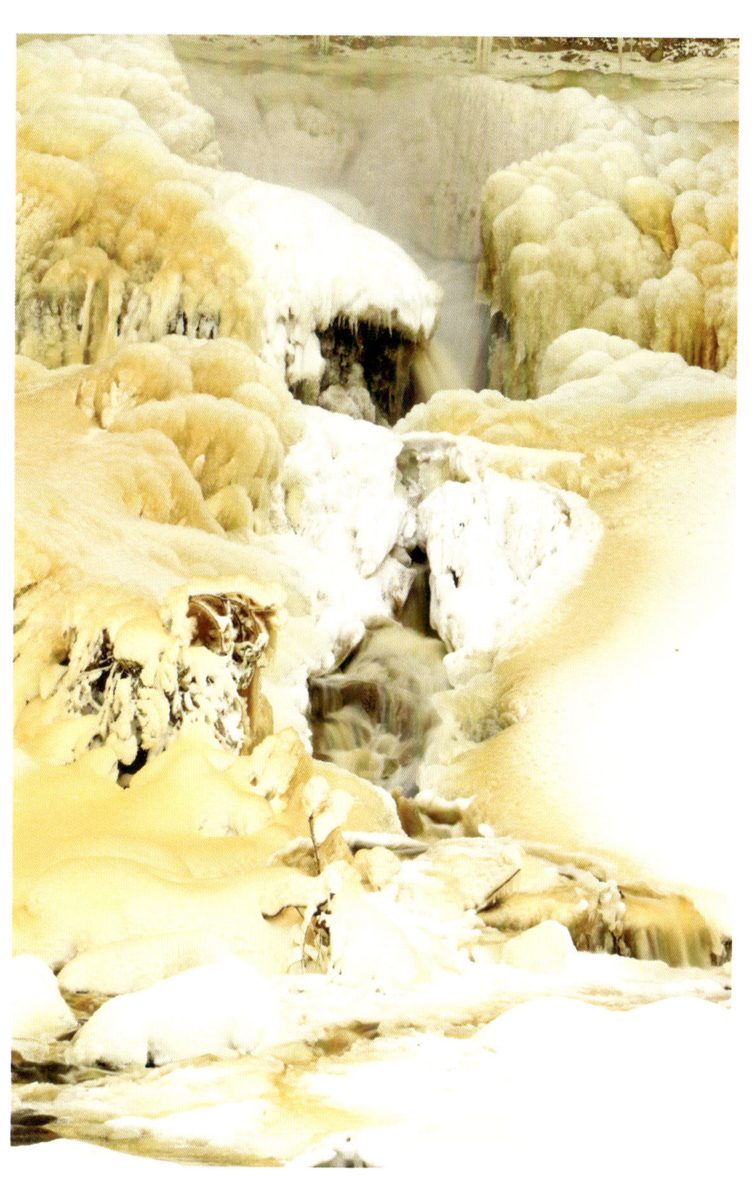

Root Beer Float

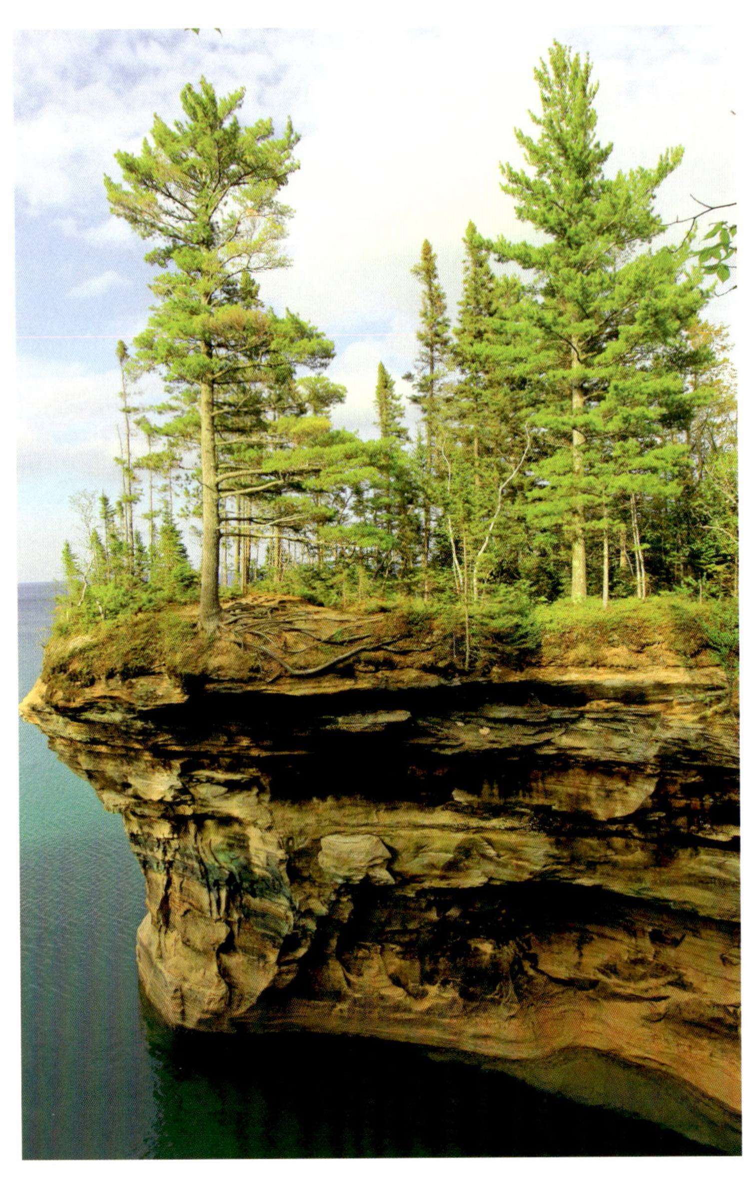

Splash of Green

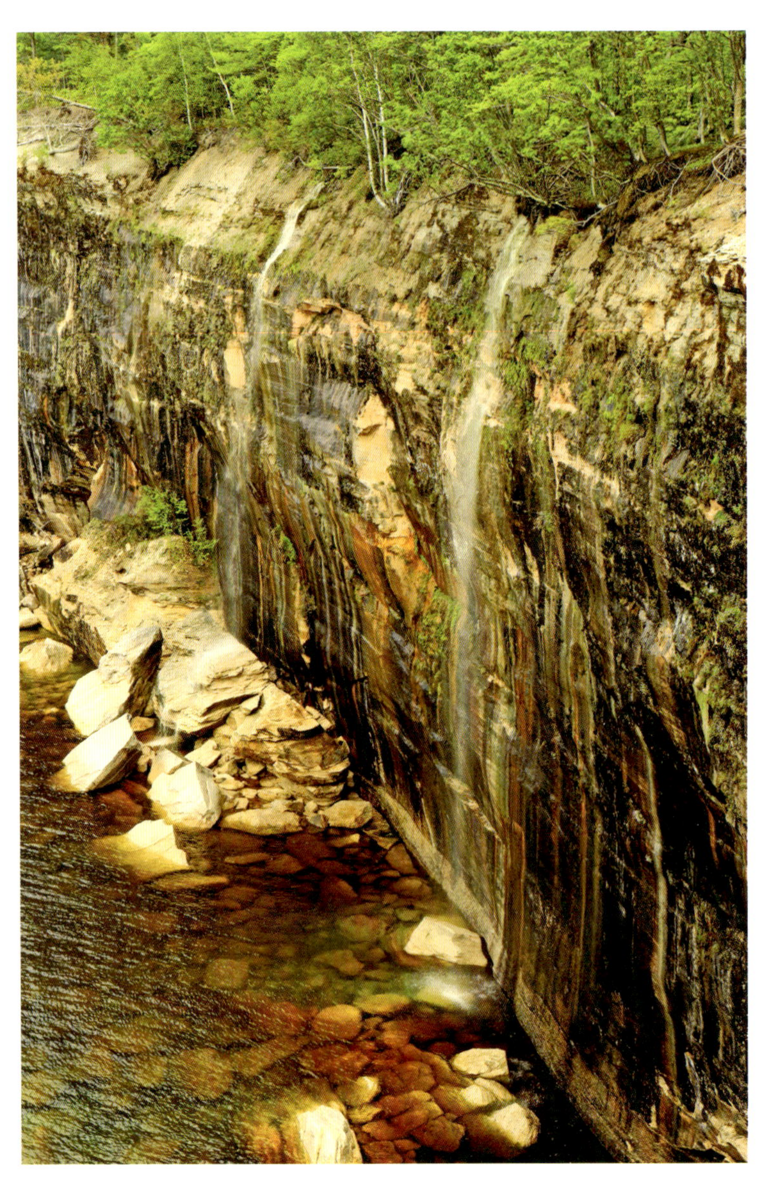

Woman in Orange Dress

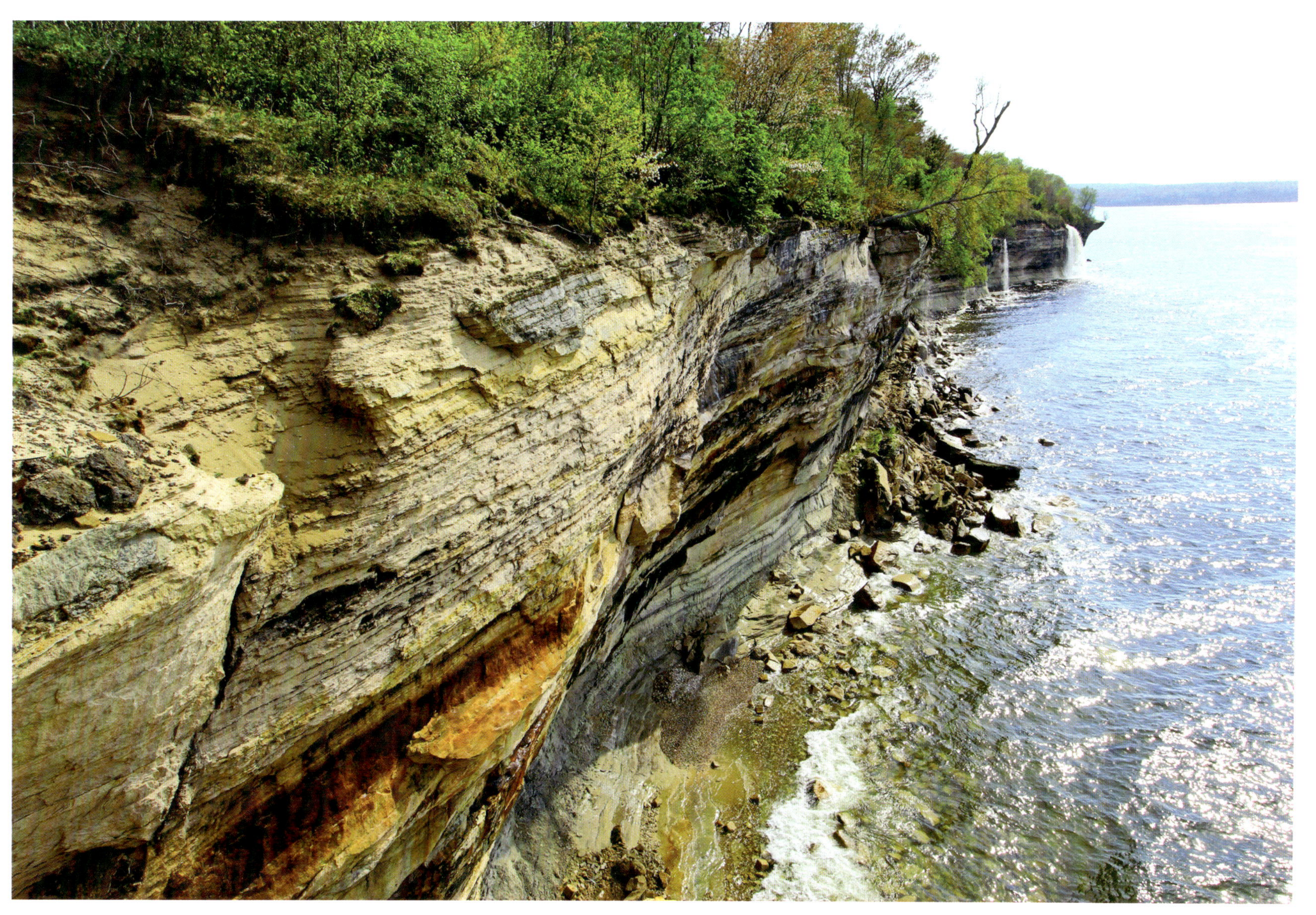

Standing on the Shoulders of Giants

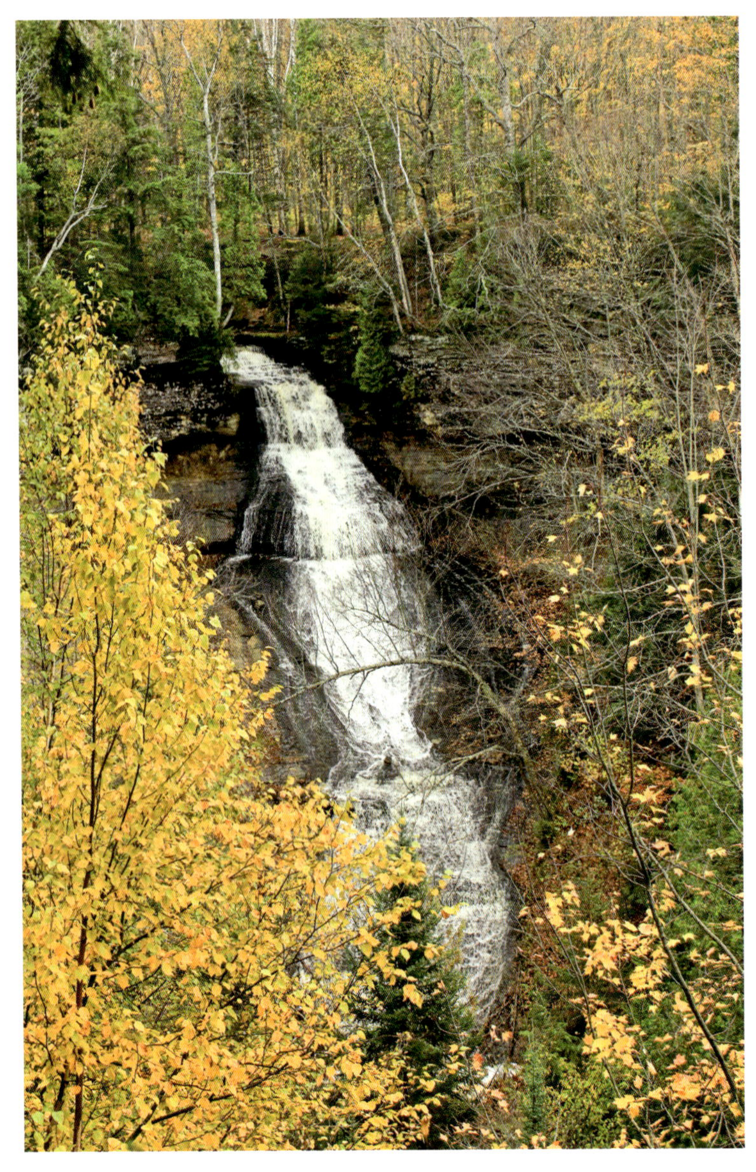

Lemon Drop: Chapel Falls

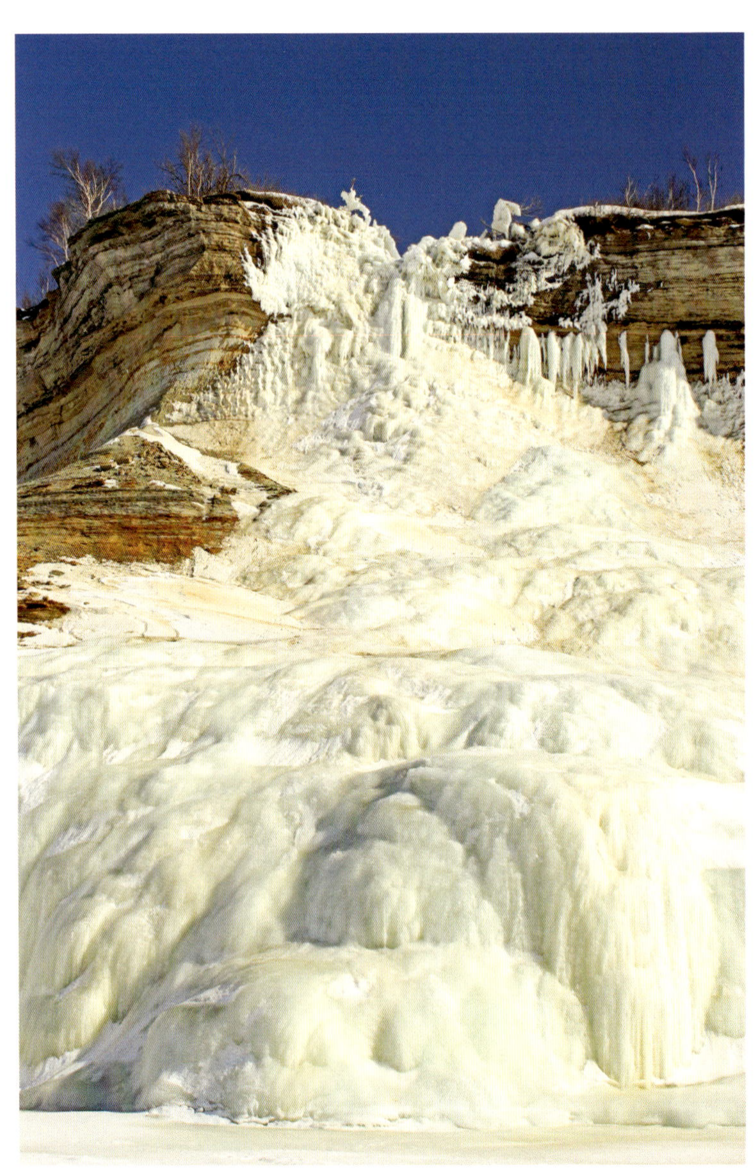

Winter Bride

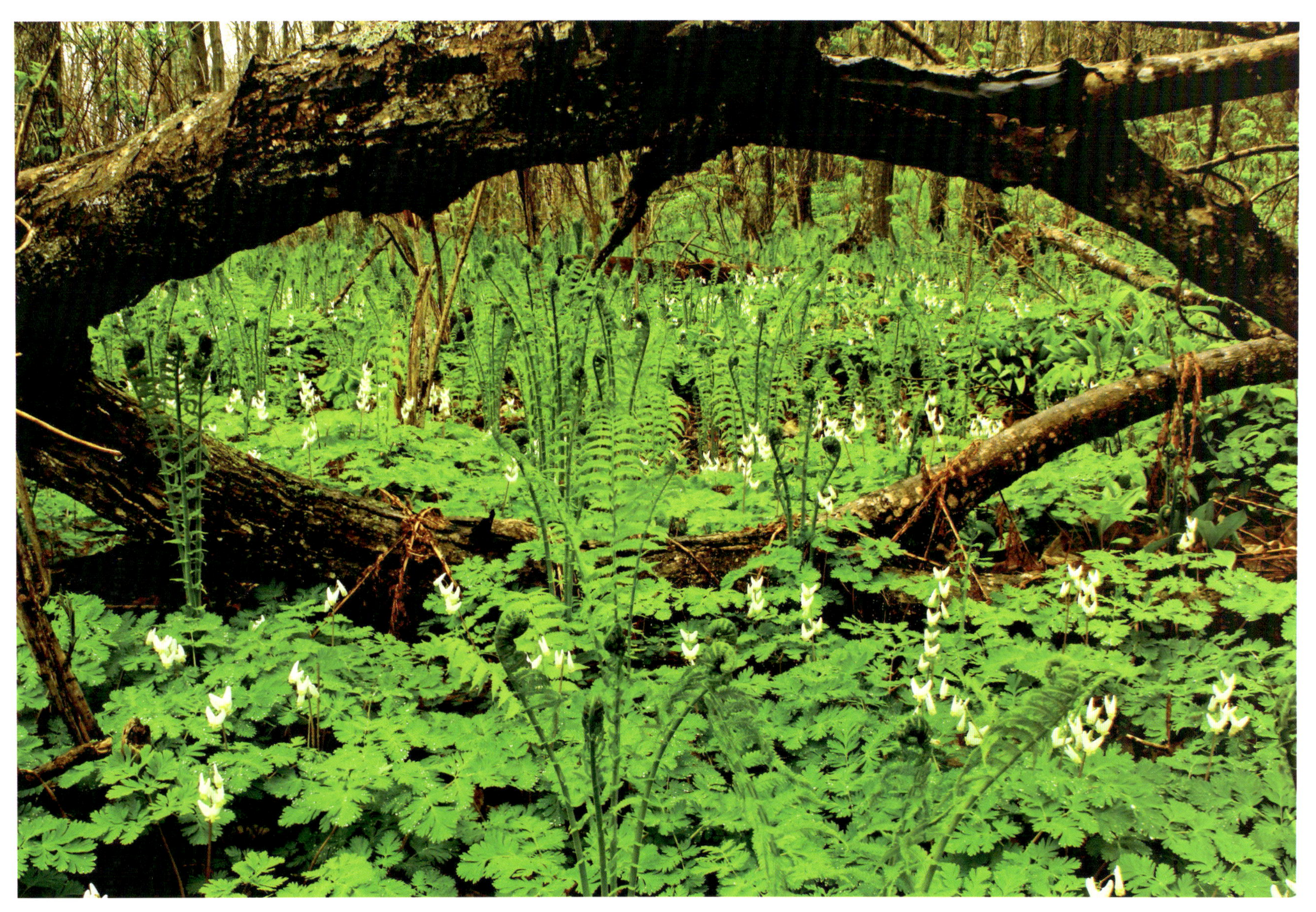

Fiddler's Eye

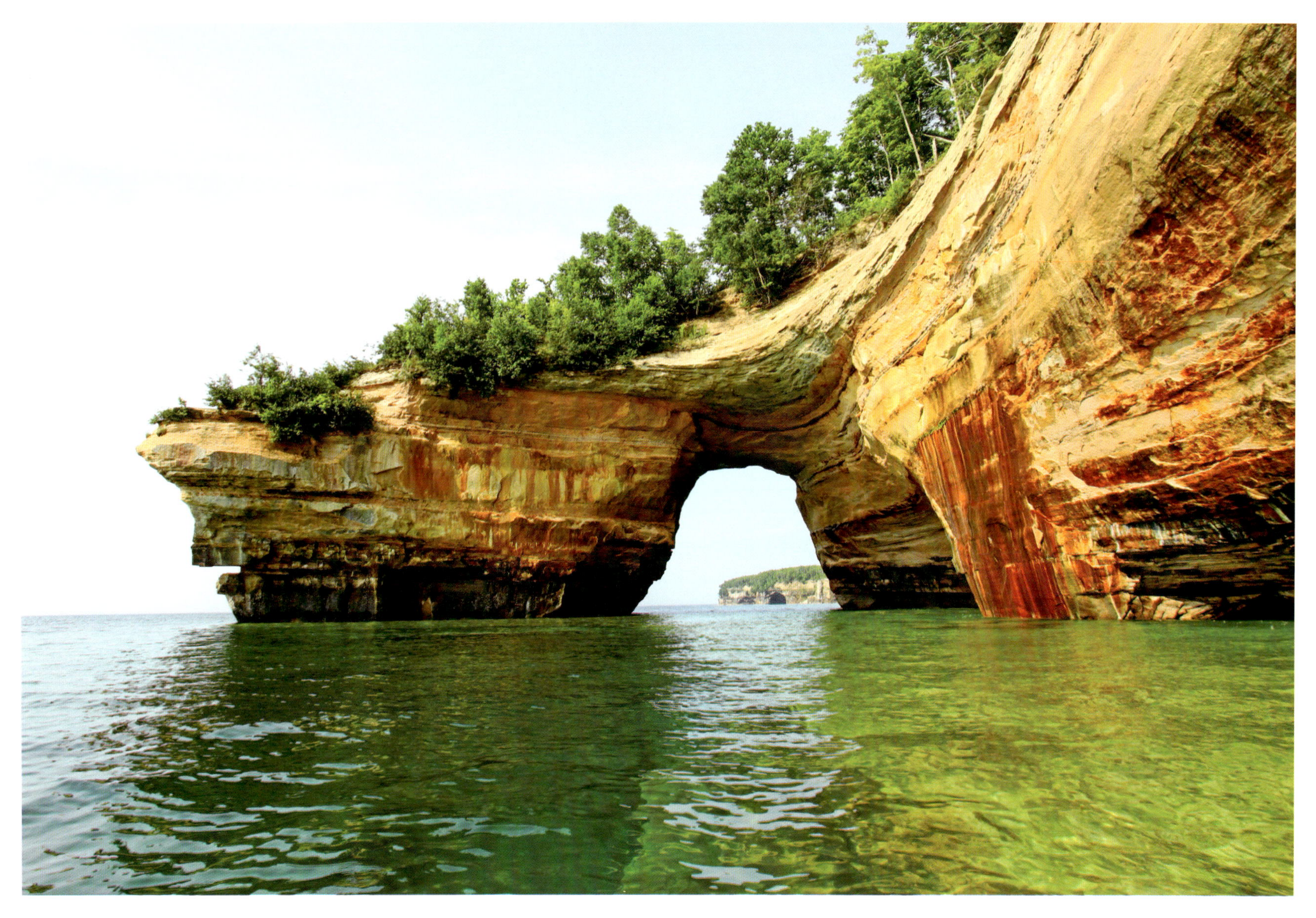

Lover's Leap

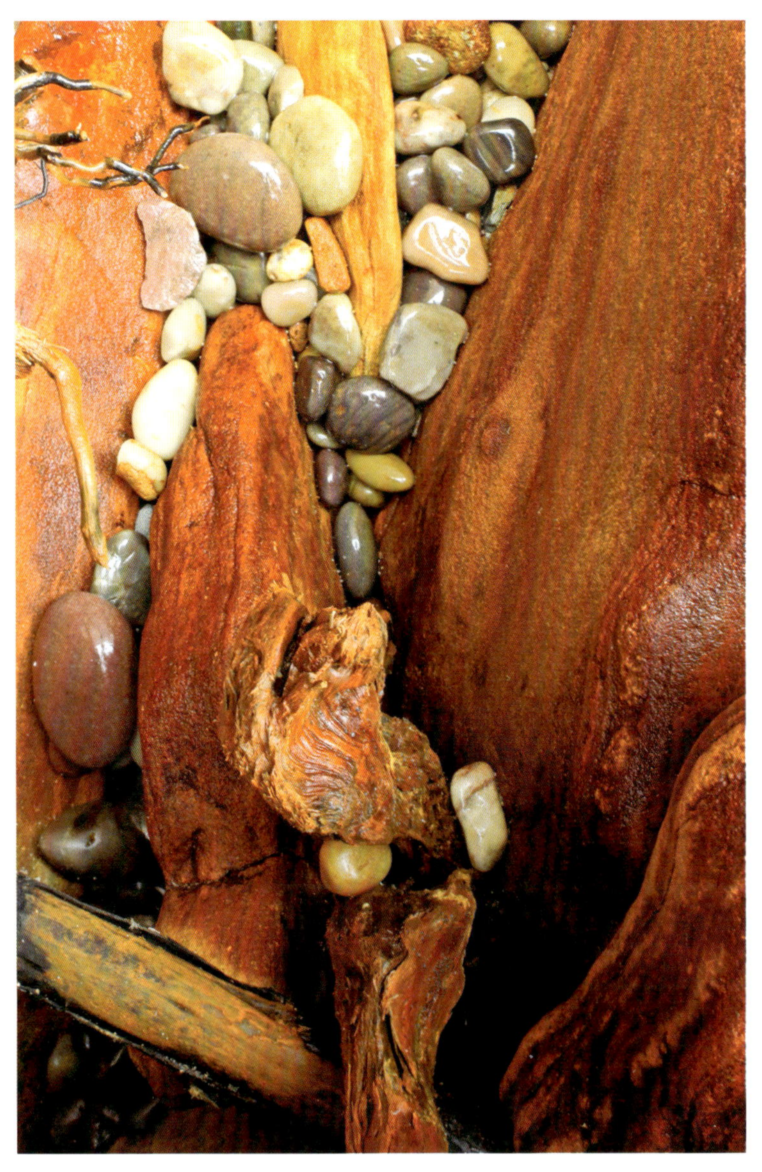

Vise Grip

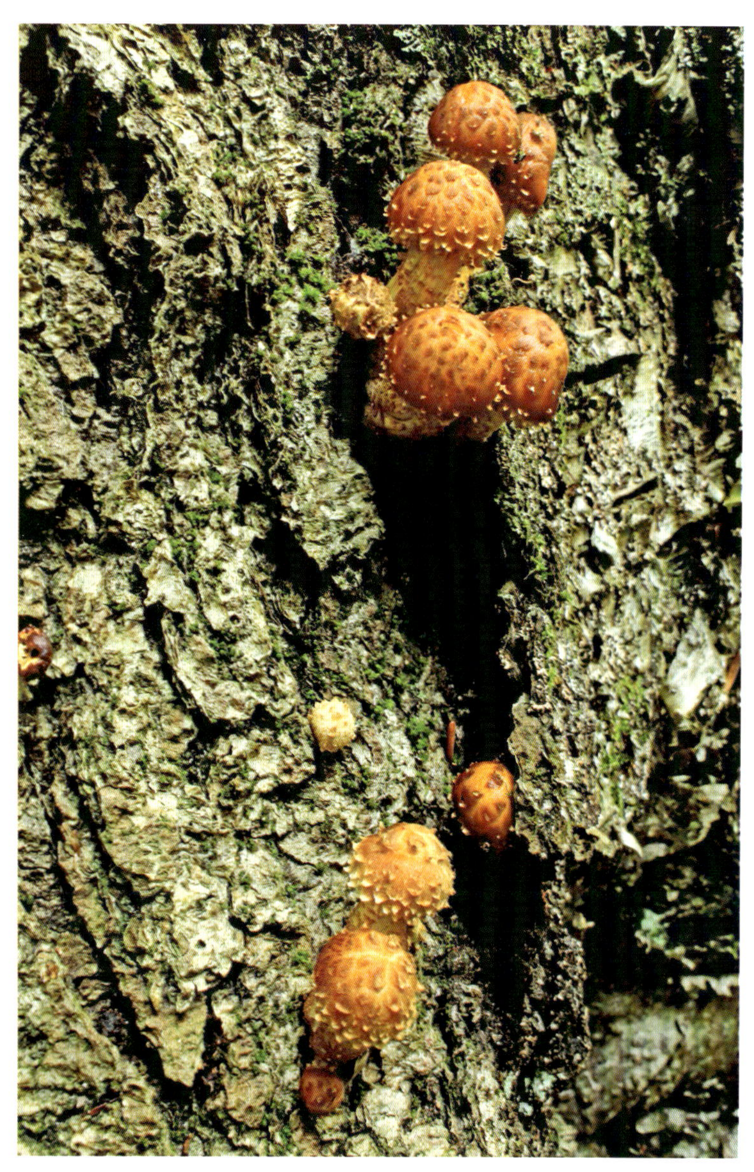

Barking Up the Wrong Tree

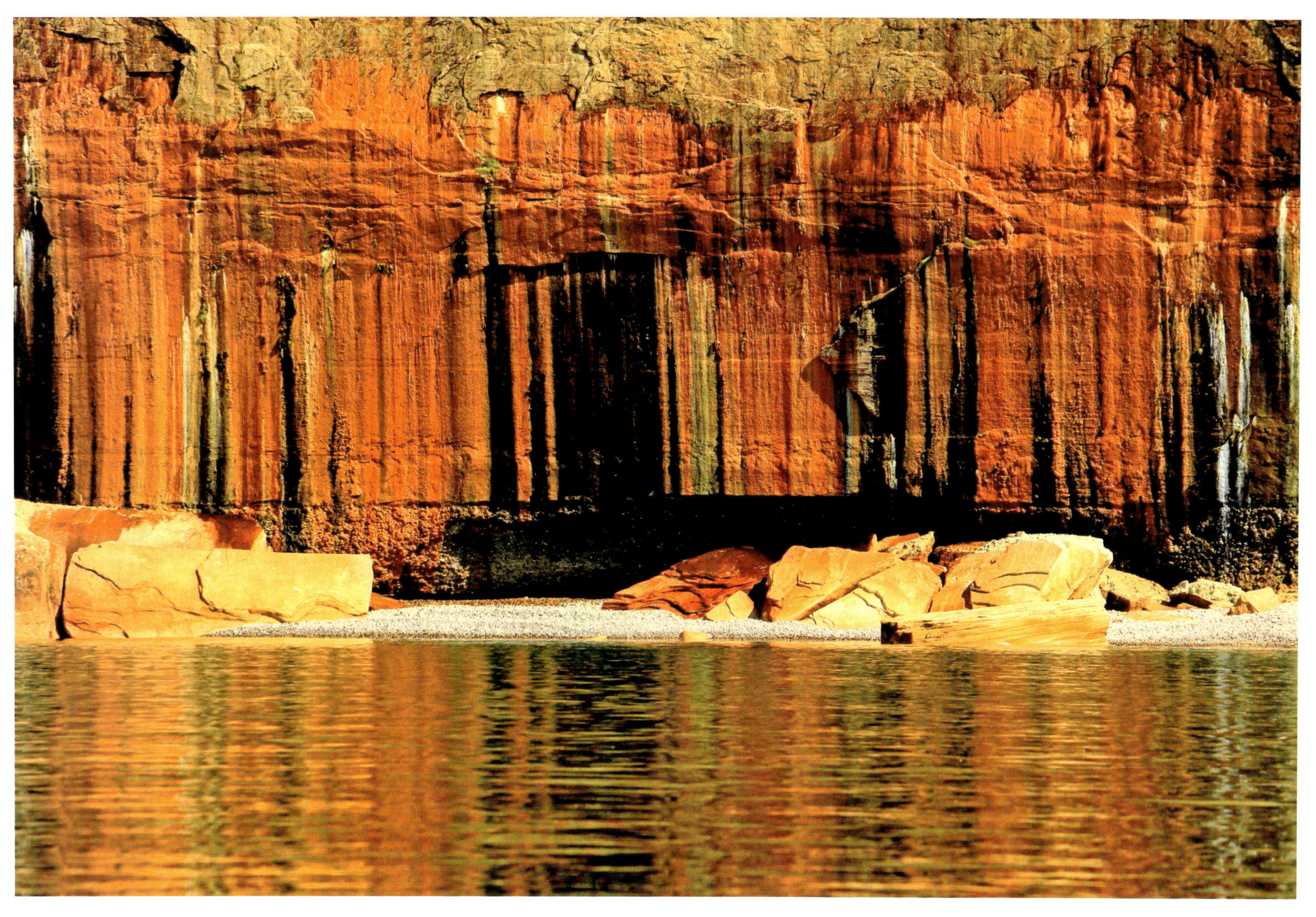

Fire Wall

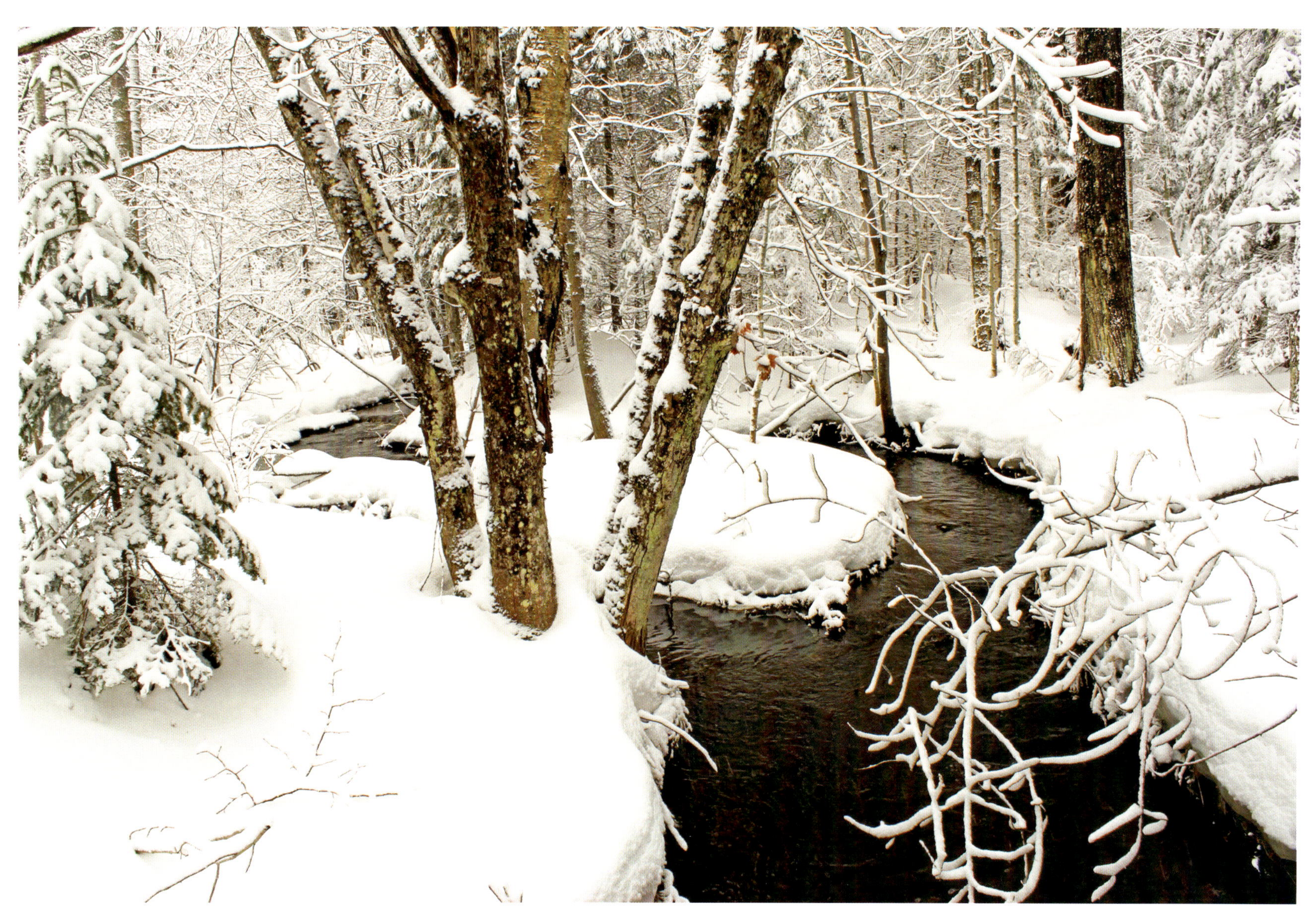

Around the Bend

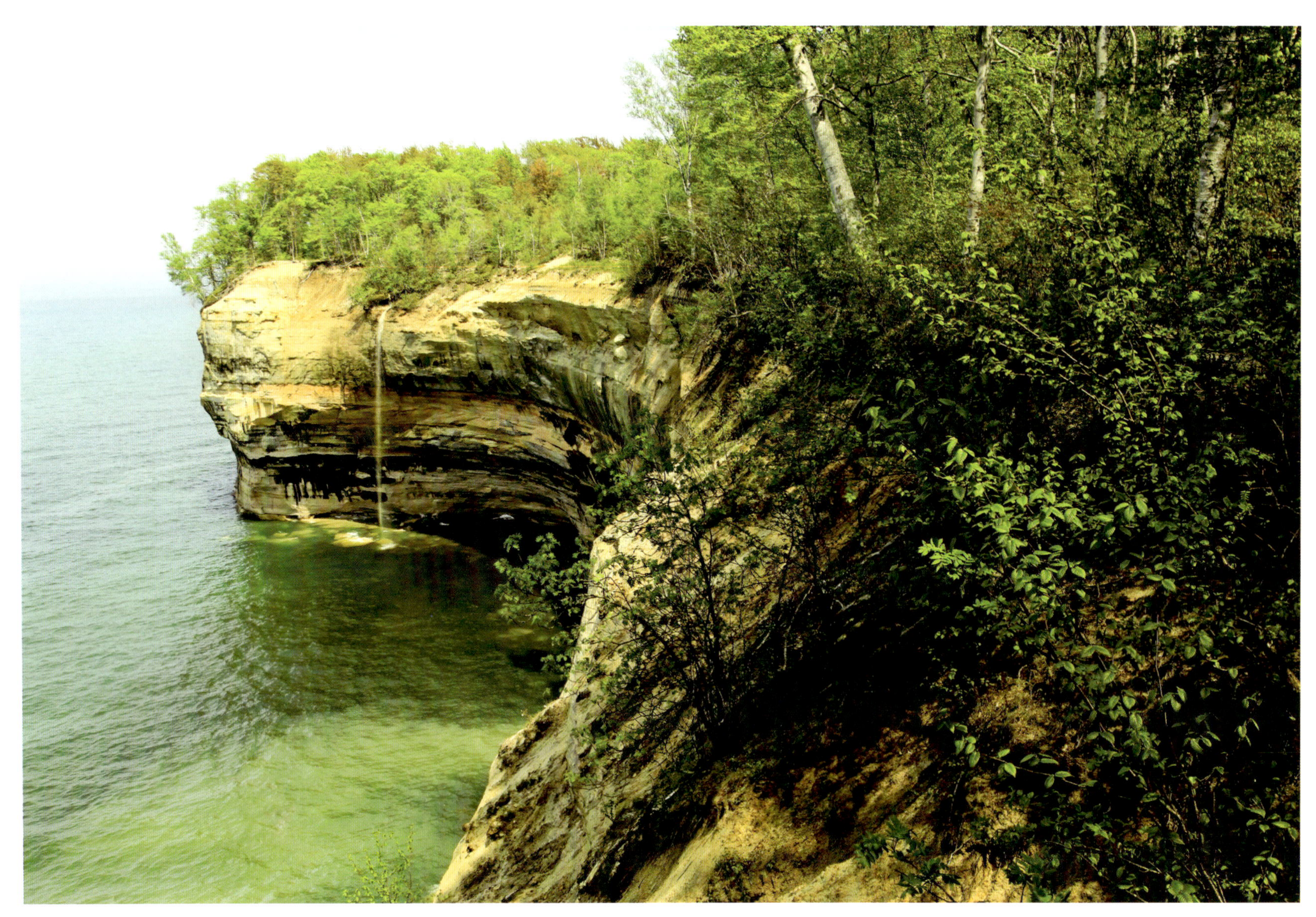

Emerald Bay: Between Chapel and Beaver Beach

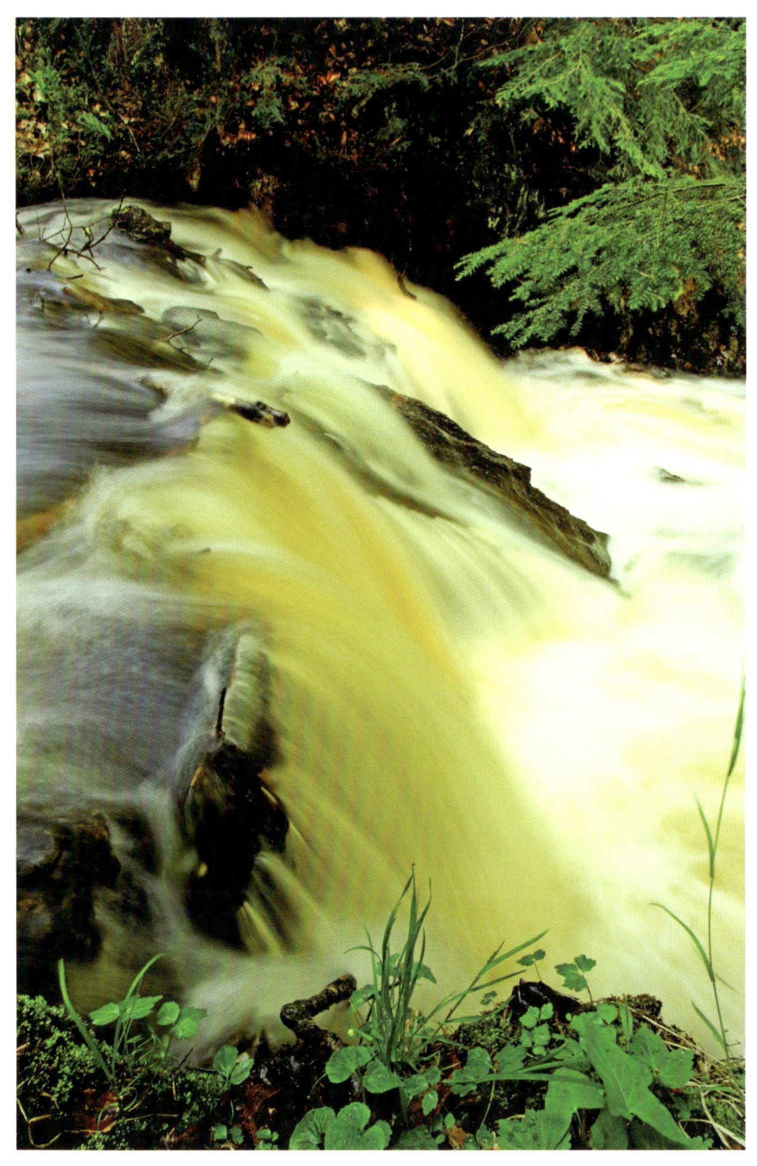

Water Slide: Chapel Falls

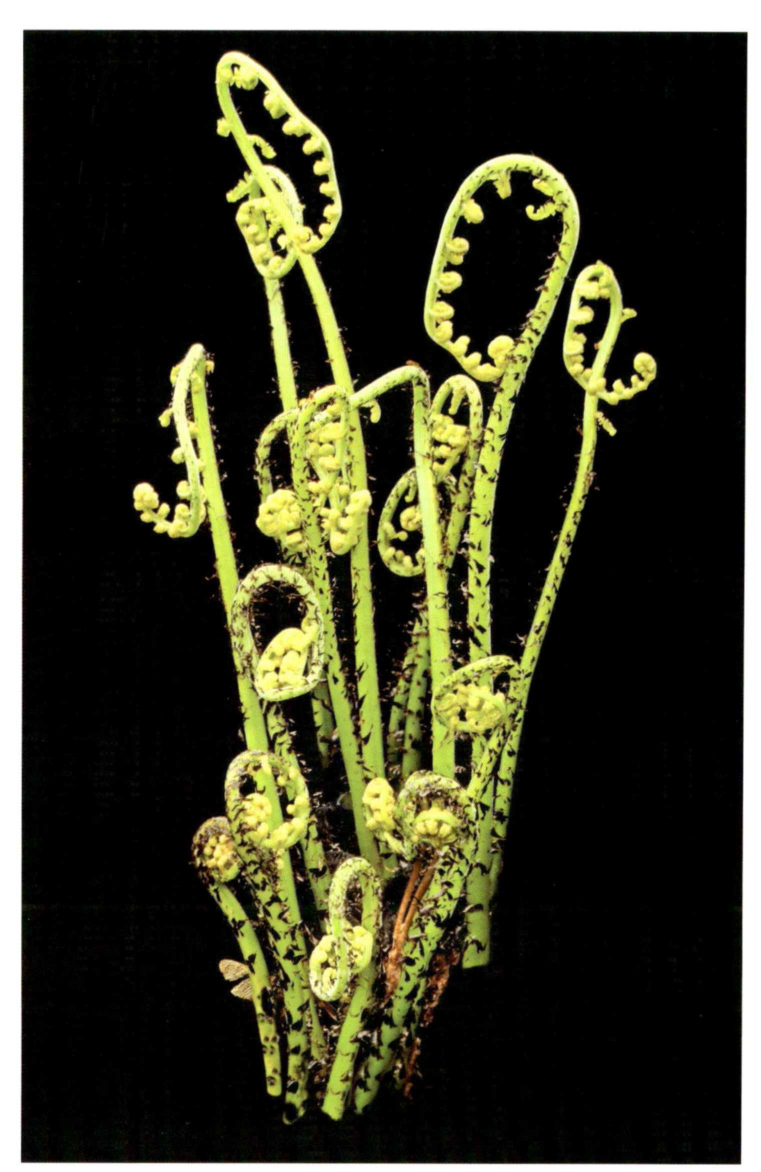

Corkscrew

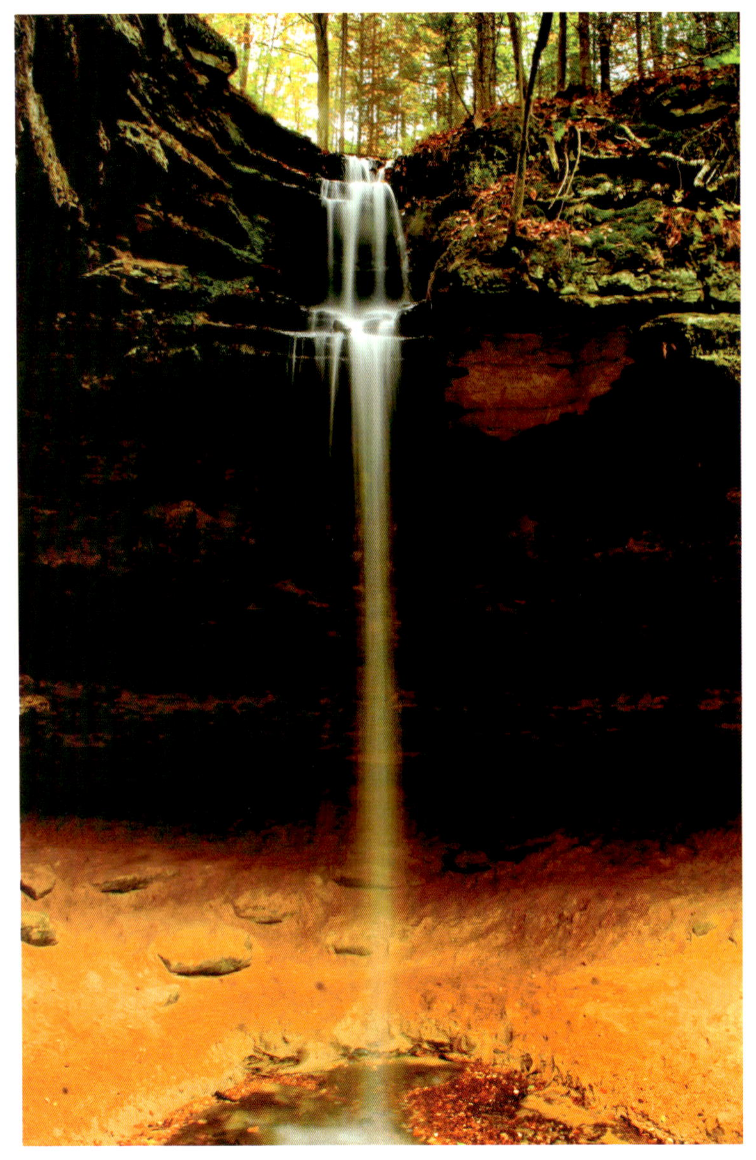

White Gold: Twin Falls

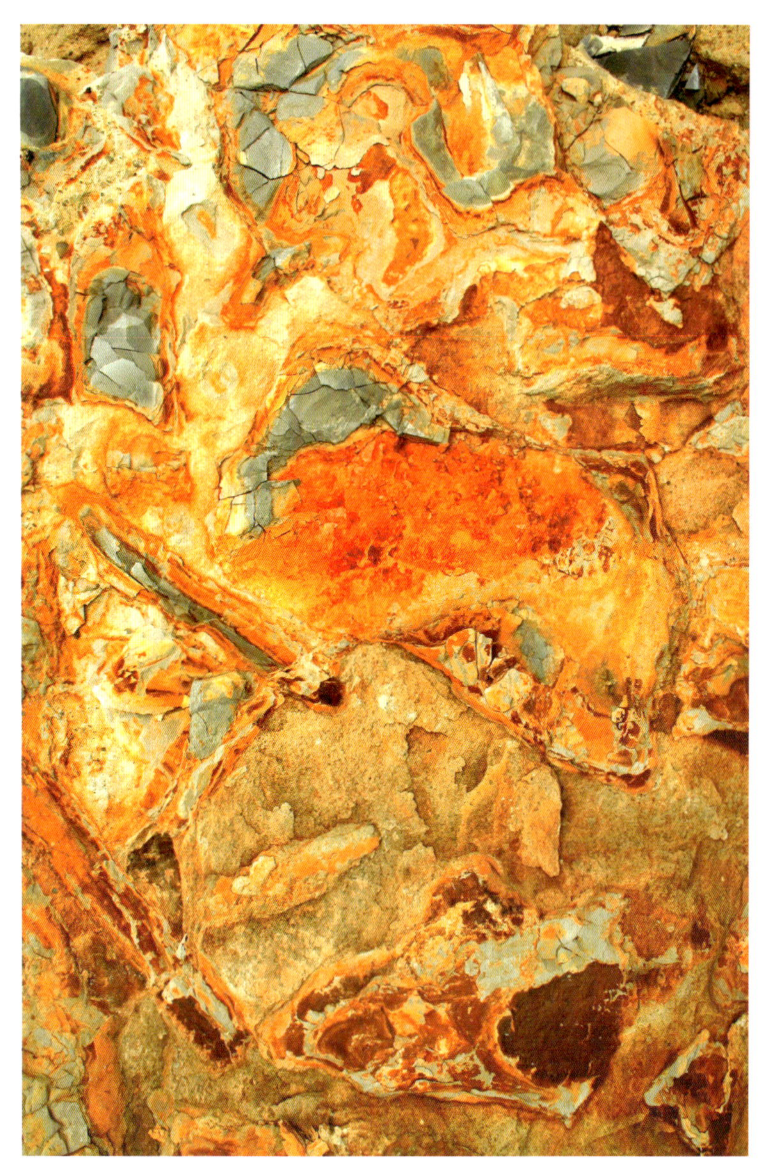

Painter's Palette

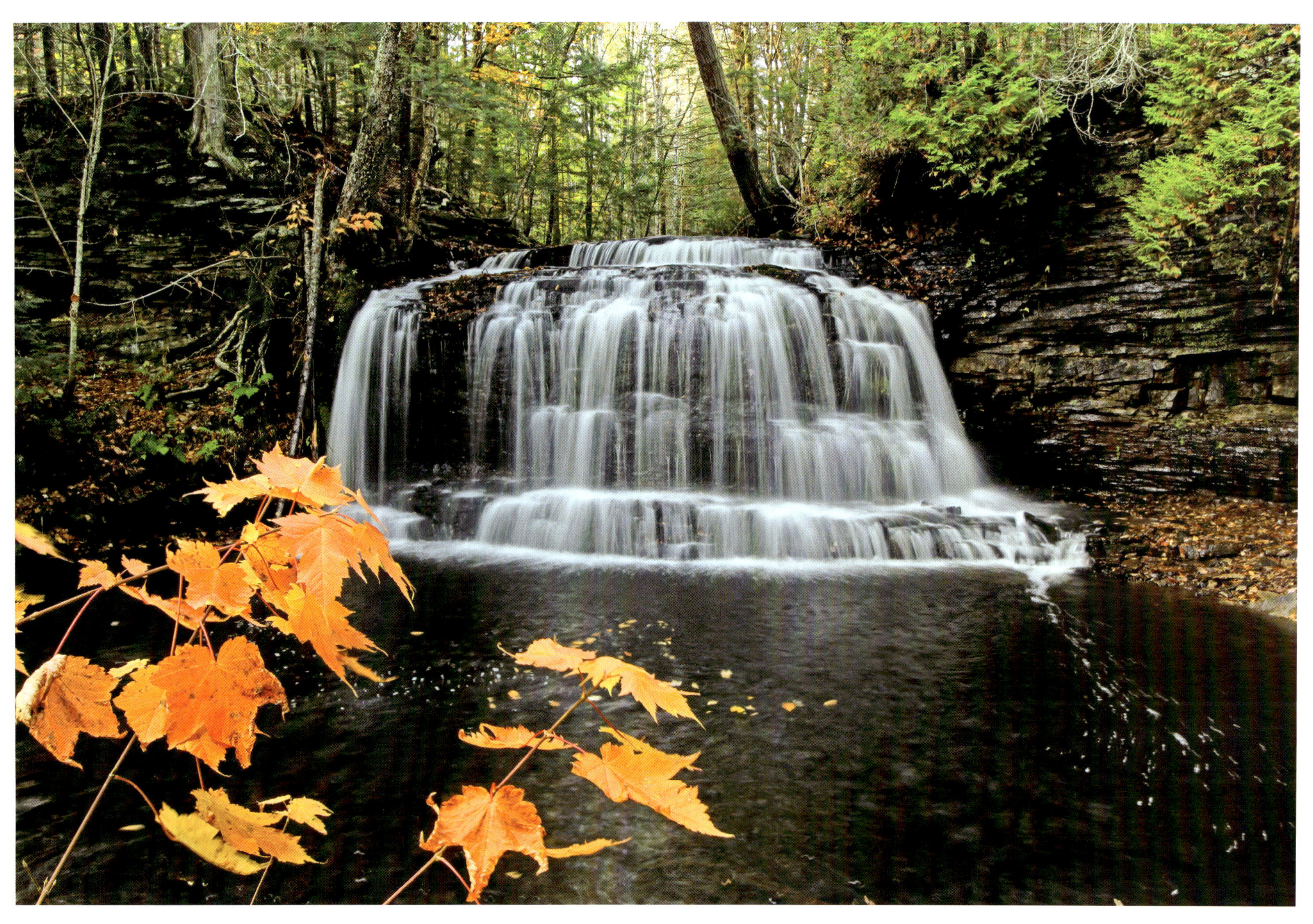

Rolling Down the River: Rock River Falls

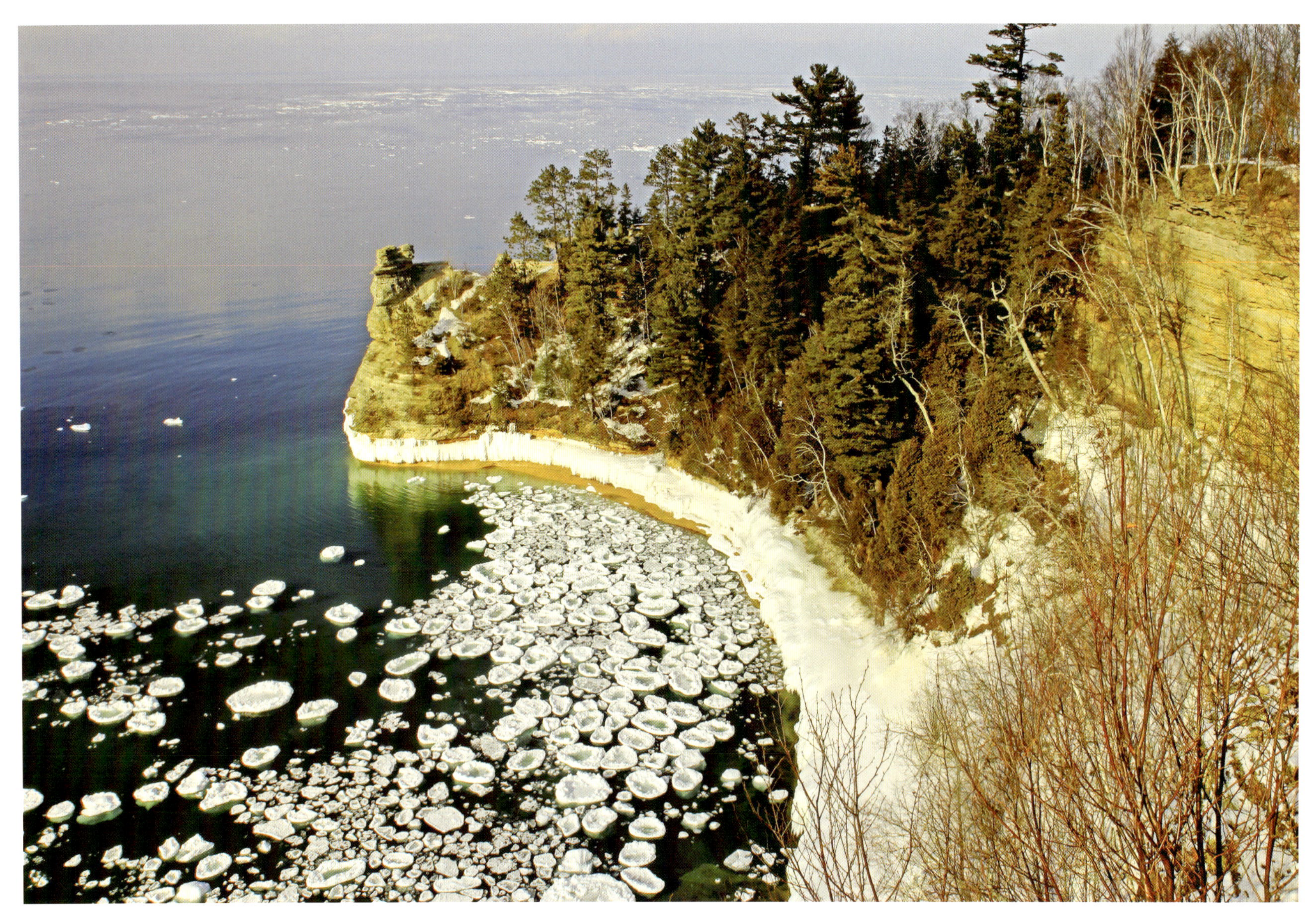

Ice Castles

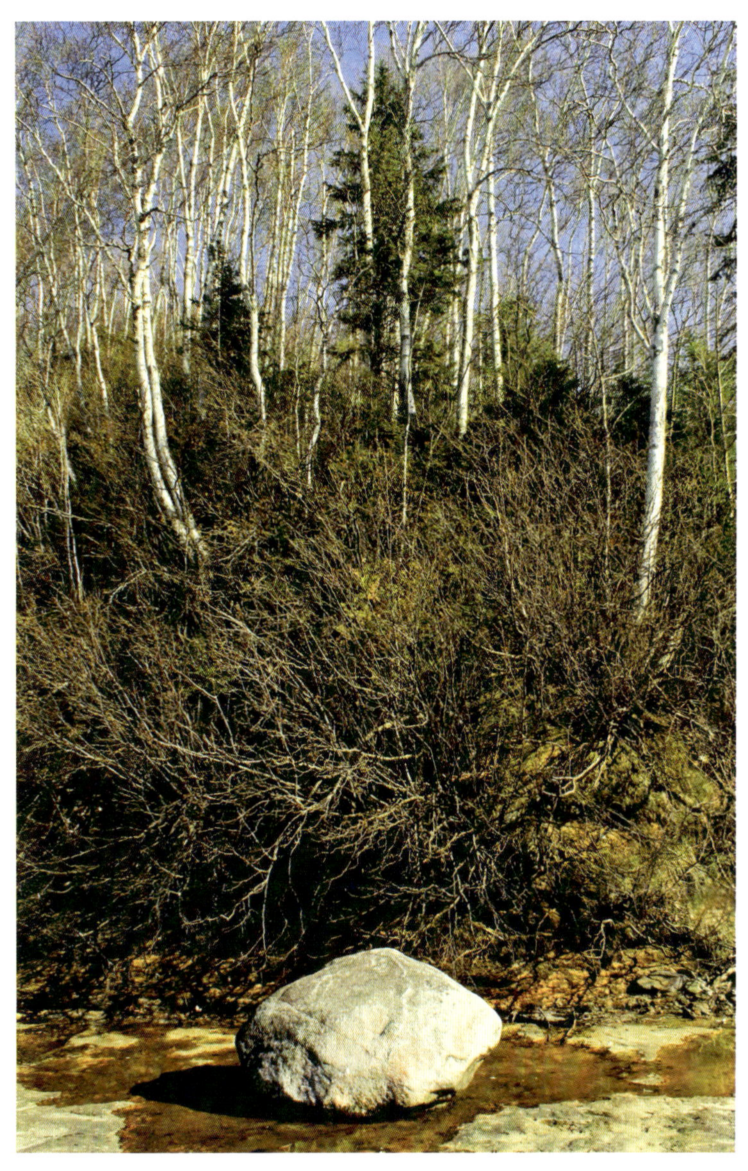

Rock Bottom

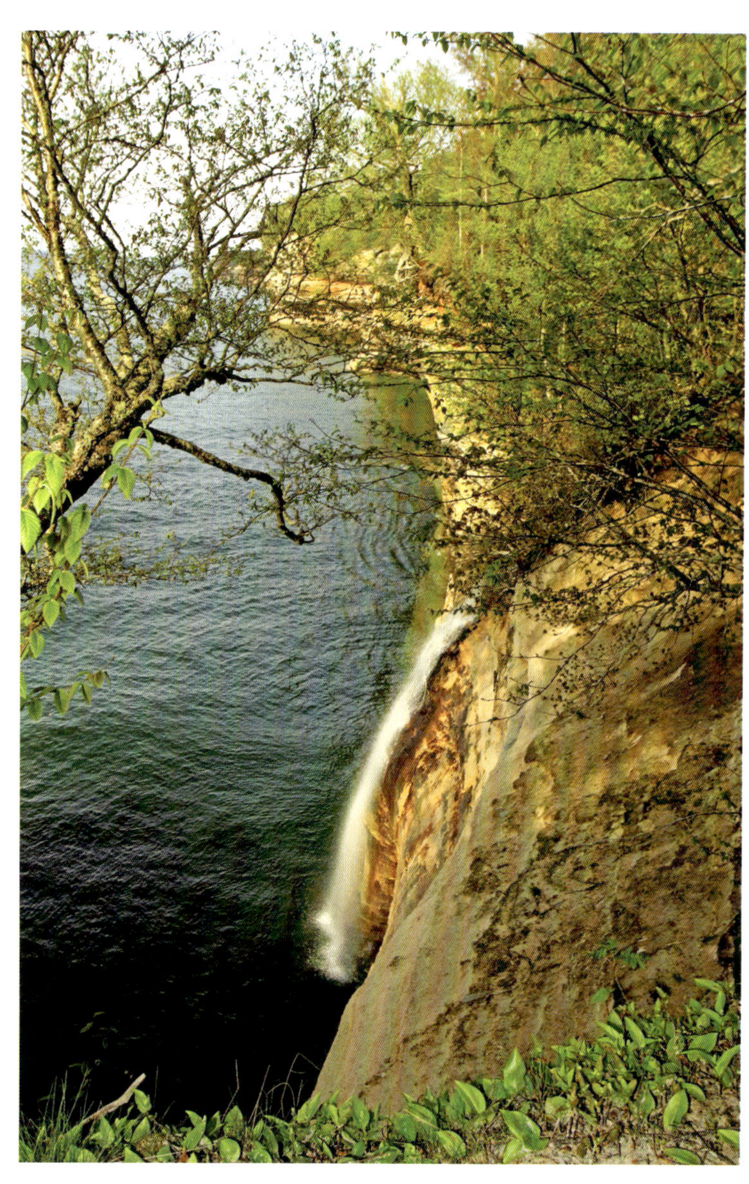

Sun Shower

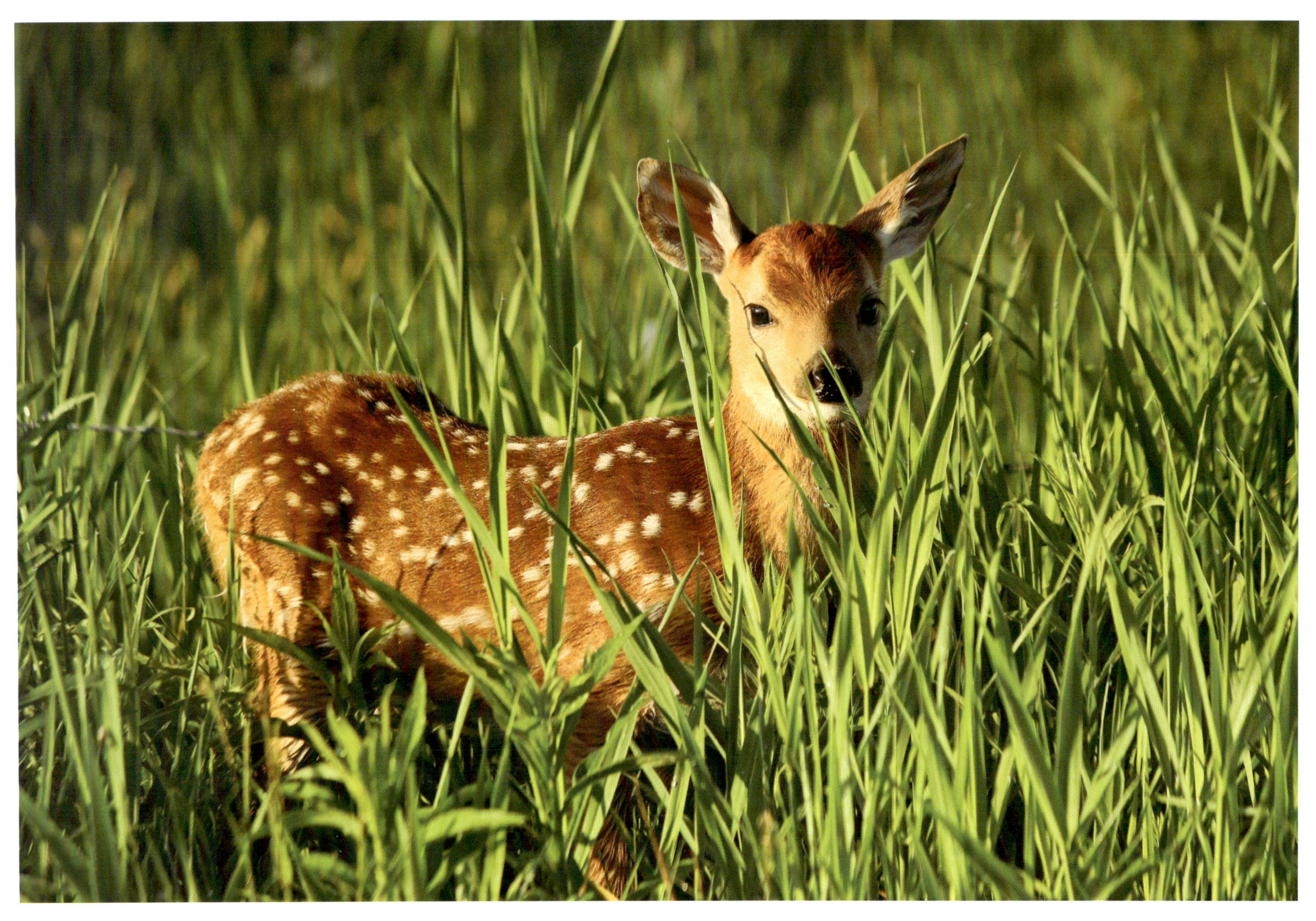

Spotted

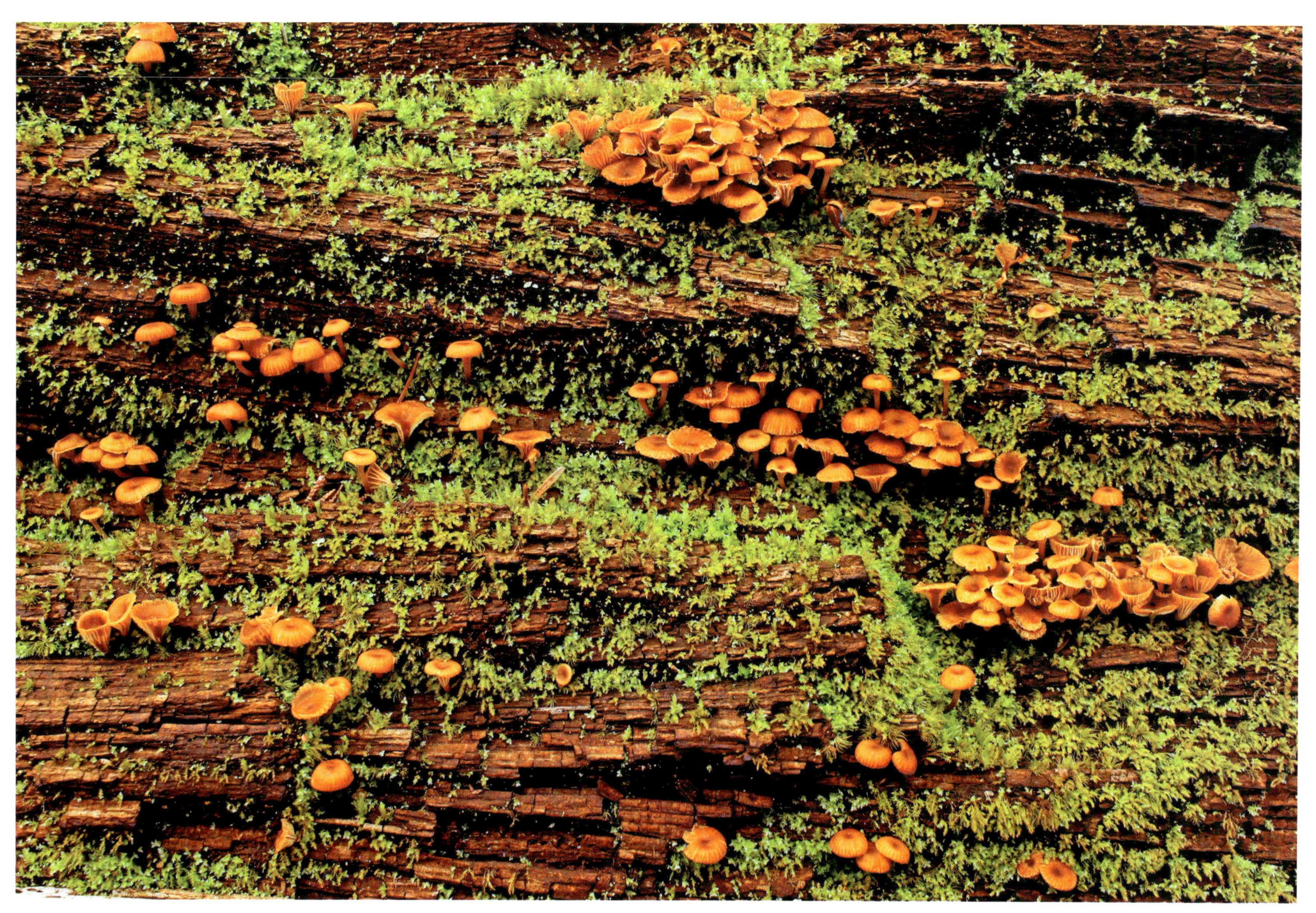

Like a Bump on a Log

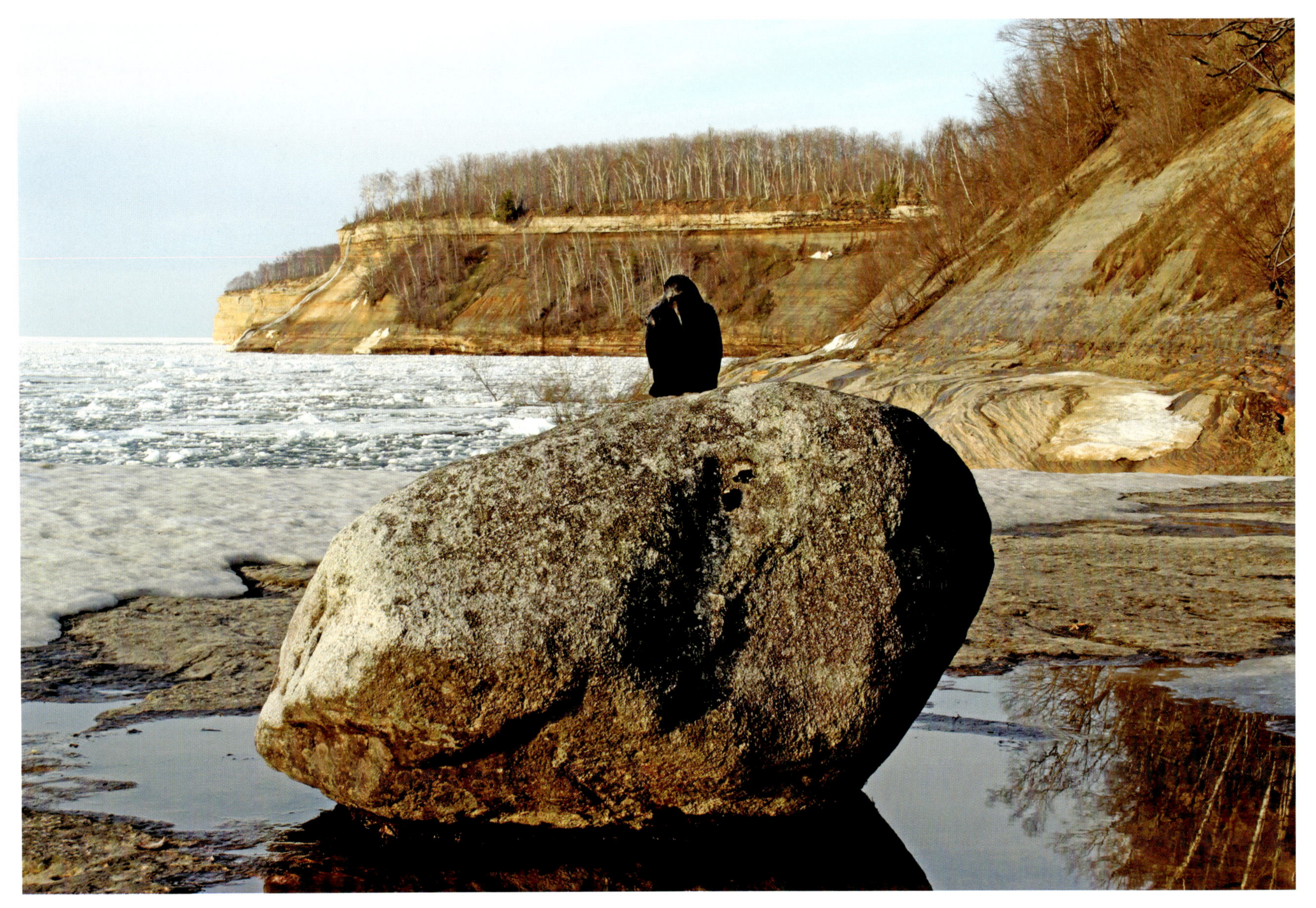

Parson's Pulpit

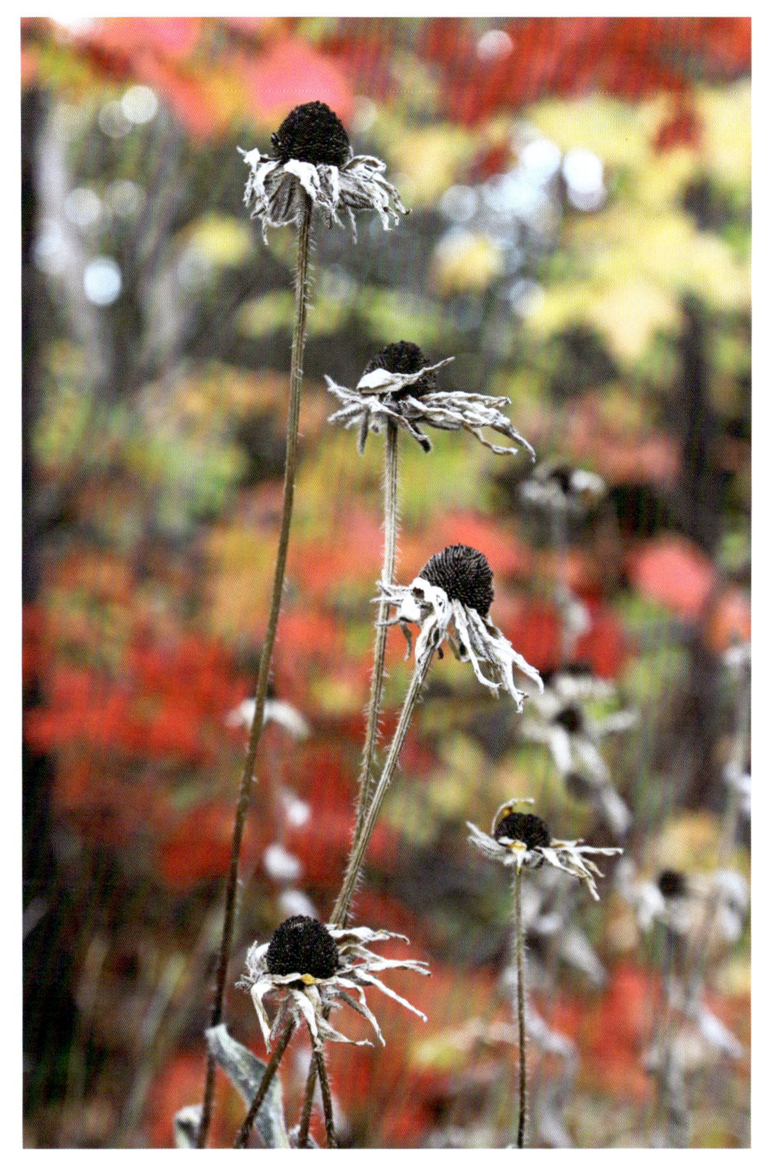

Growing Old Gracefully

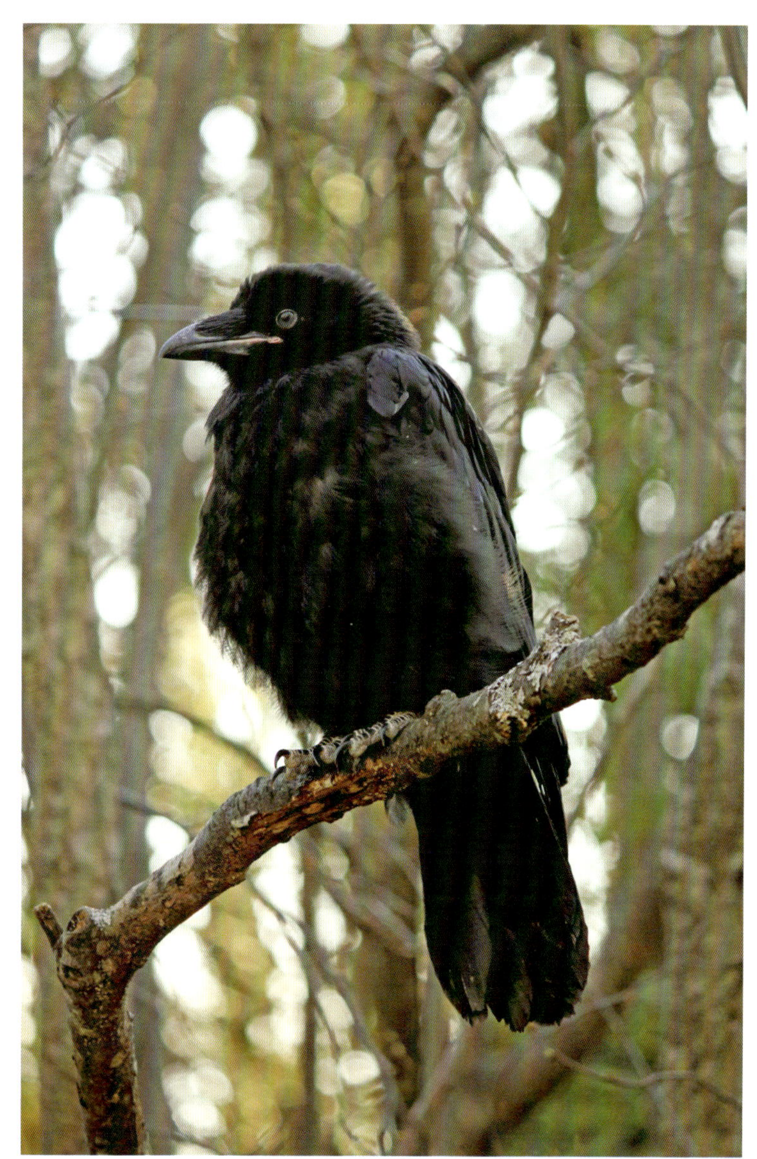

Linda

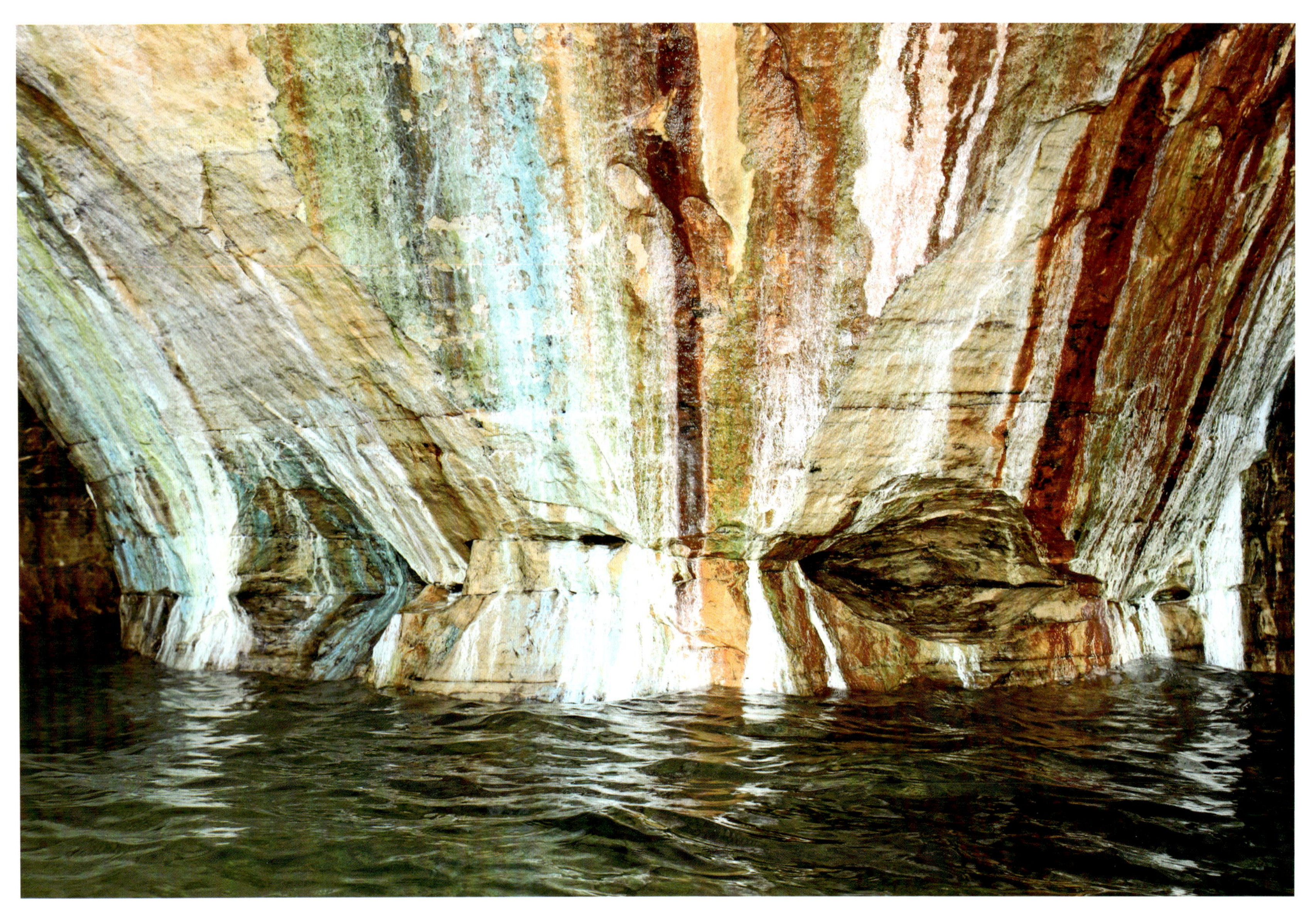

Masquerade

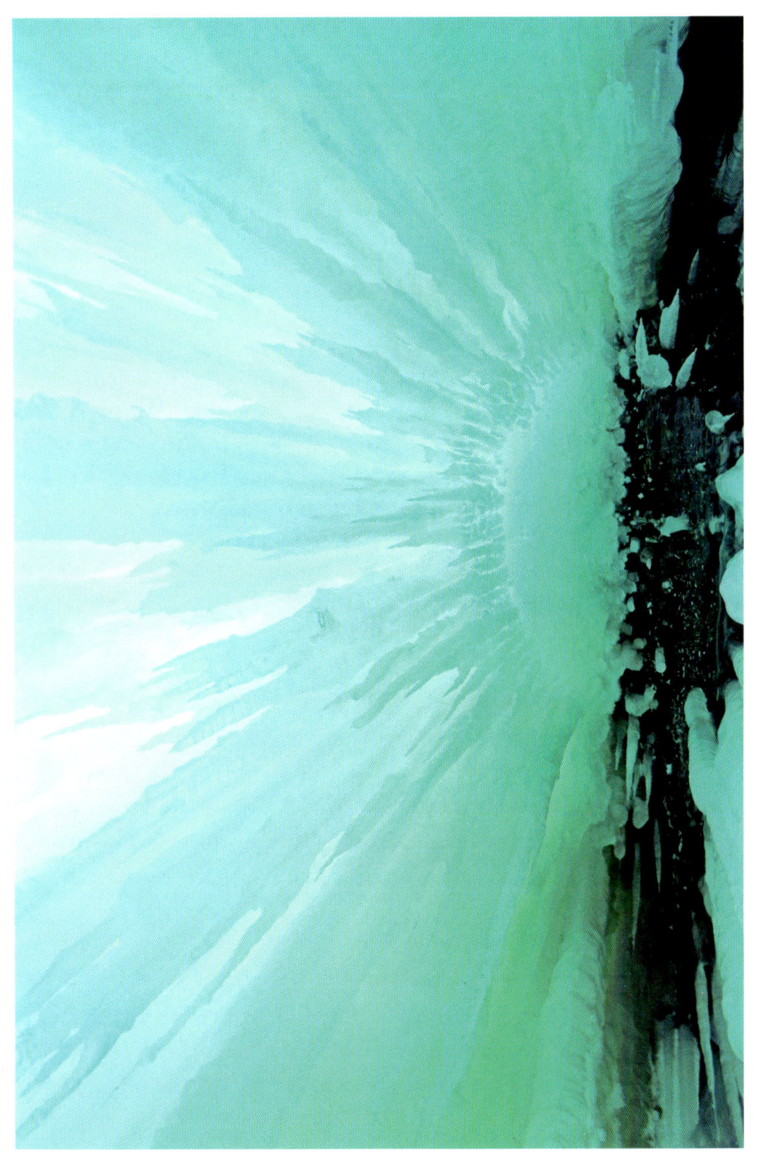

Blue Rays

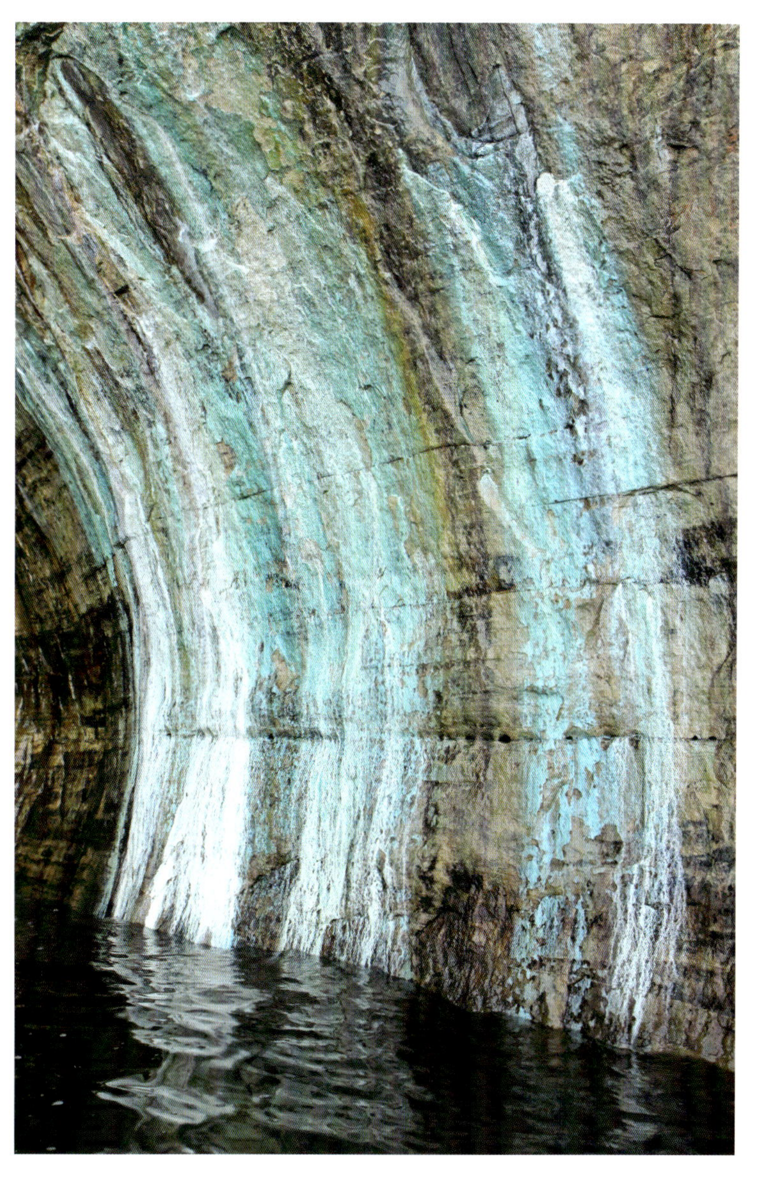

Out of the Blue

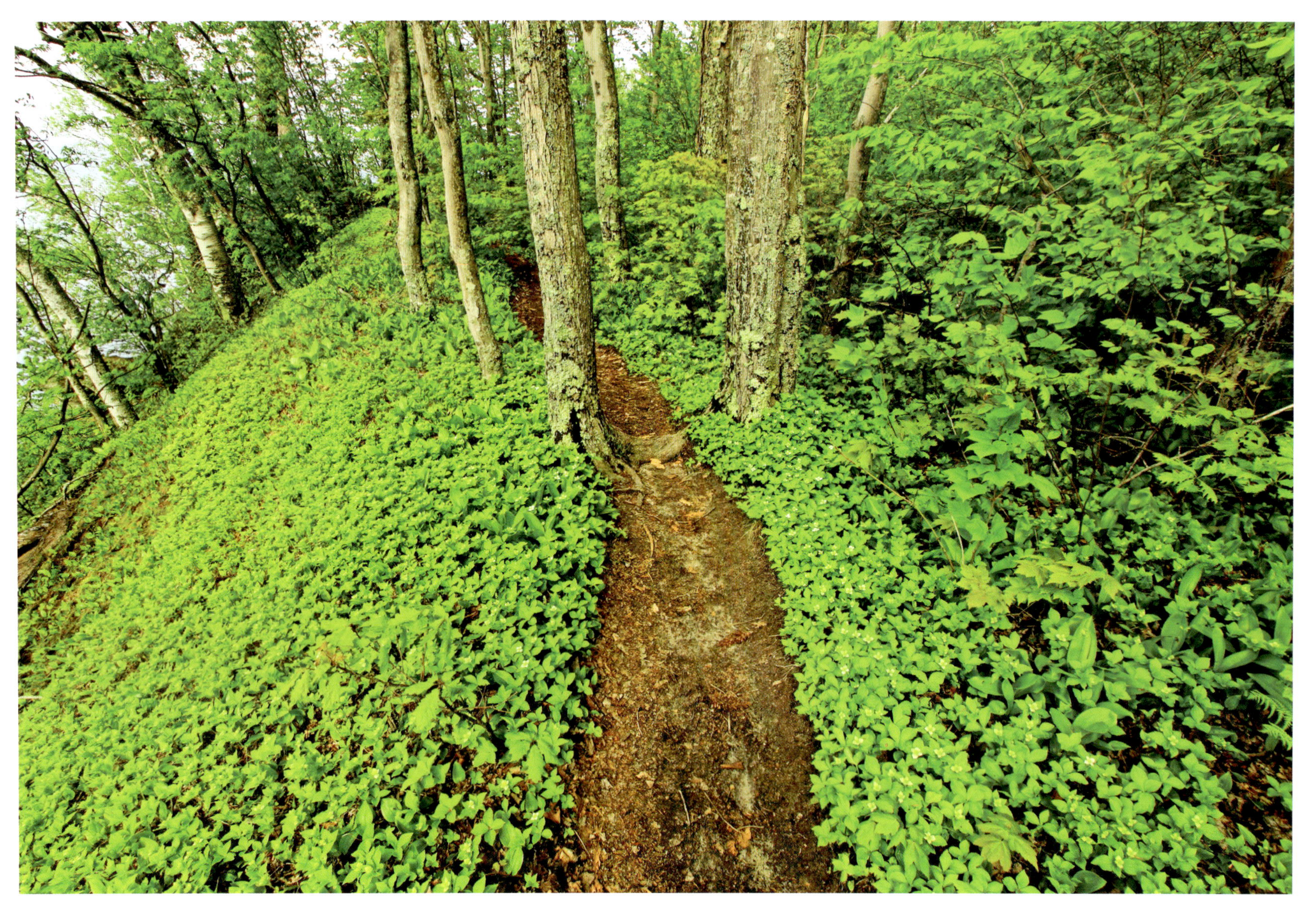

Bunch Berry Ridge

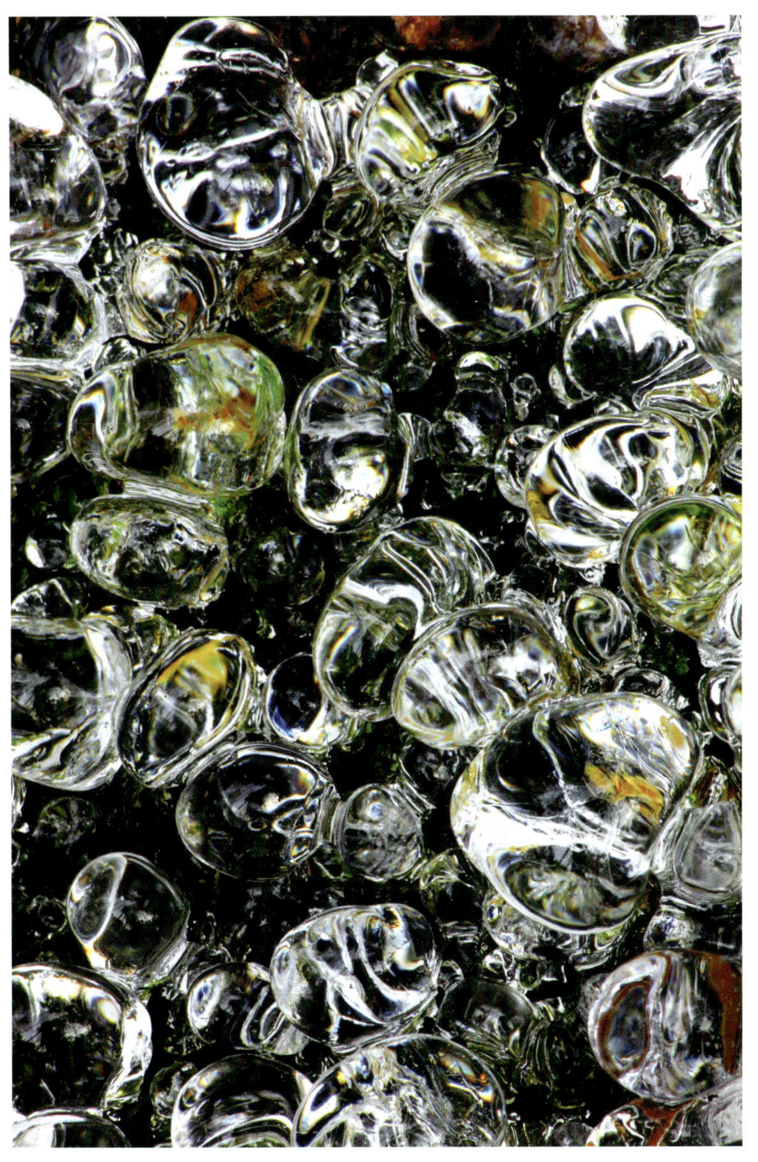

Crystal Balls

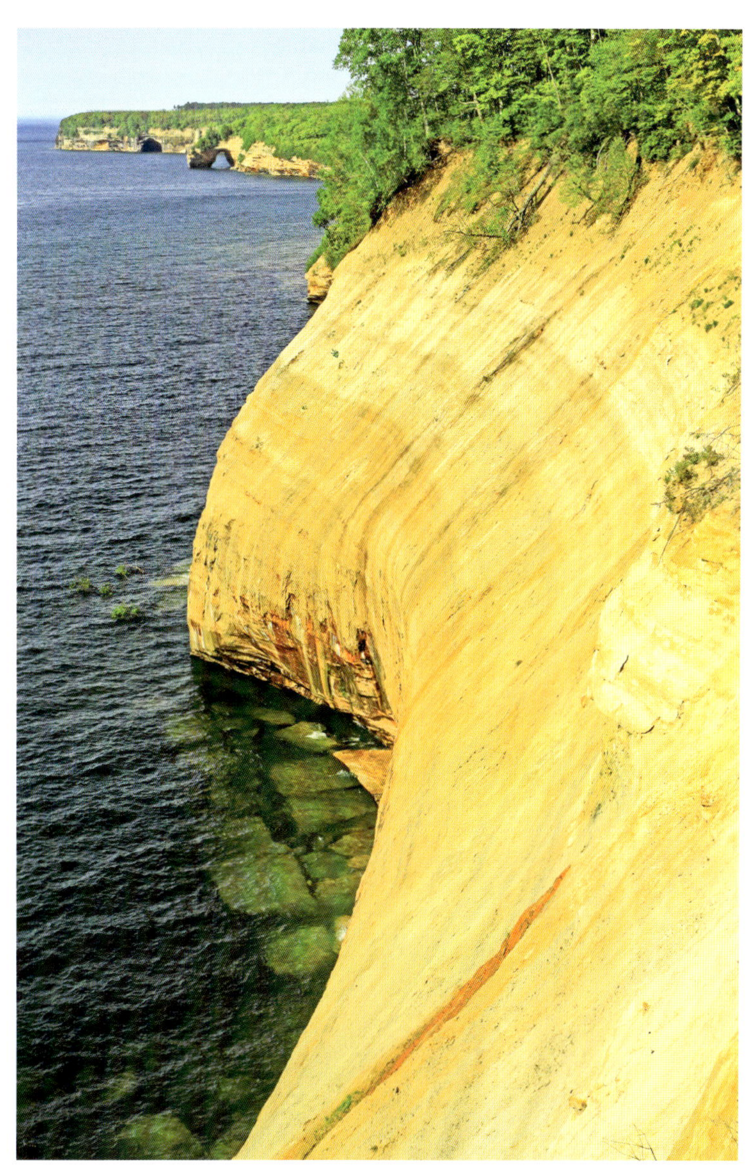

Fear of Falling

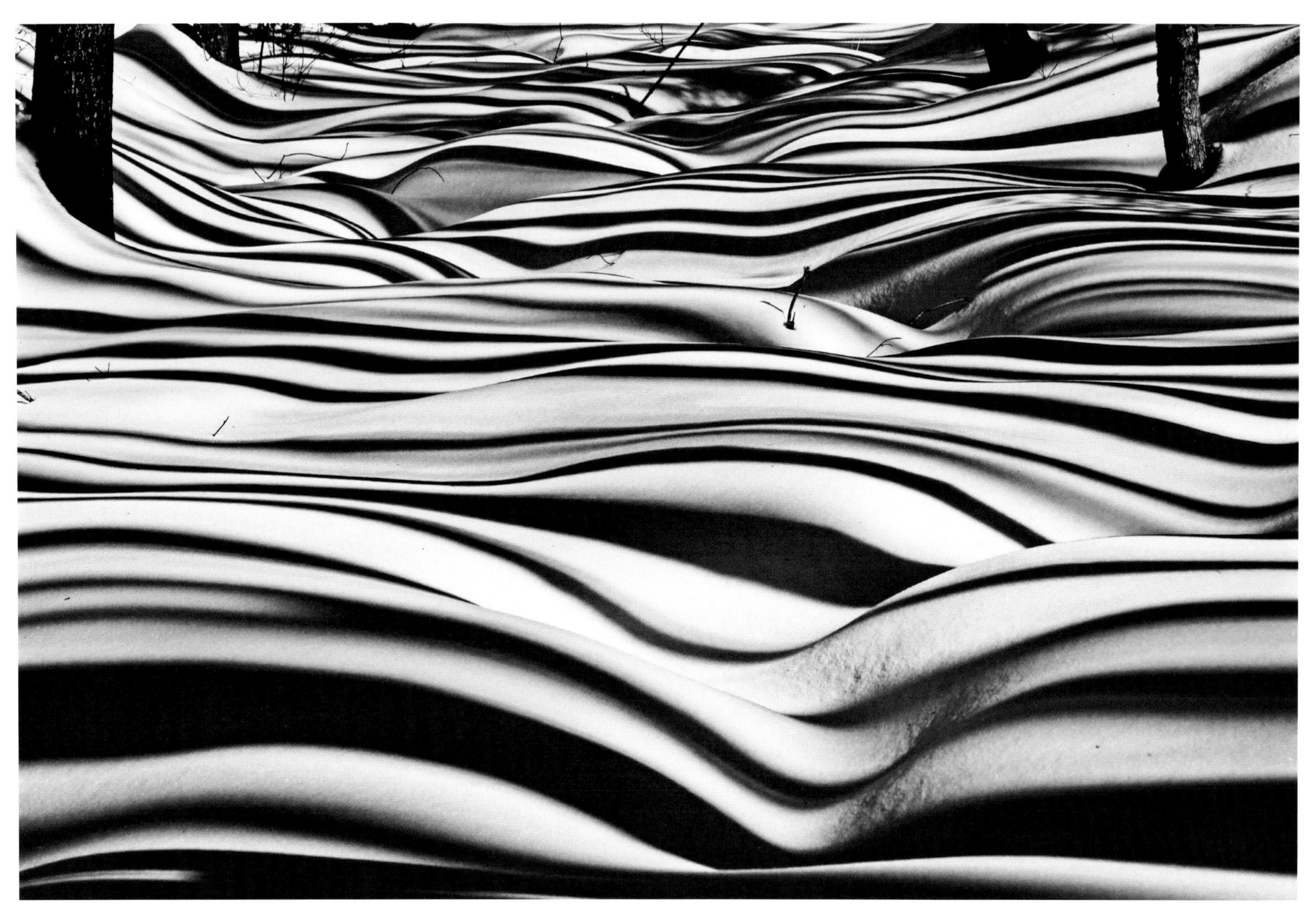

Zebra Stripes: Snowshoeing to Chapel Rock

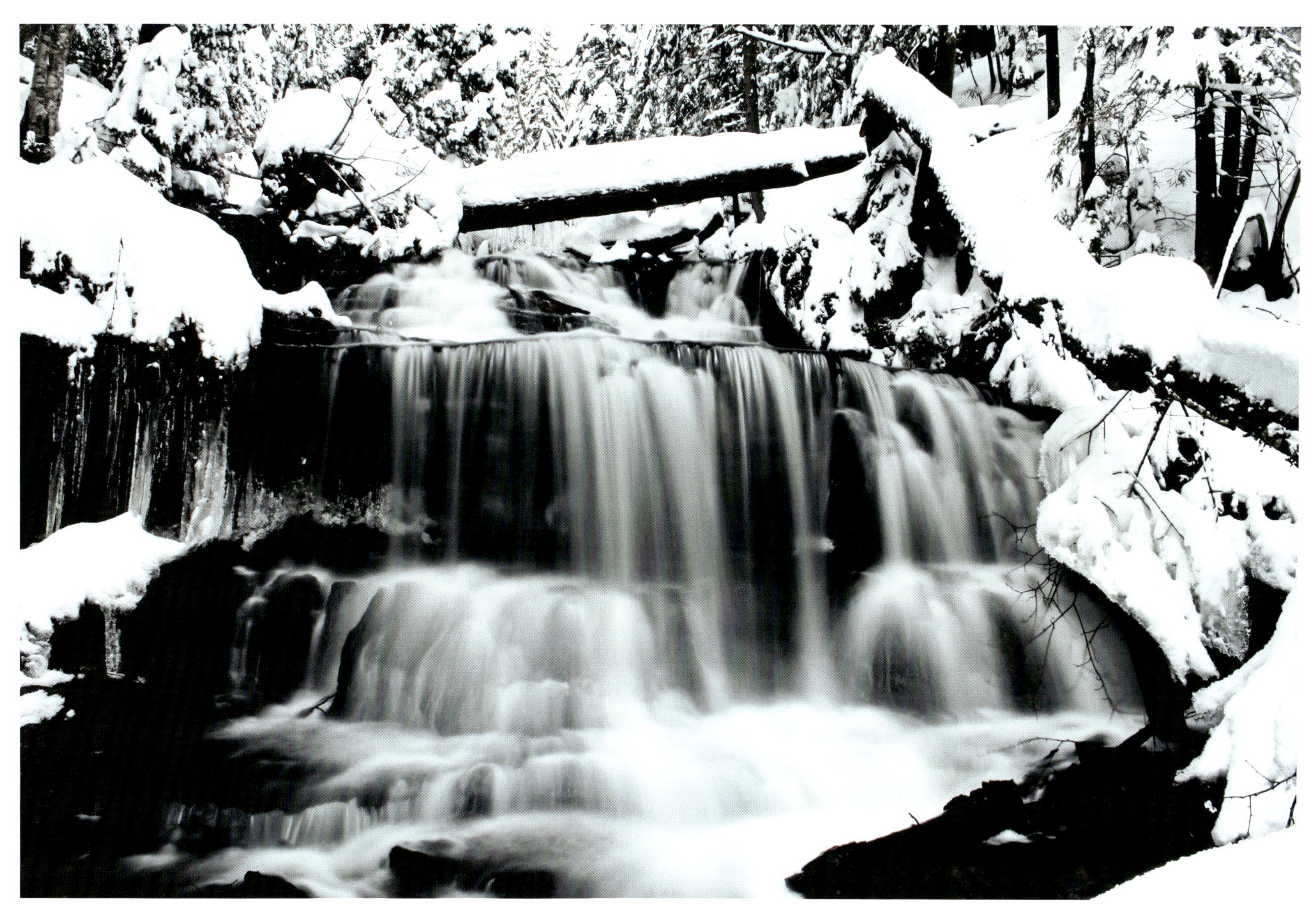

Snow White: Wagner Falls

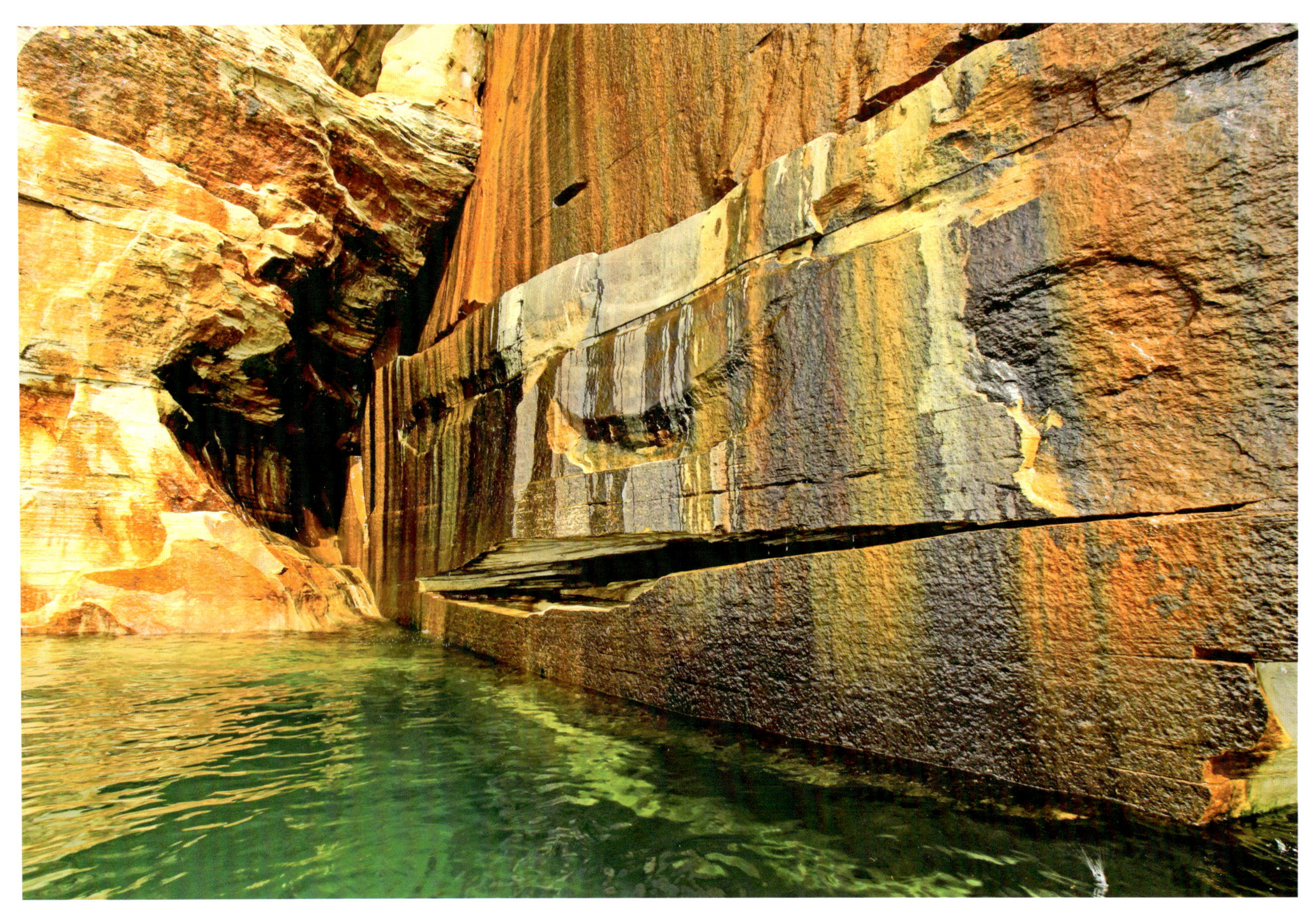

Counter Balance

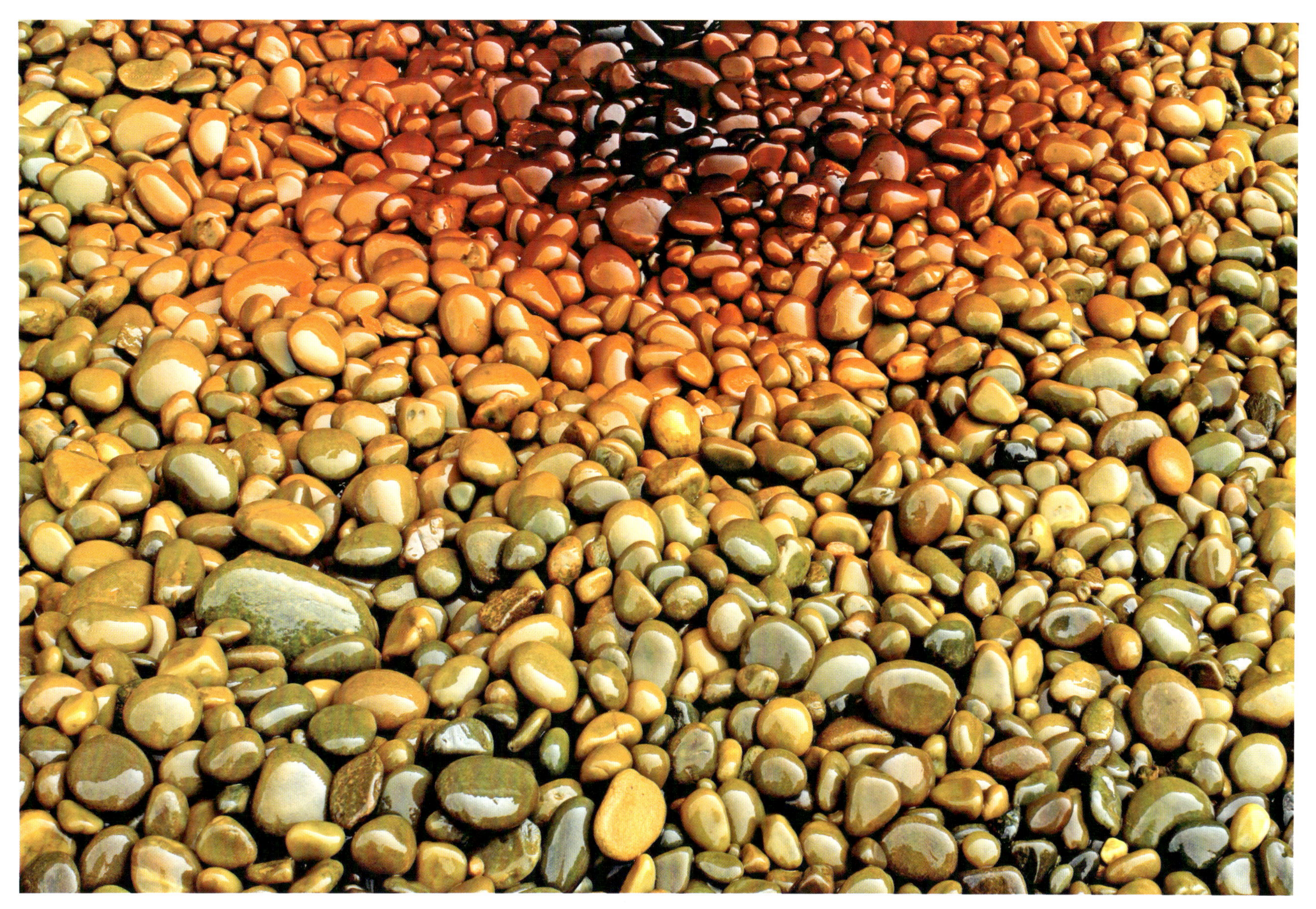

Rainbow Rocks

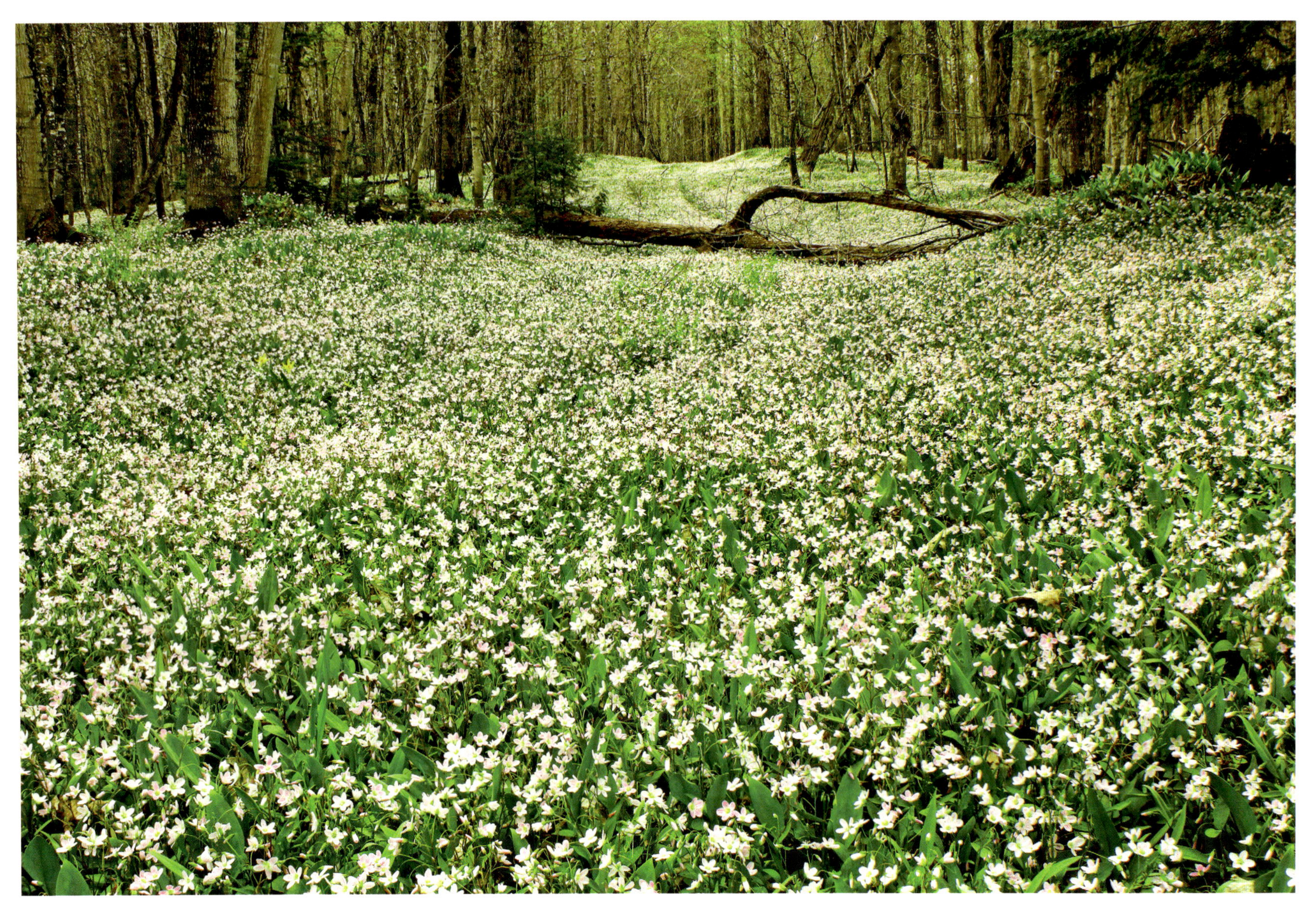

Road Less Traveled

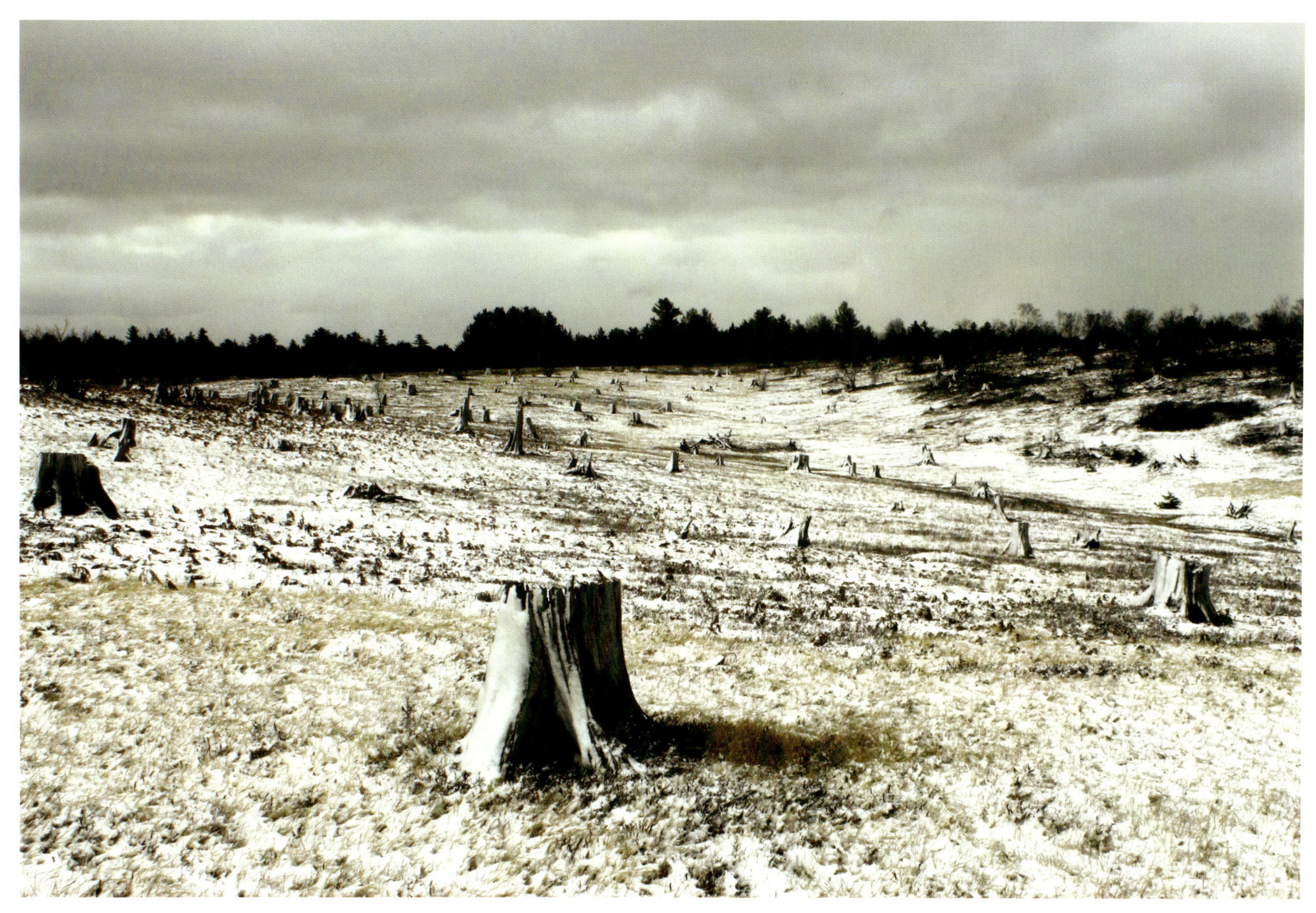

High Plains Drifter: Kingston Plains

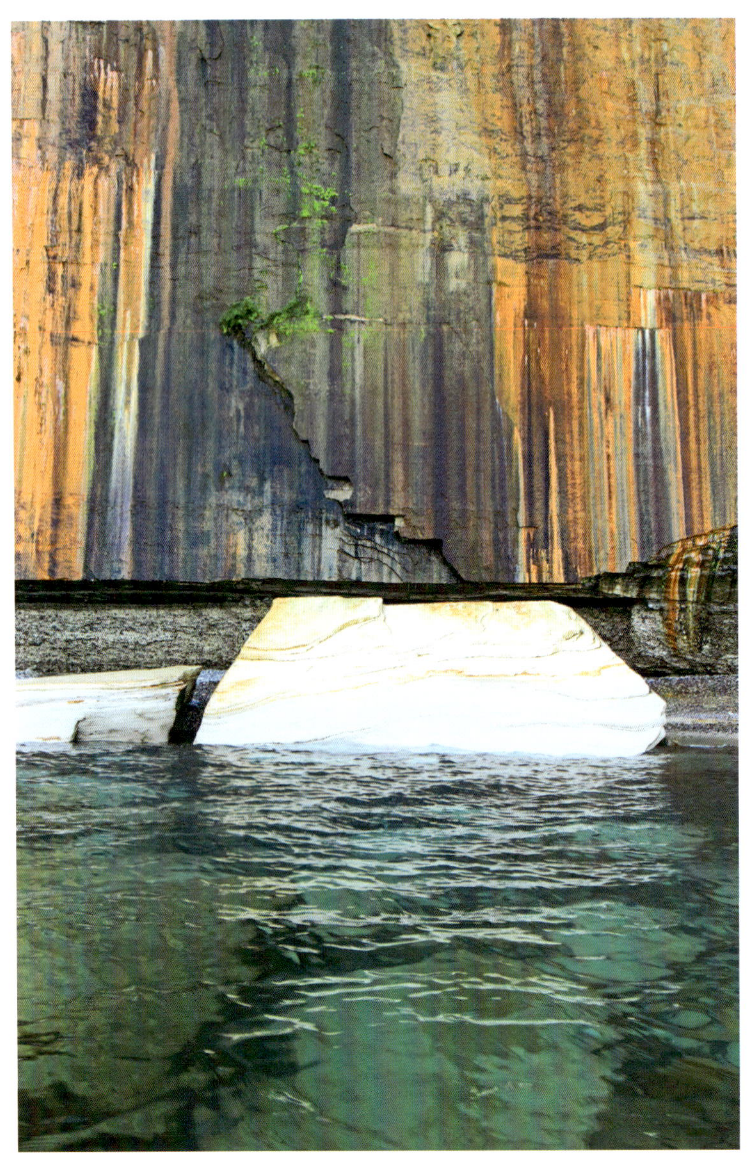

Manganese Madness

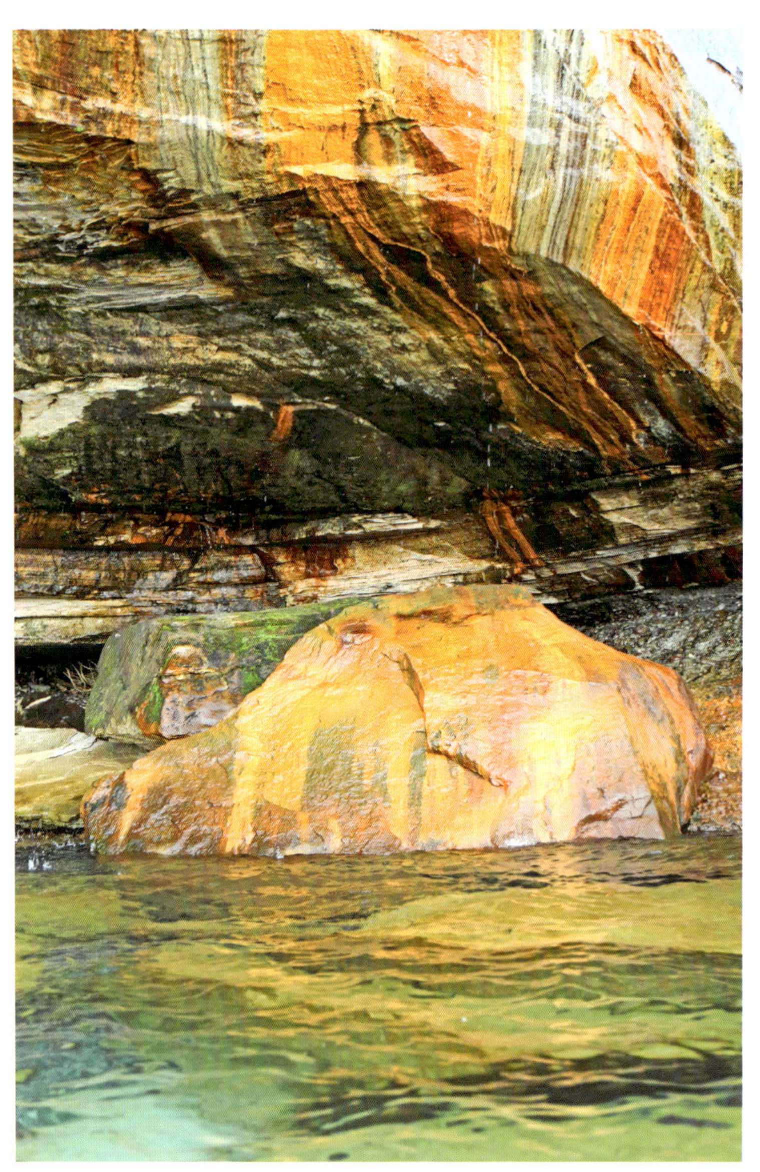

Orange Crush

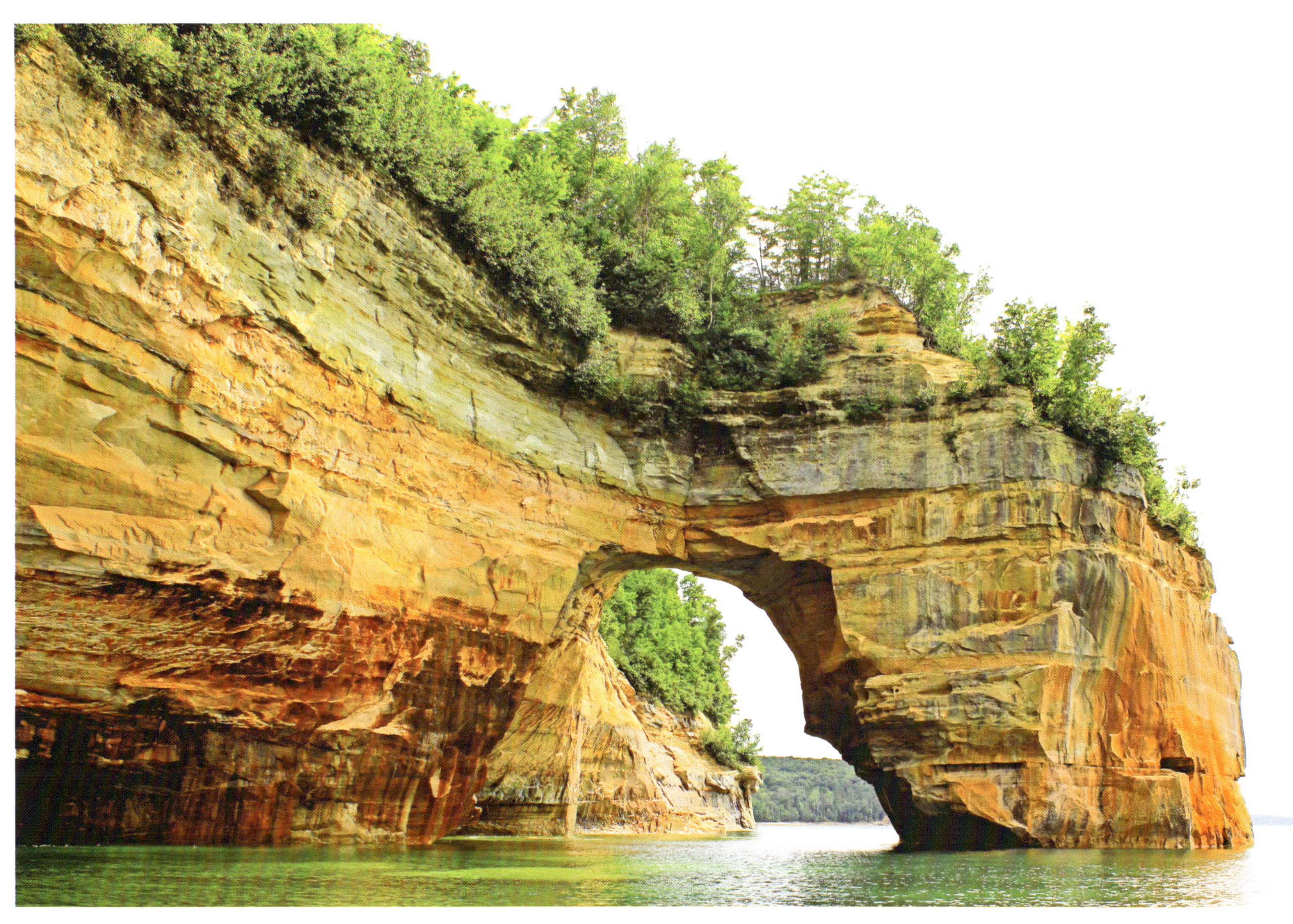

Water Under the Bridge

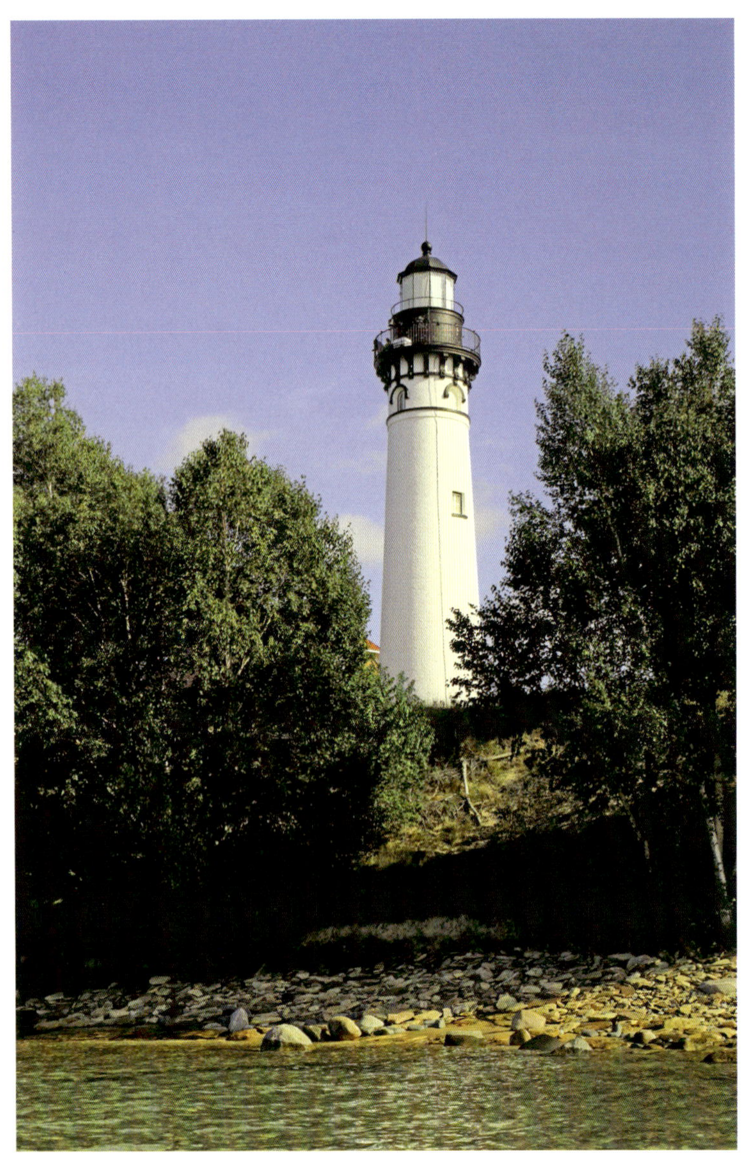

Keeping Vigil:
AuSable Lighthouse

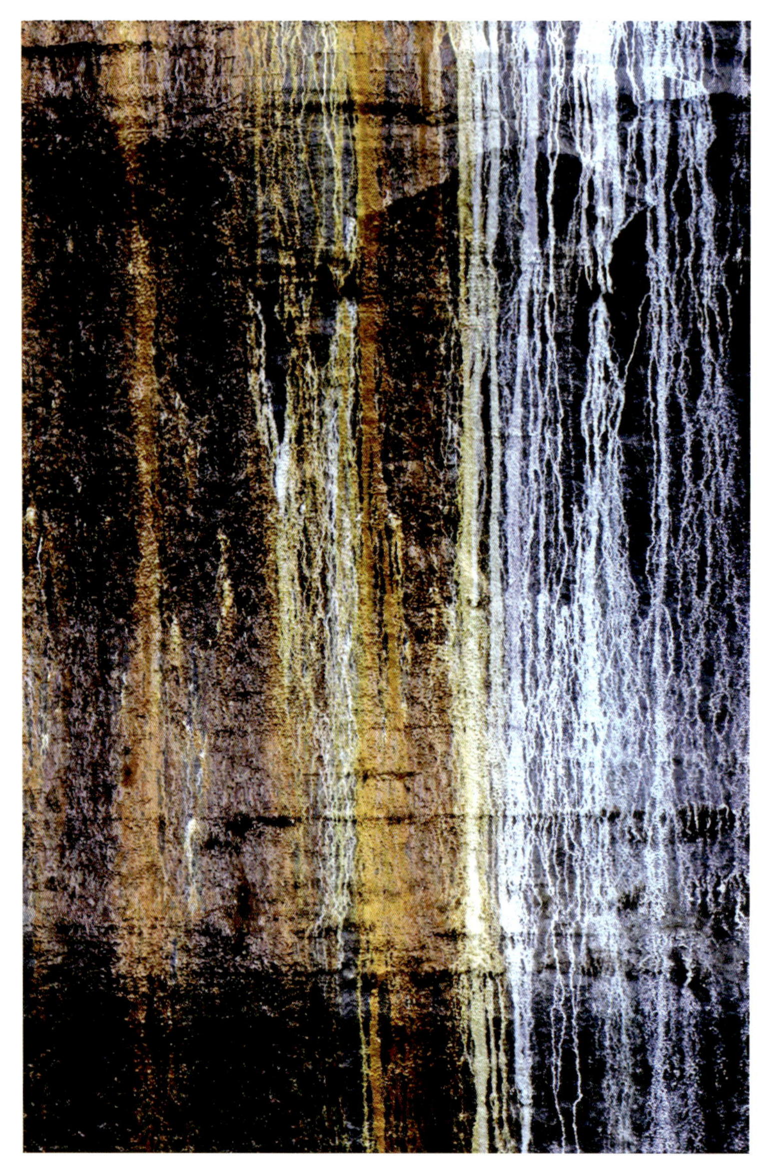

Blue Tears

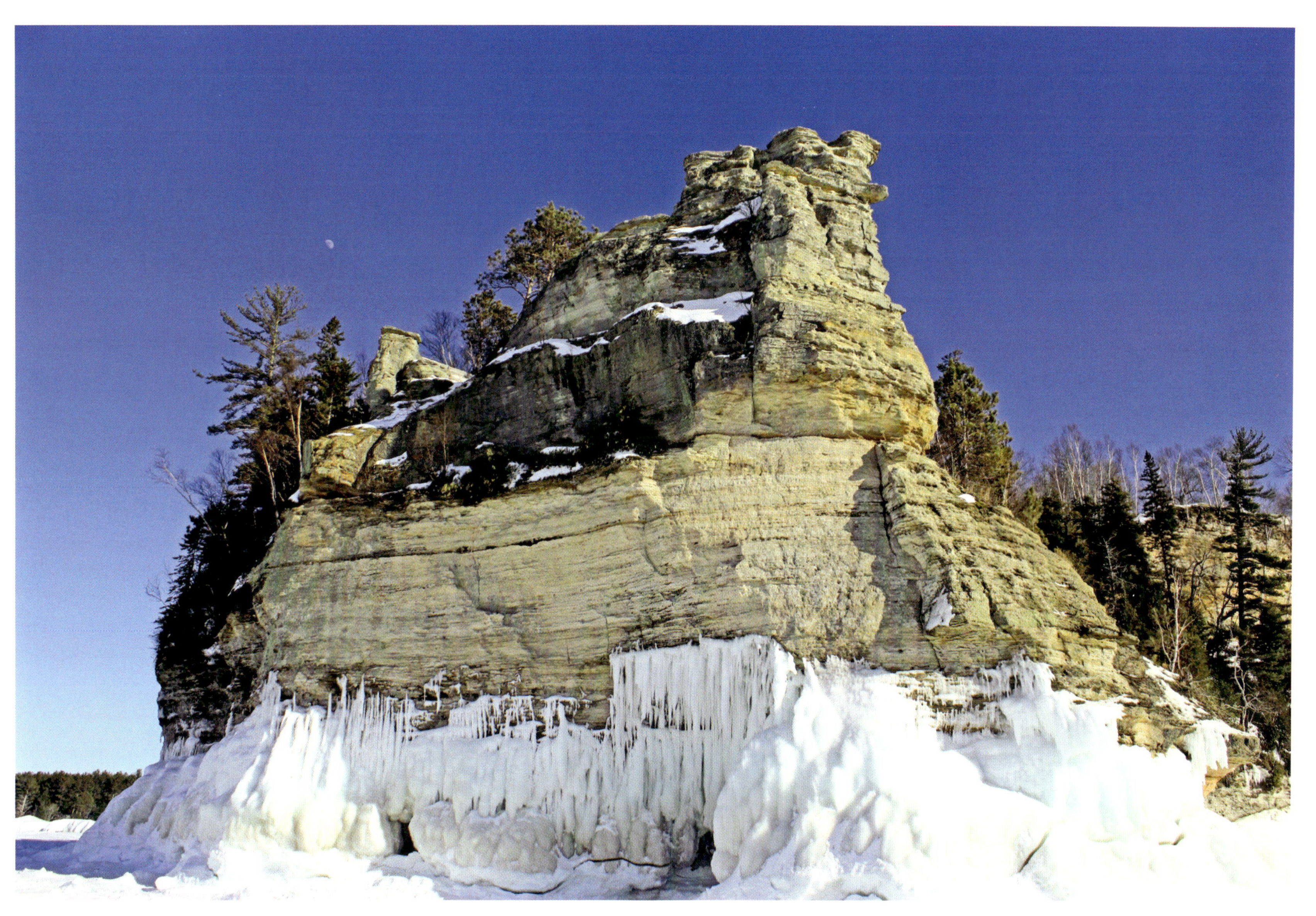

Once in a Blue Moon

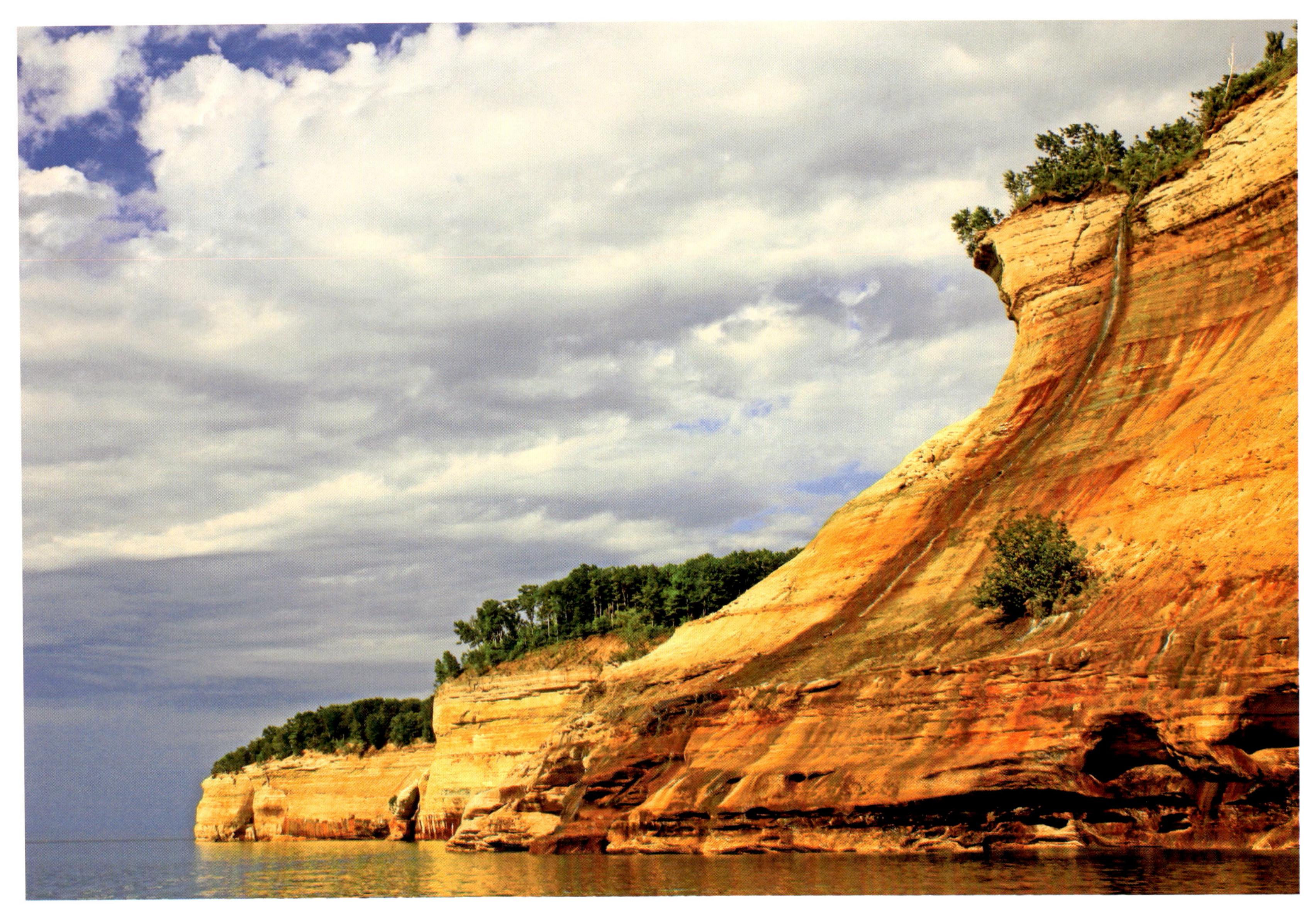

Sunset Bride: Bridal Veil Falls

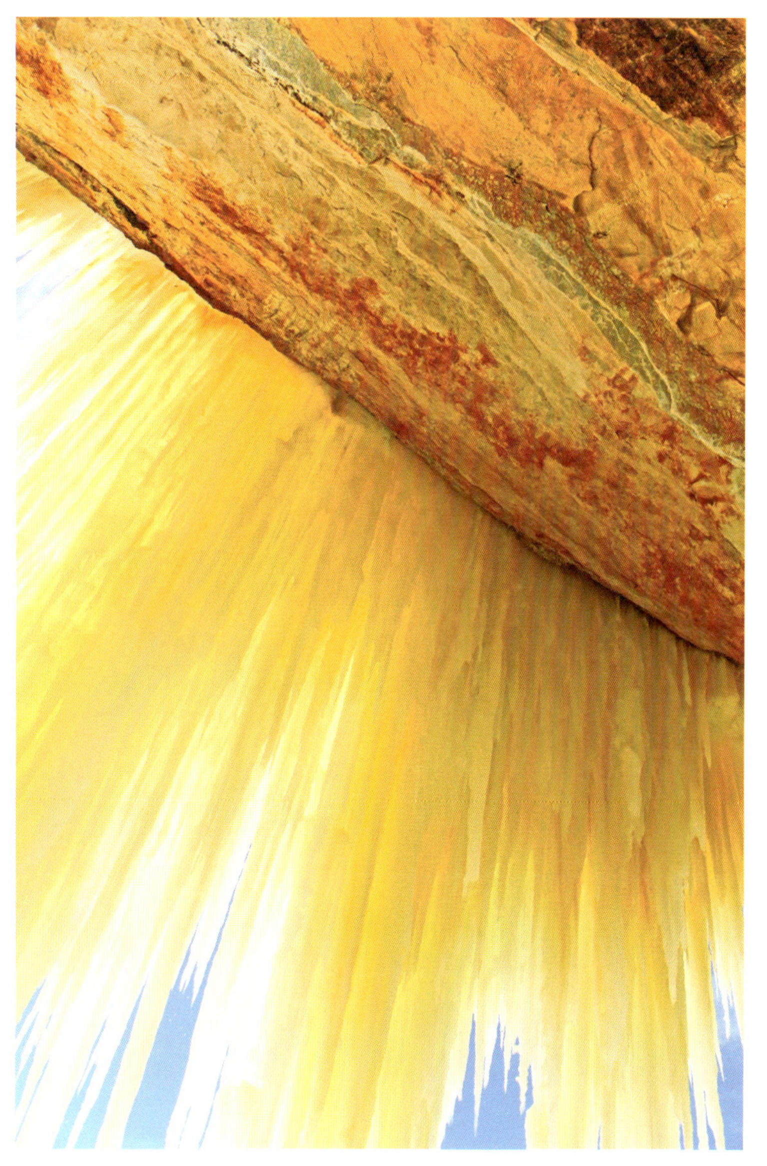

Sunny Side Up

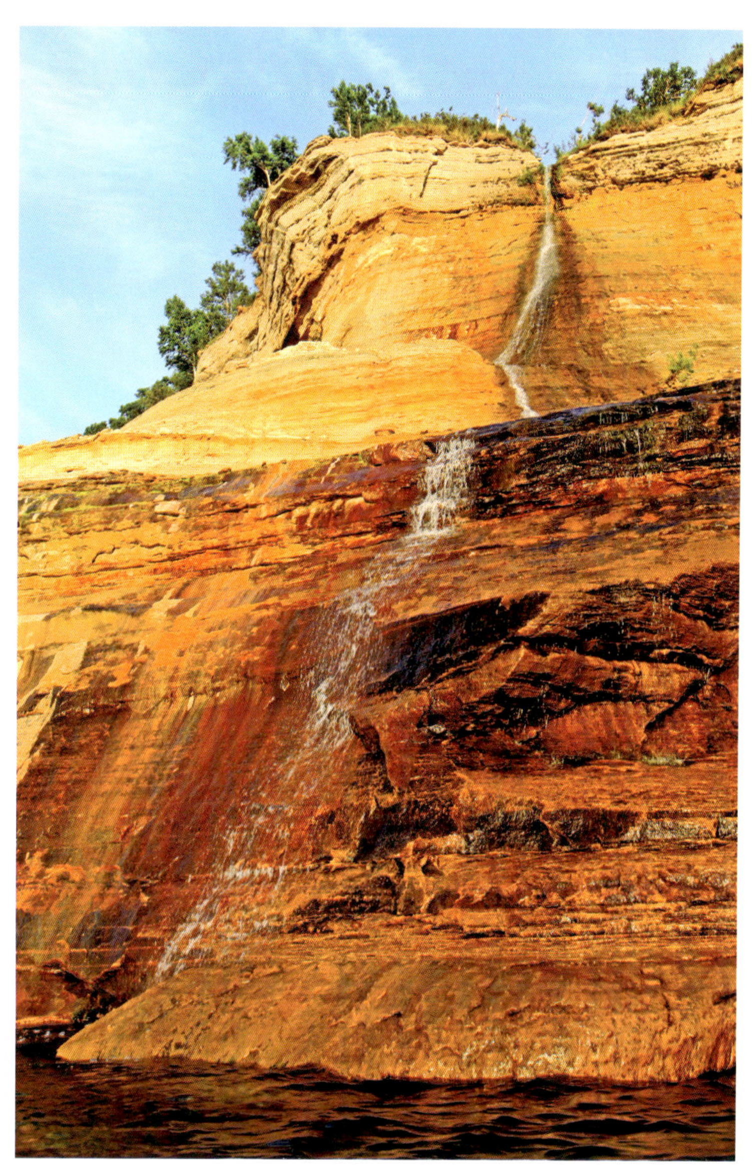

Zig Zag

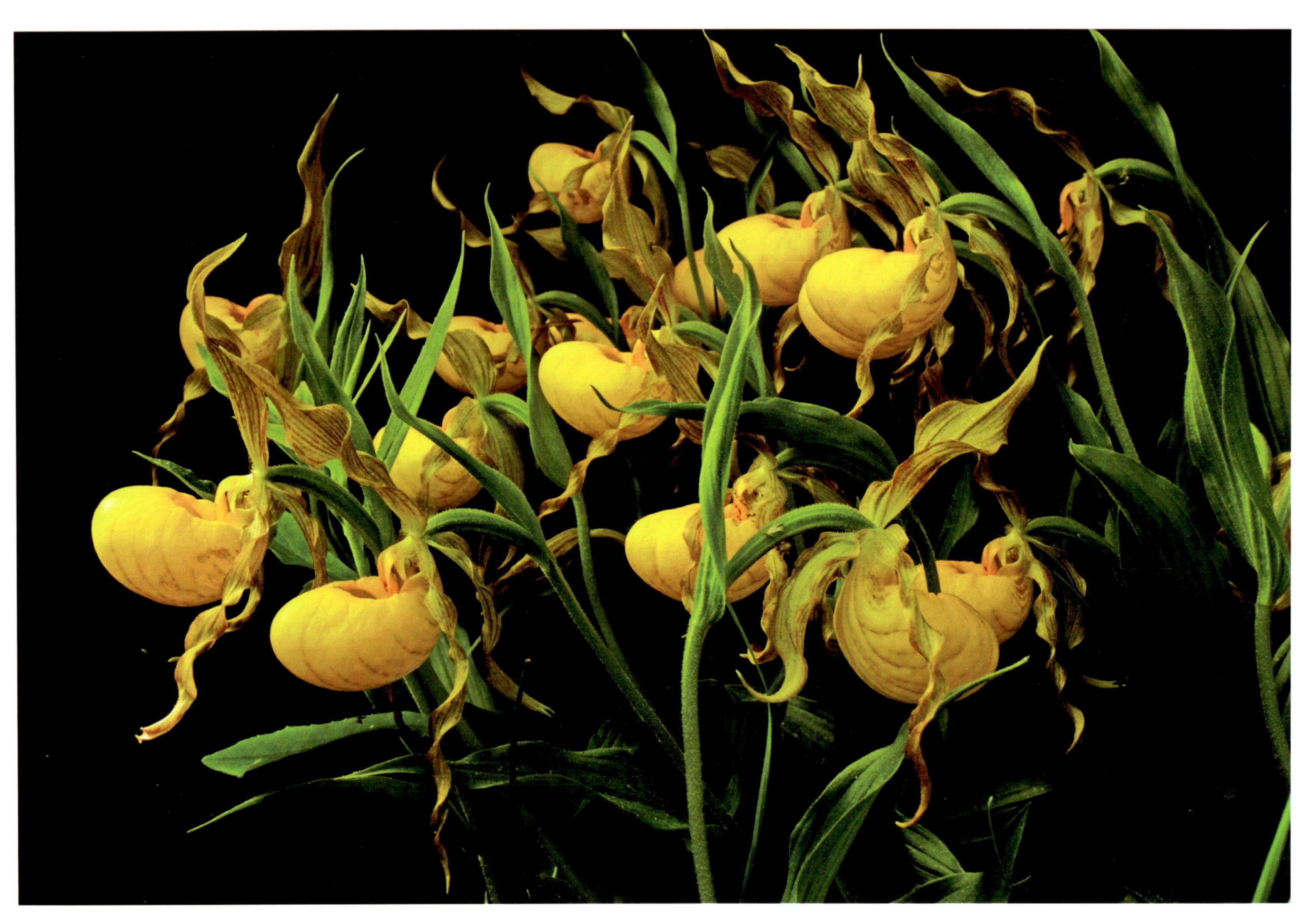

Nine Ladies Dancing

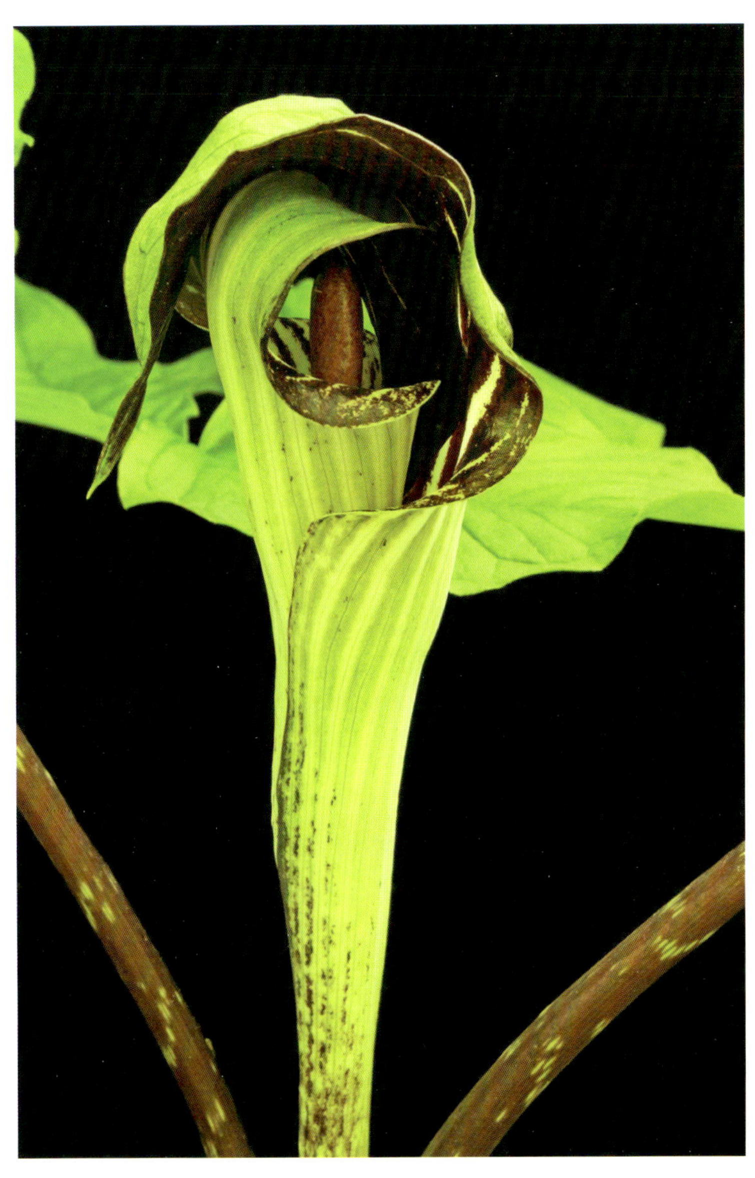

Jack-in-the-Pulpit

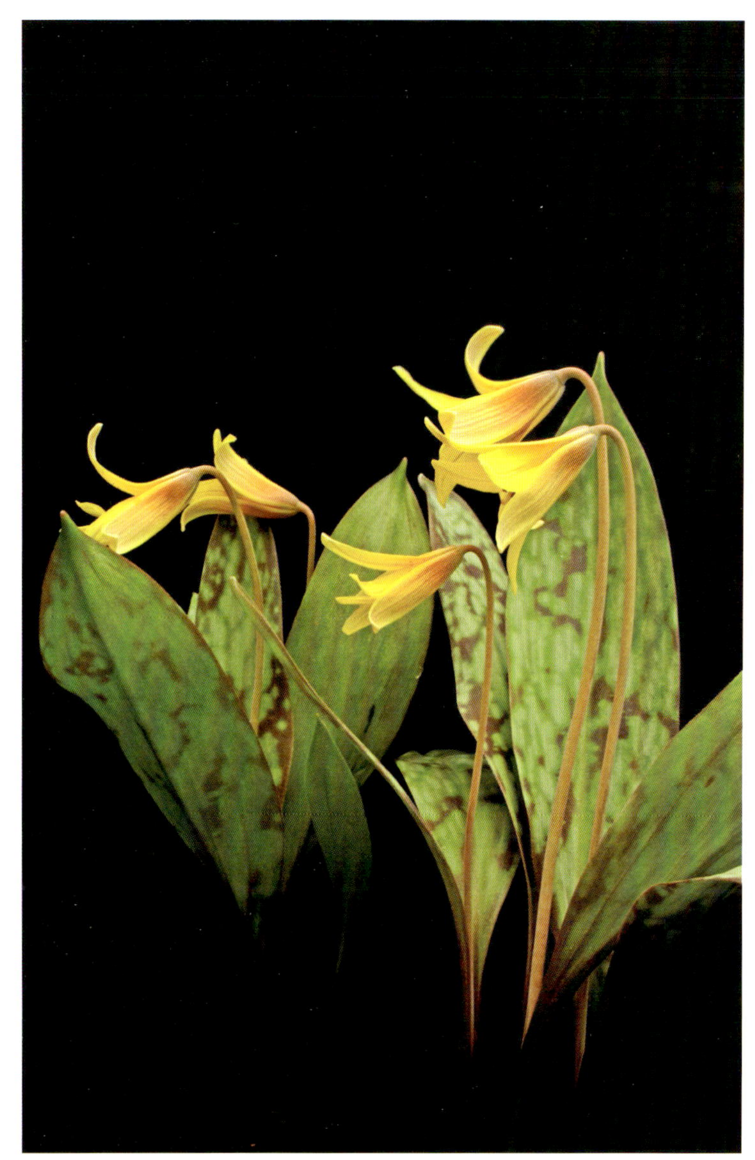

Trumpeting Trout Lilies

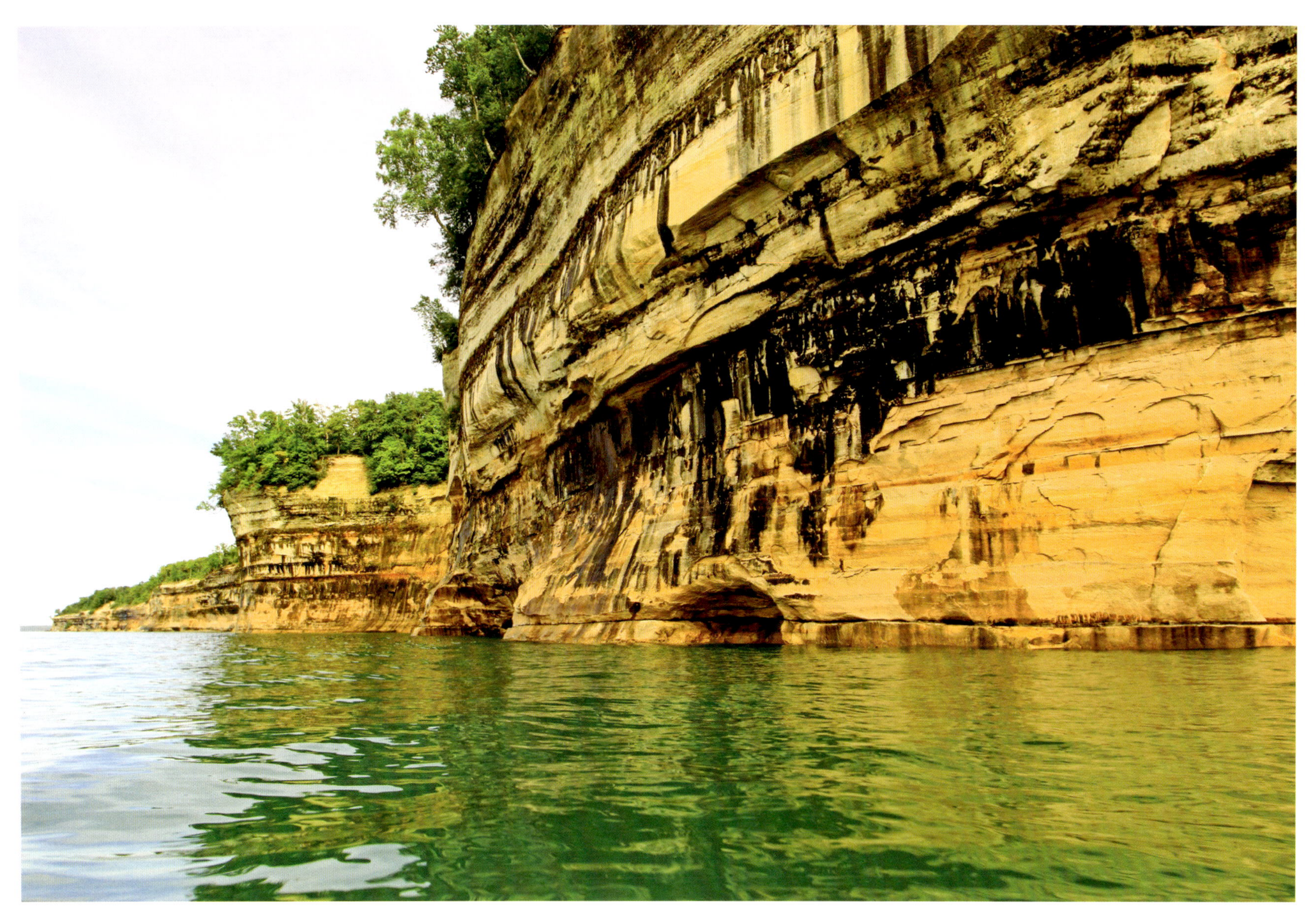

Paradise Found

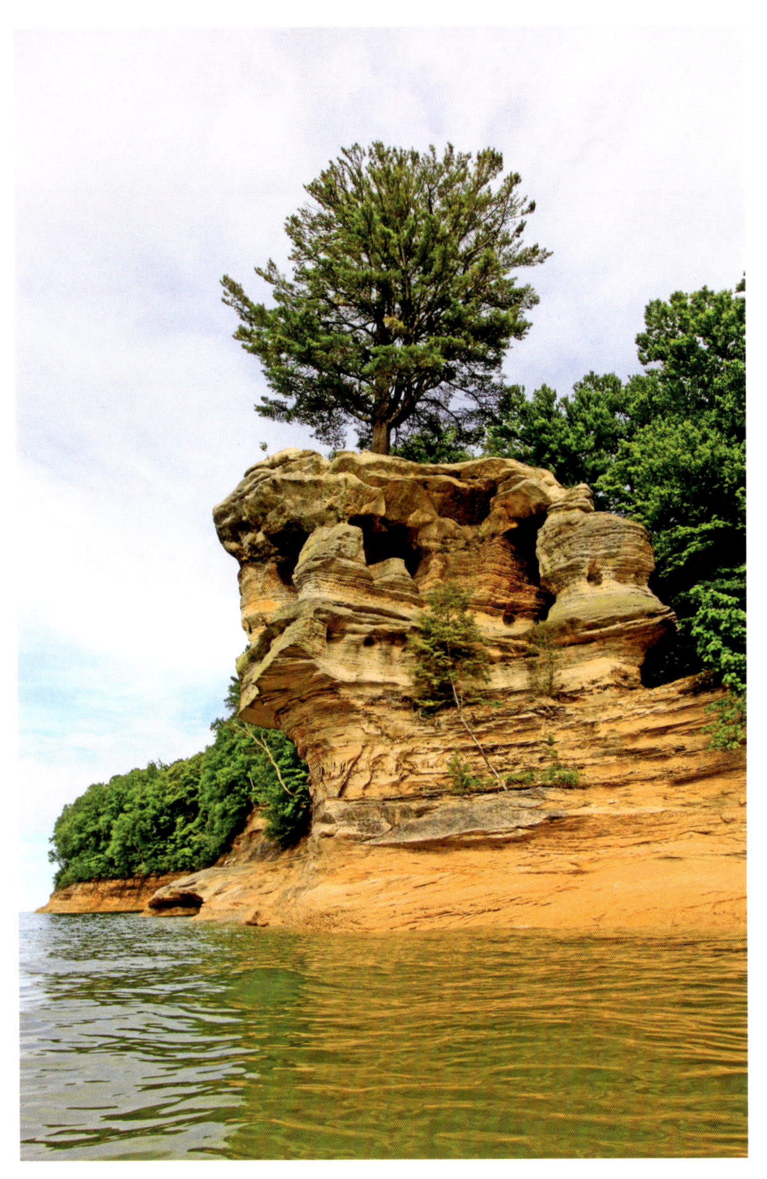

Standing Tall:
Chapel Rock

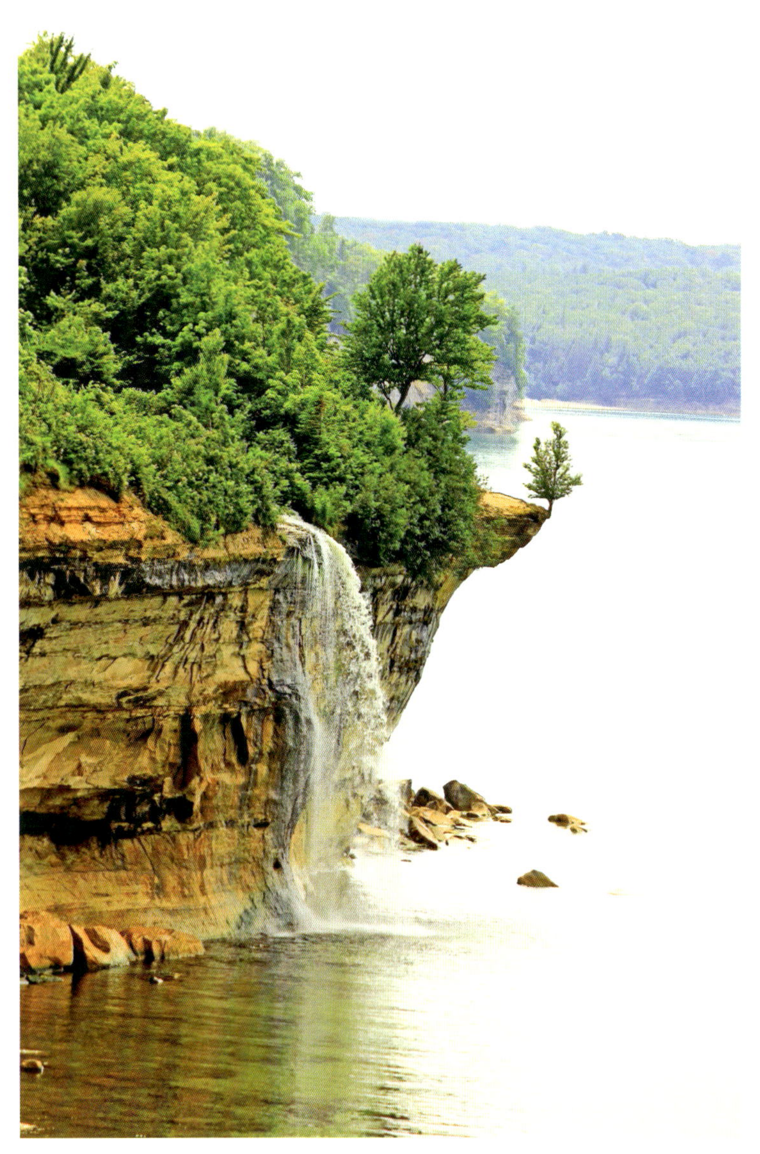

Living on the Edge

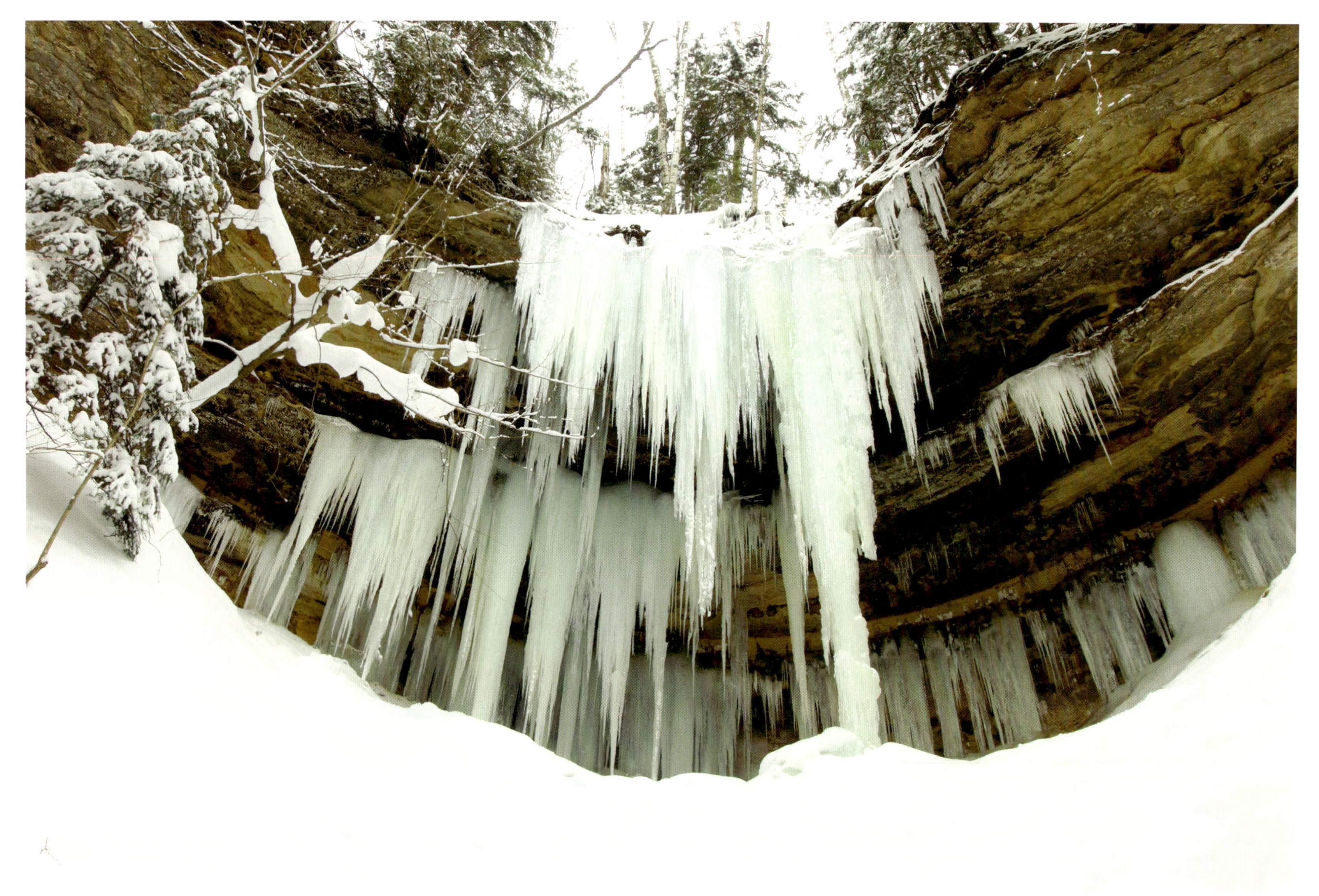

Cathedral: Sand Point

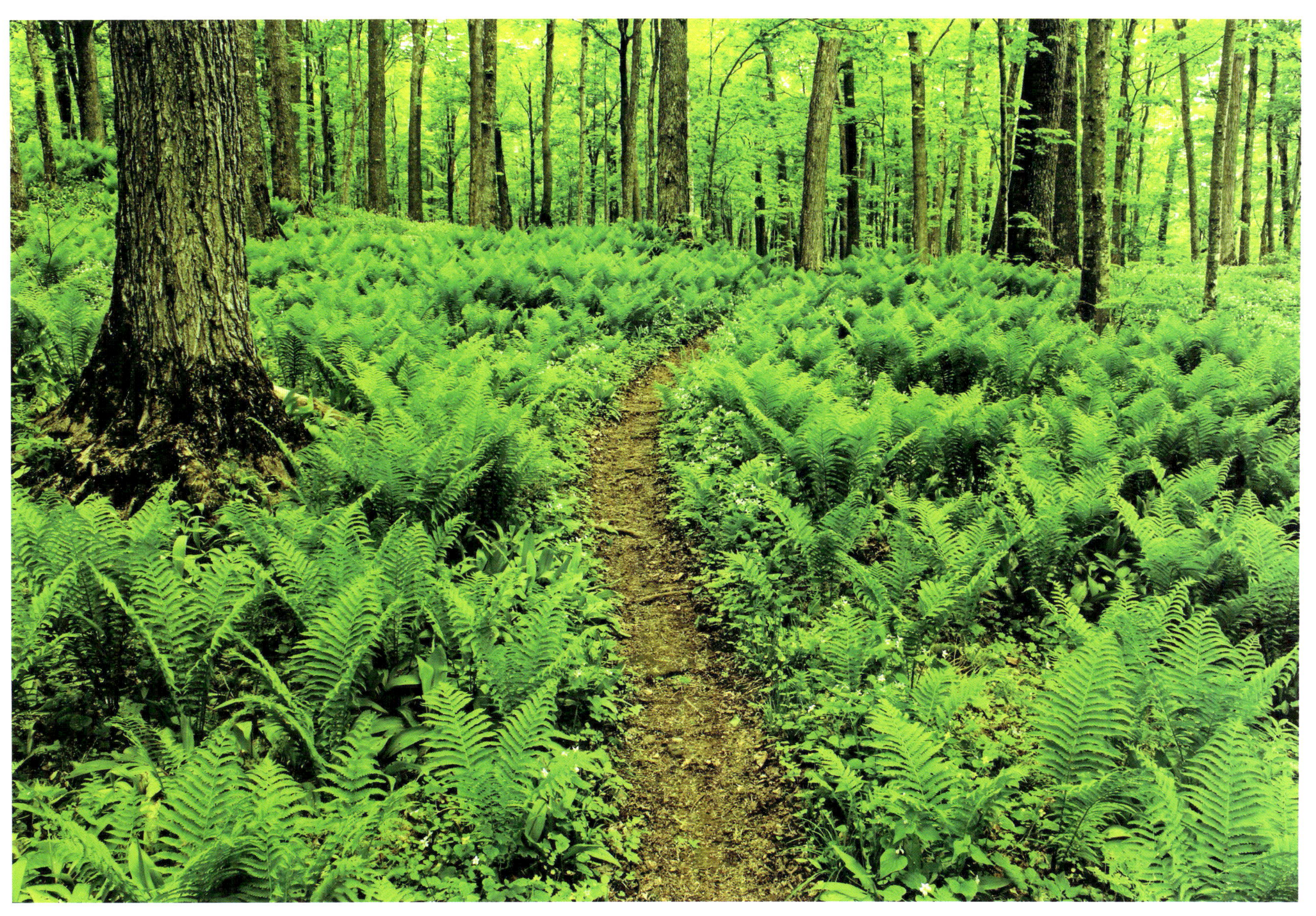

Fan Fare

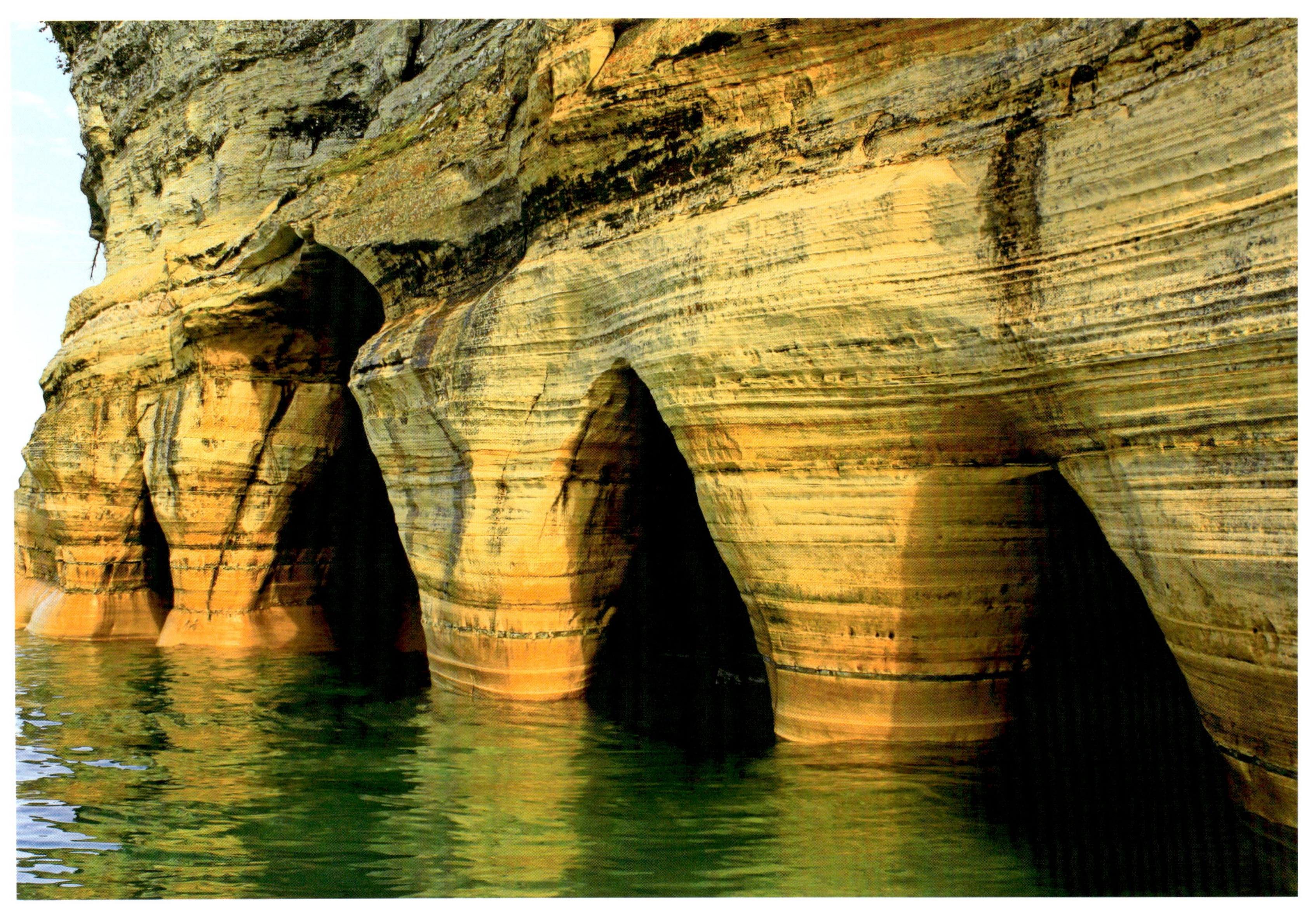

Tunnel Vision

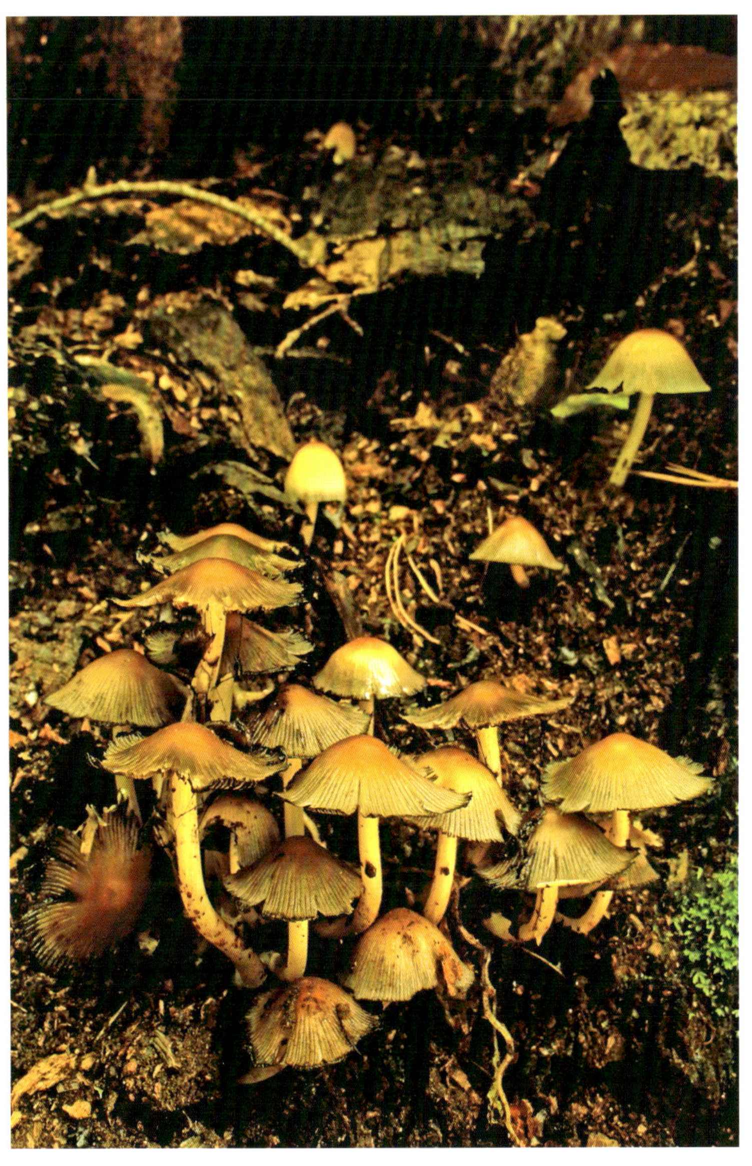

Fungus Among Us

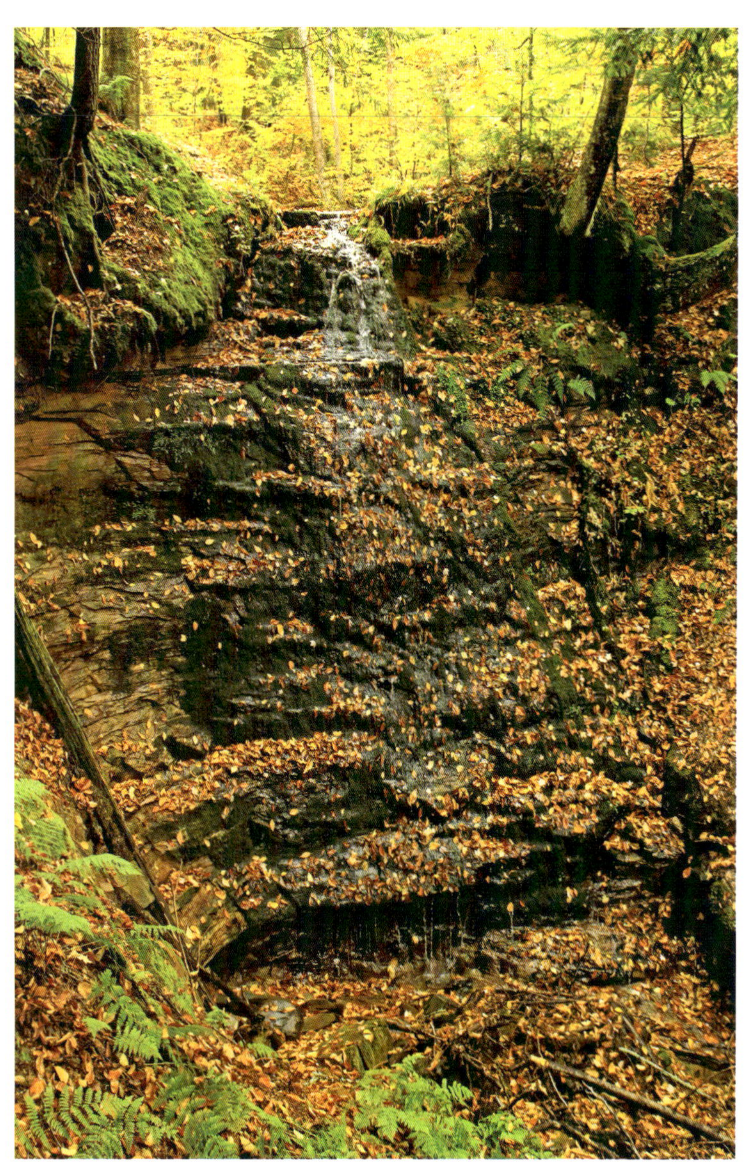

Falling into Place:
Silver Bell Falls

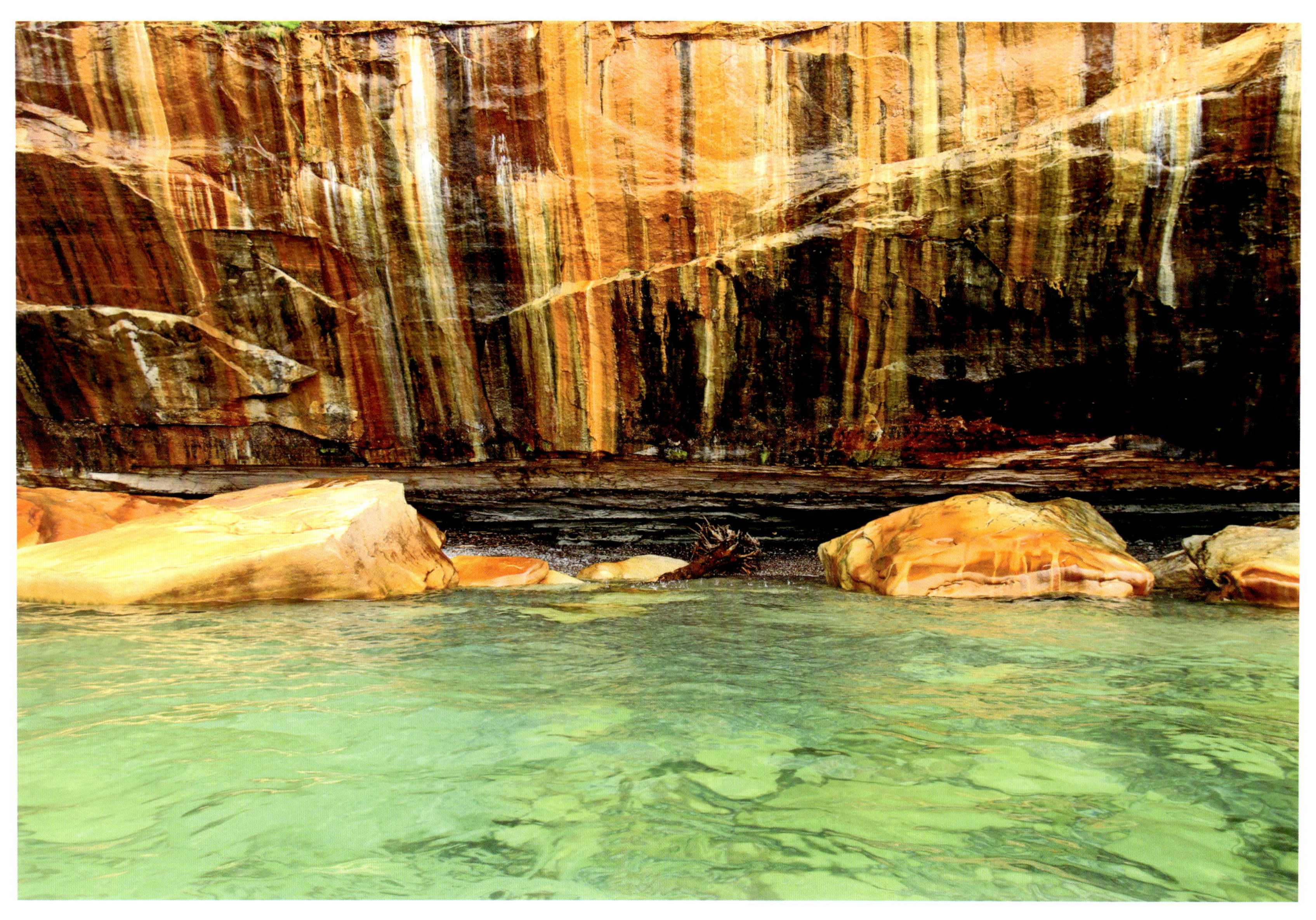

Aquamarine

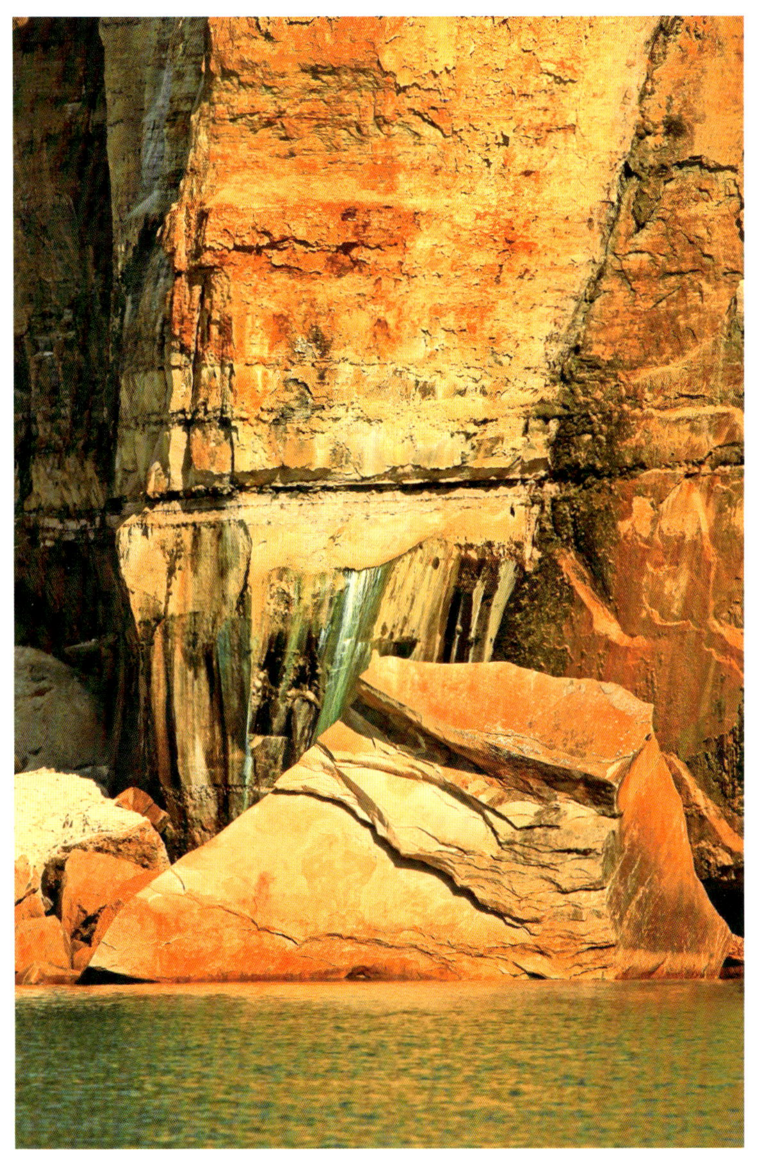

Blue Streak

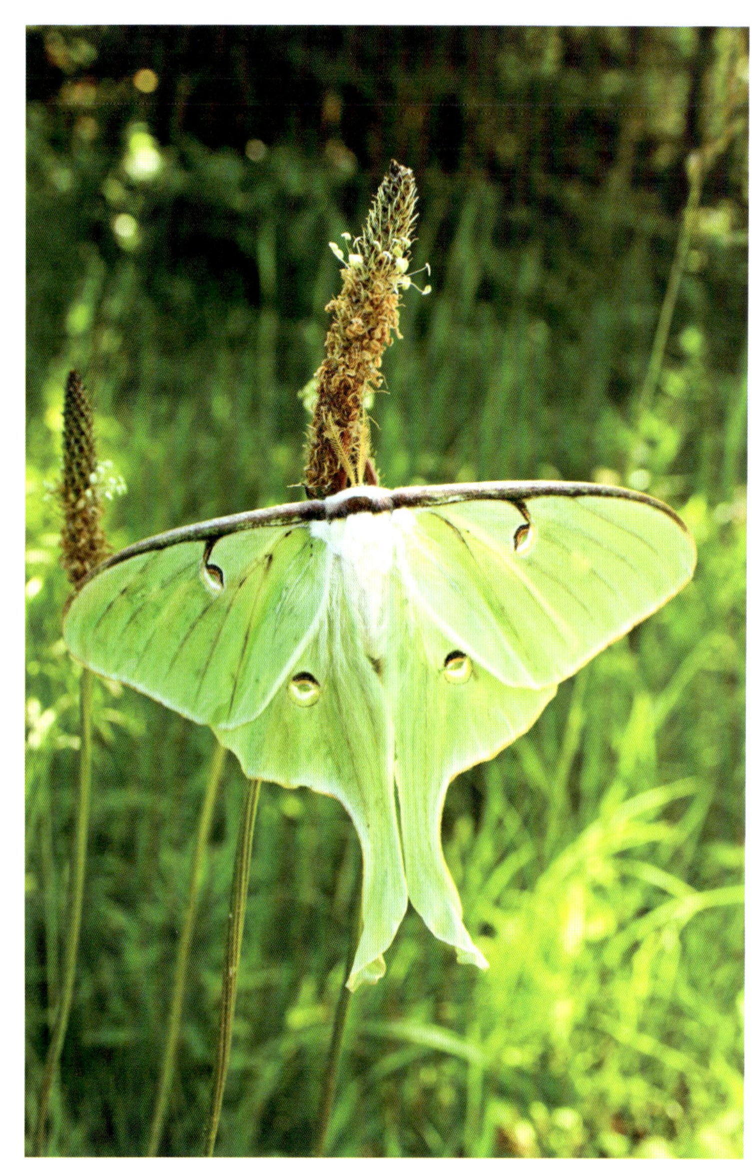

Luna by Day

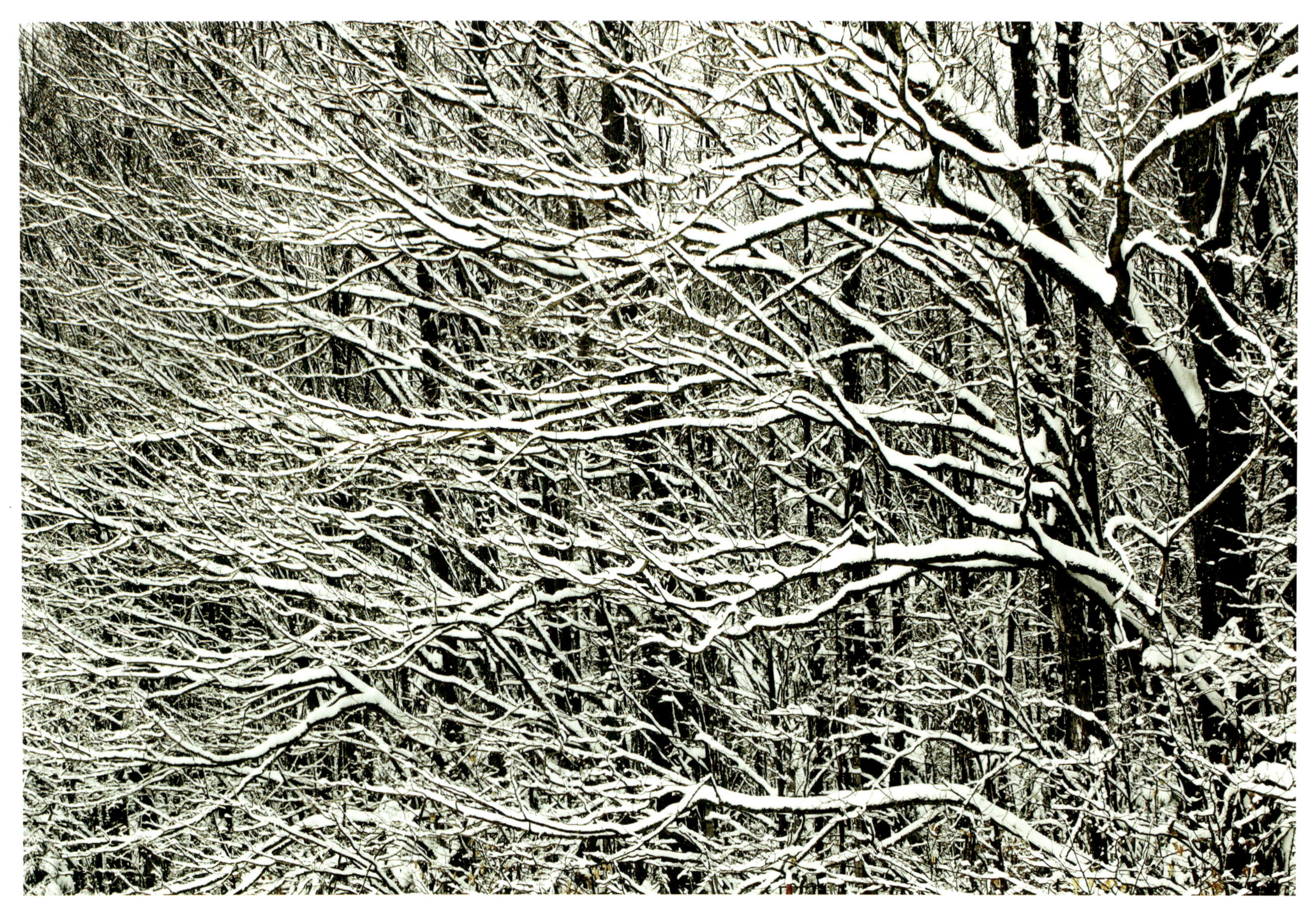

Branching Out

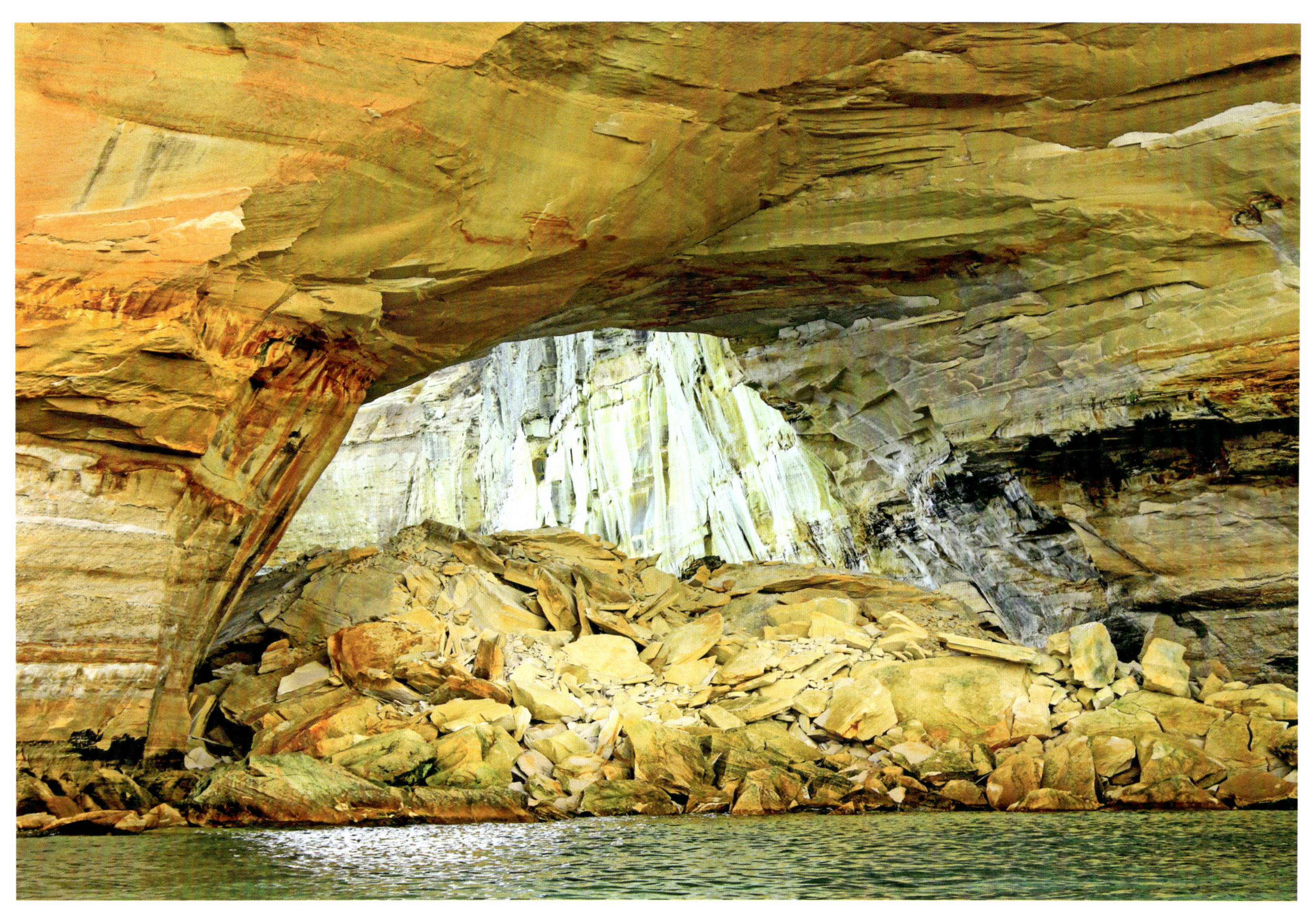

Carved in Stone: Grand Portal Point

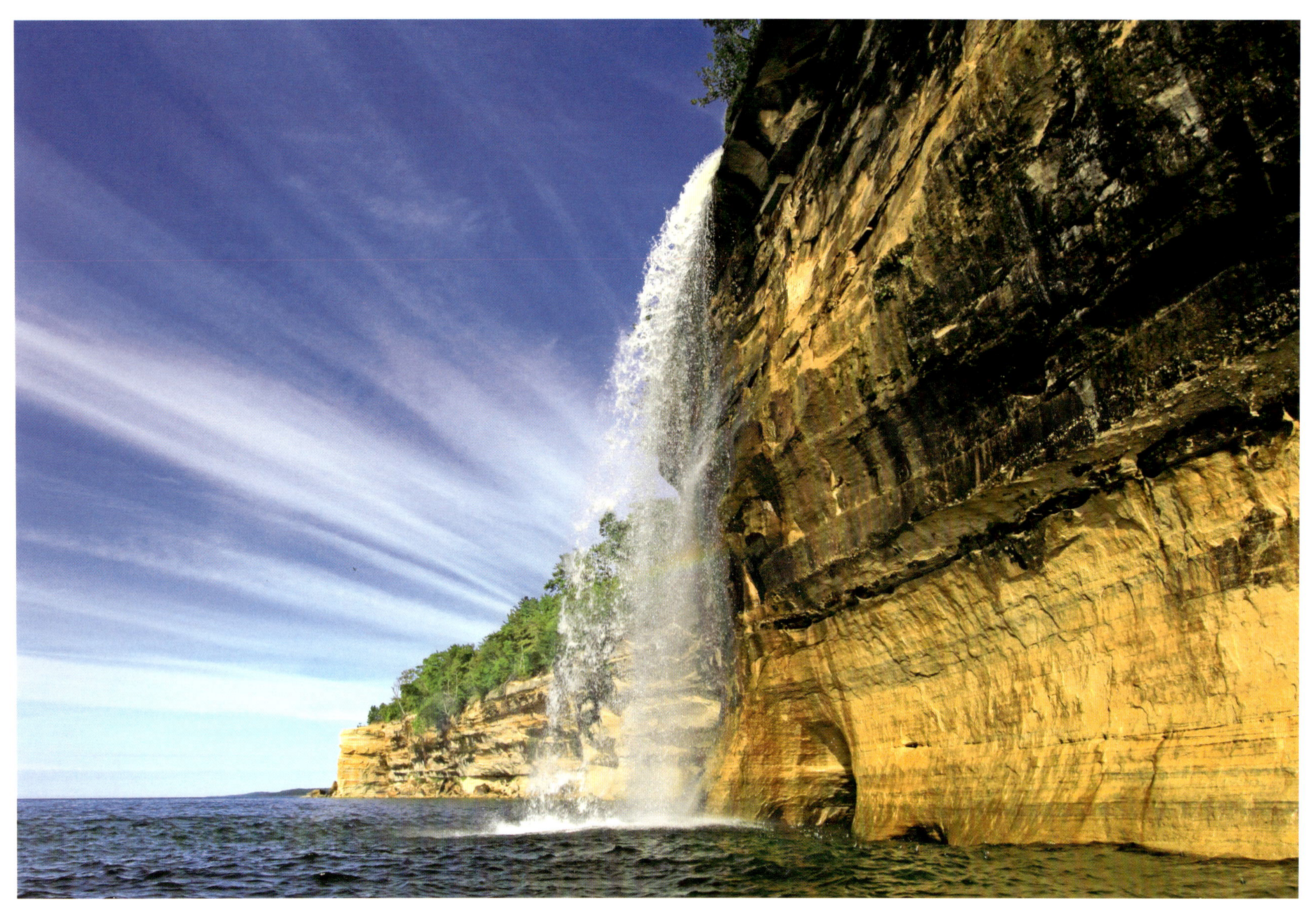

Rainbow Connection

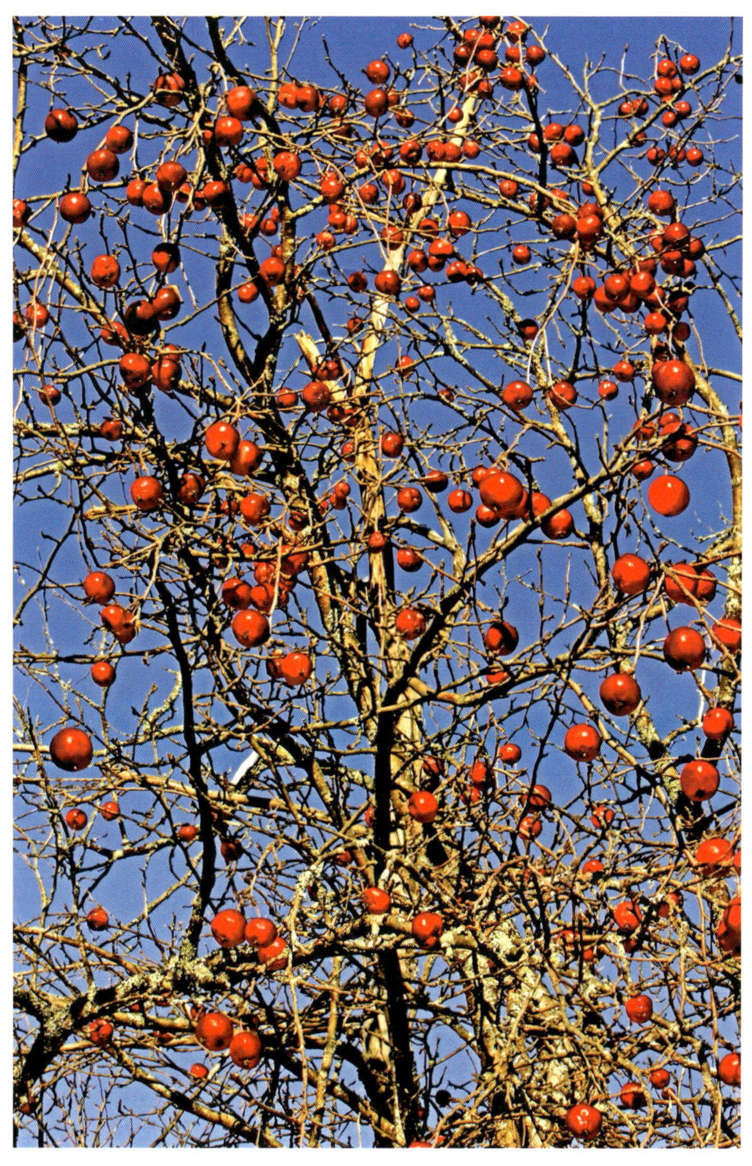

Not Far From the Tree

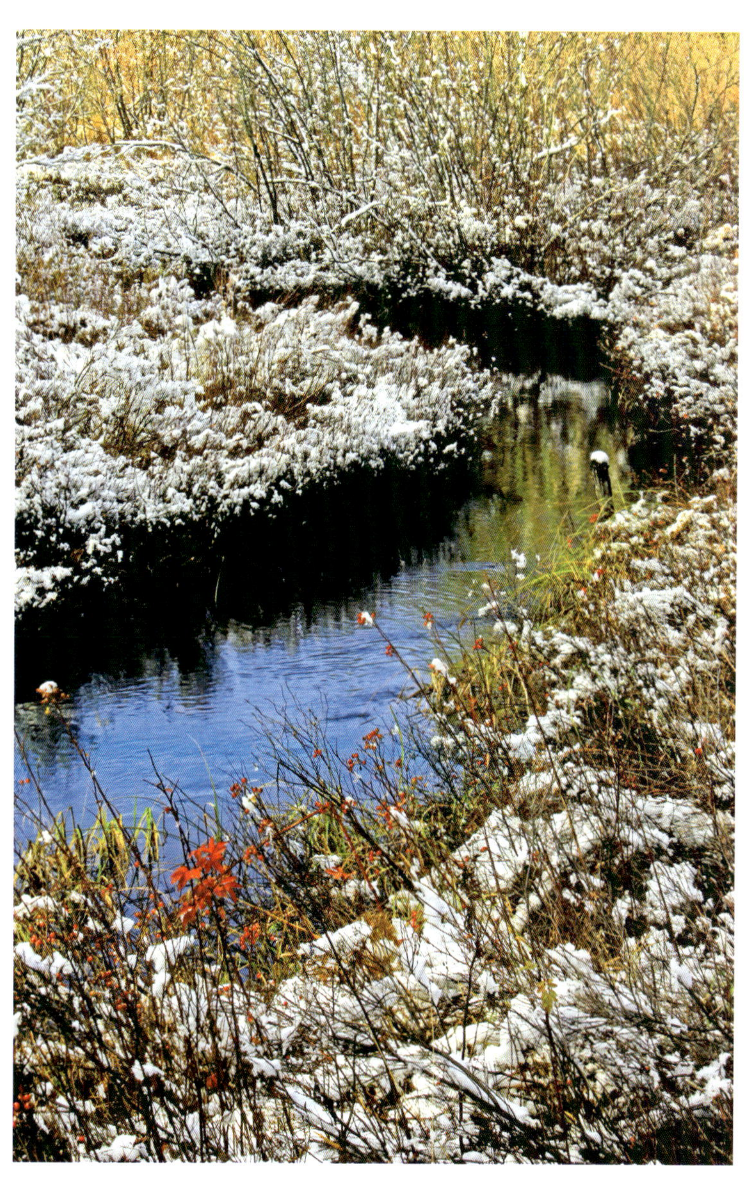

Cotton Fields

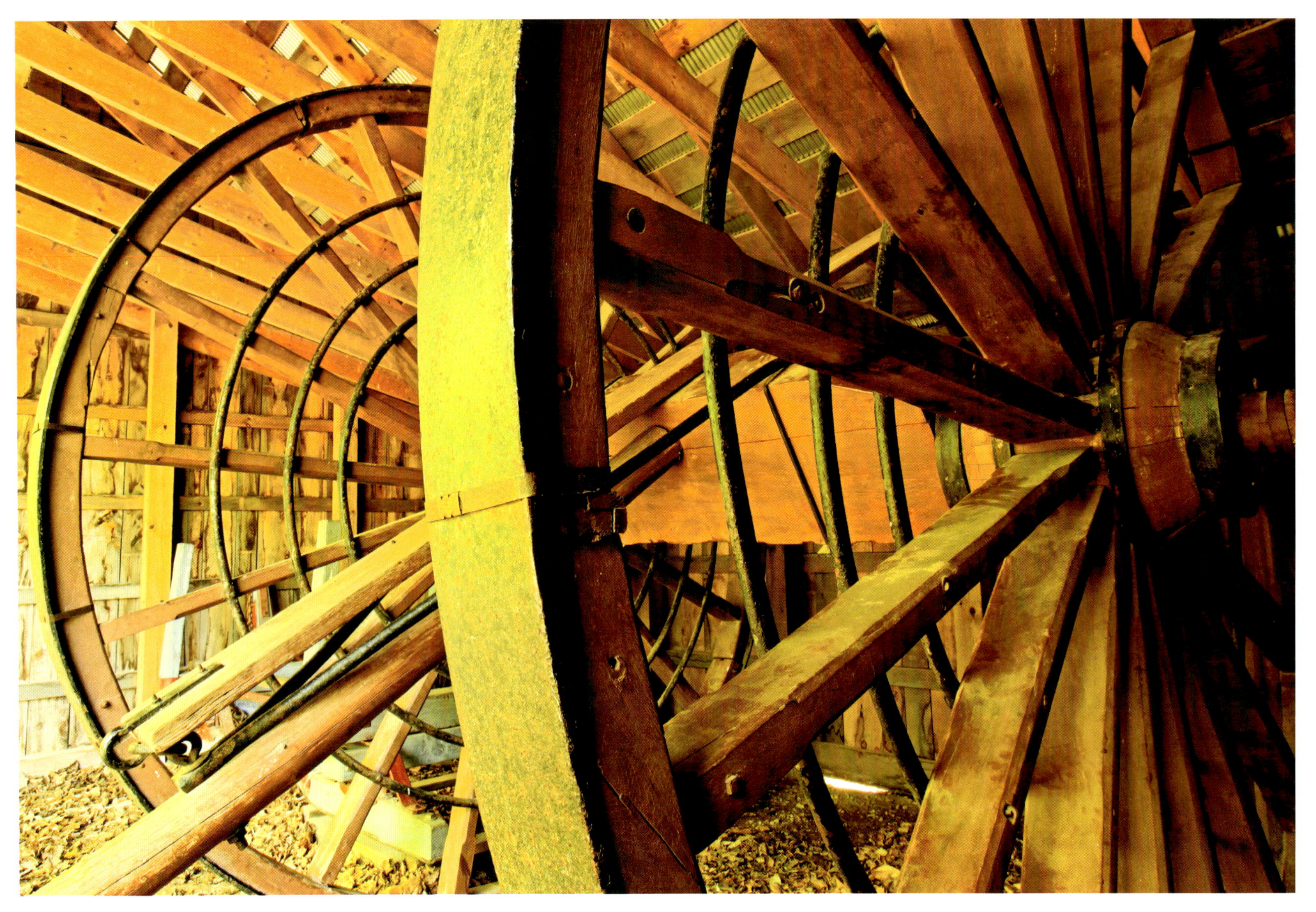

Big Wheels Keep on Turning: Log Slide Area

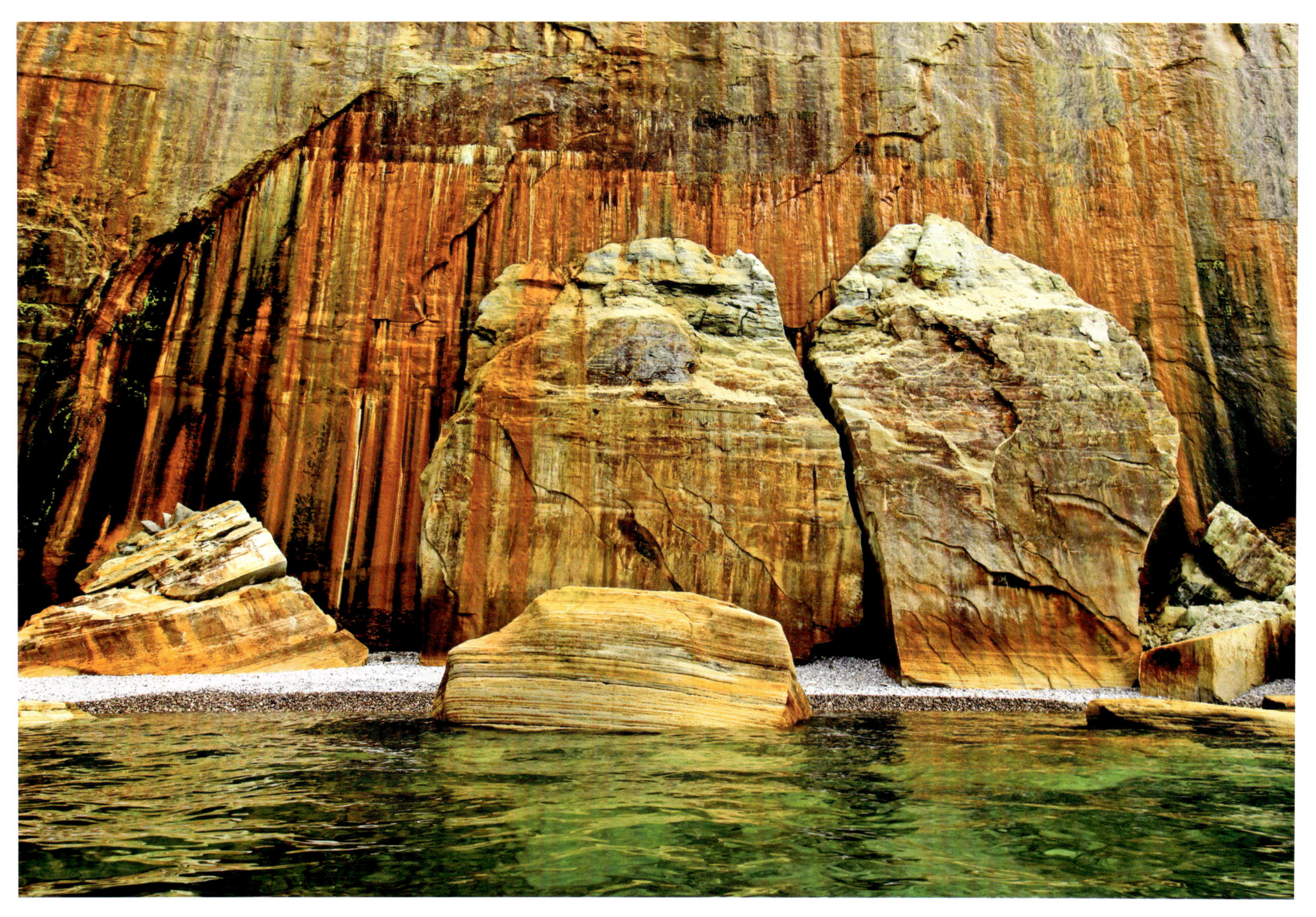

Back Against the Wall

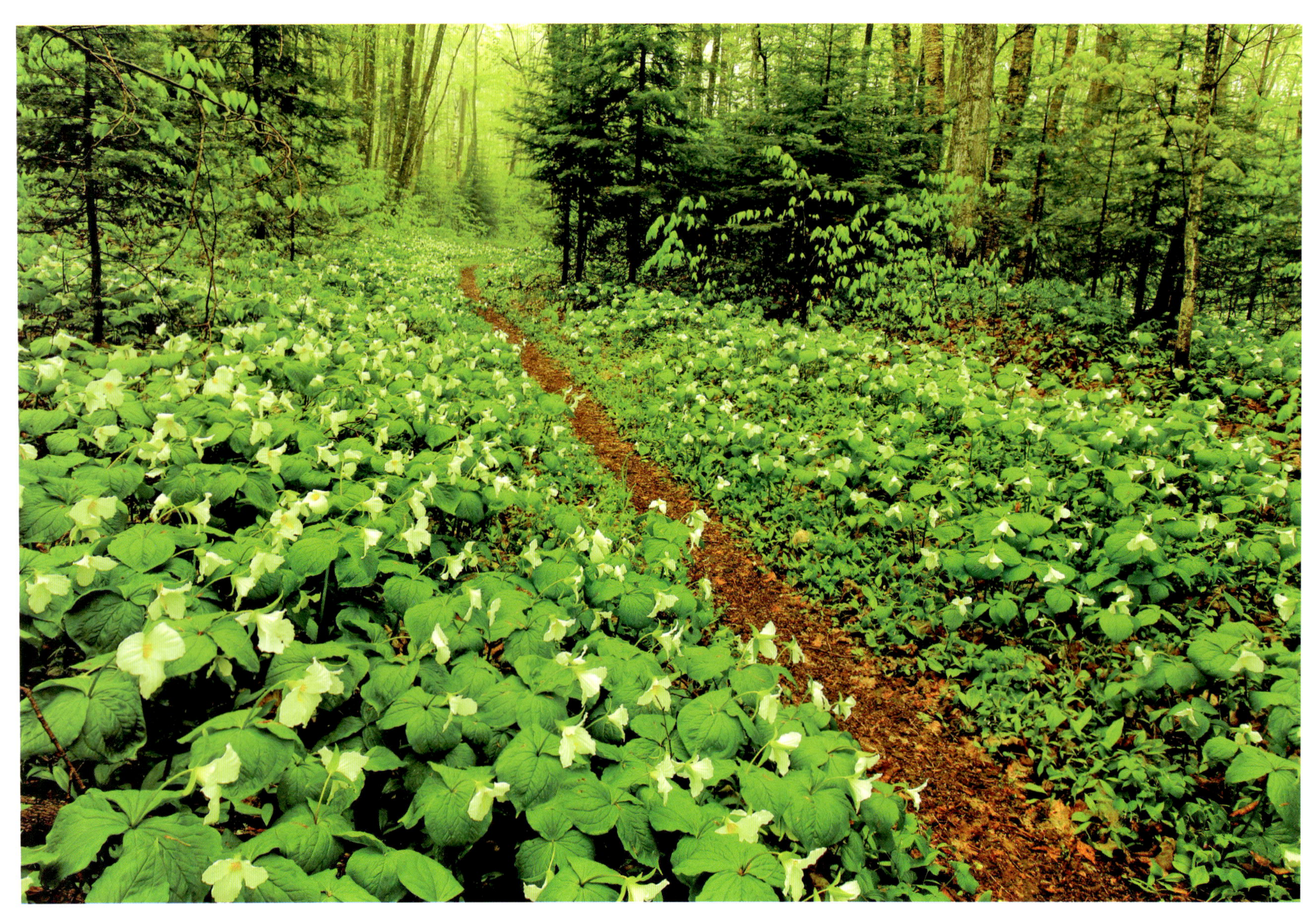

A Trillion Trilliums

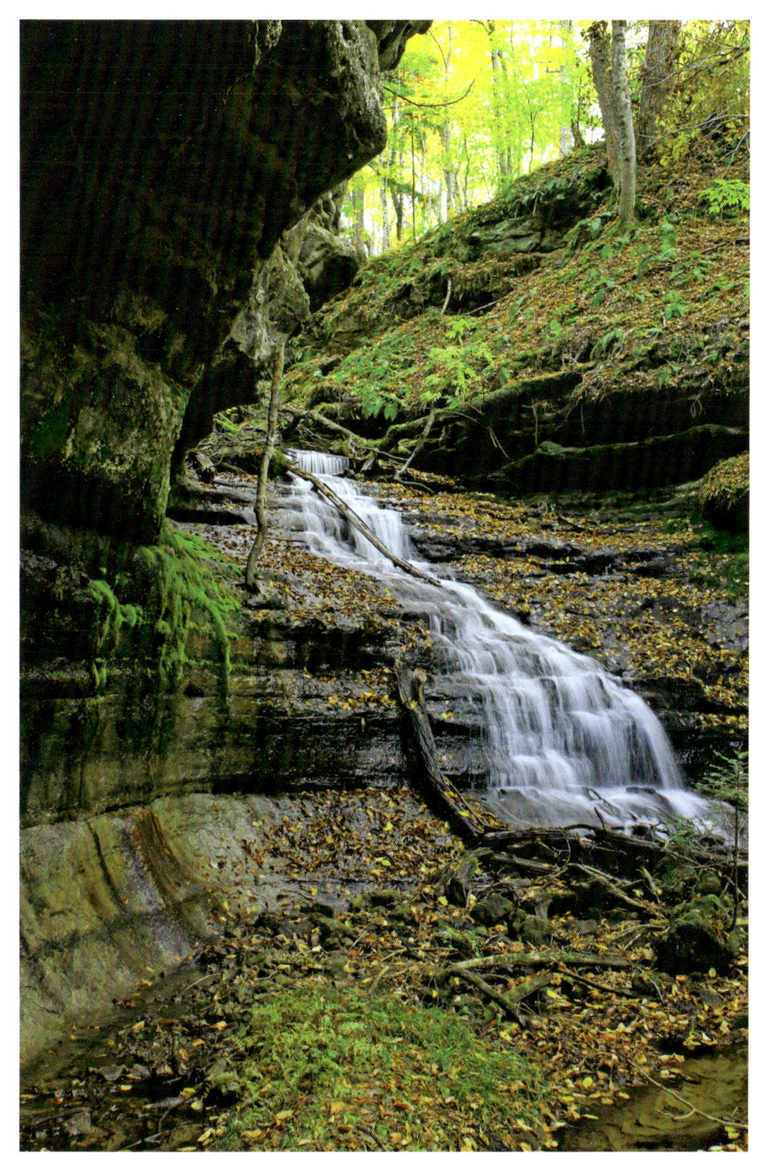

Falling Between the Cracks
Chapel Creek Falls

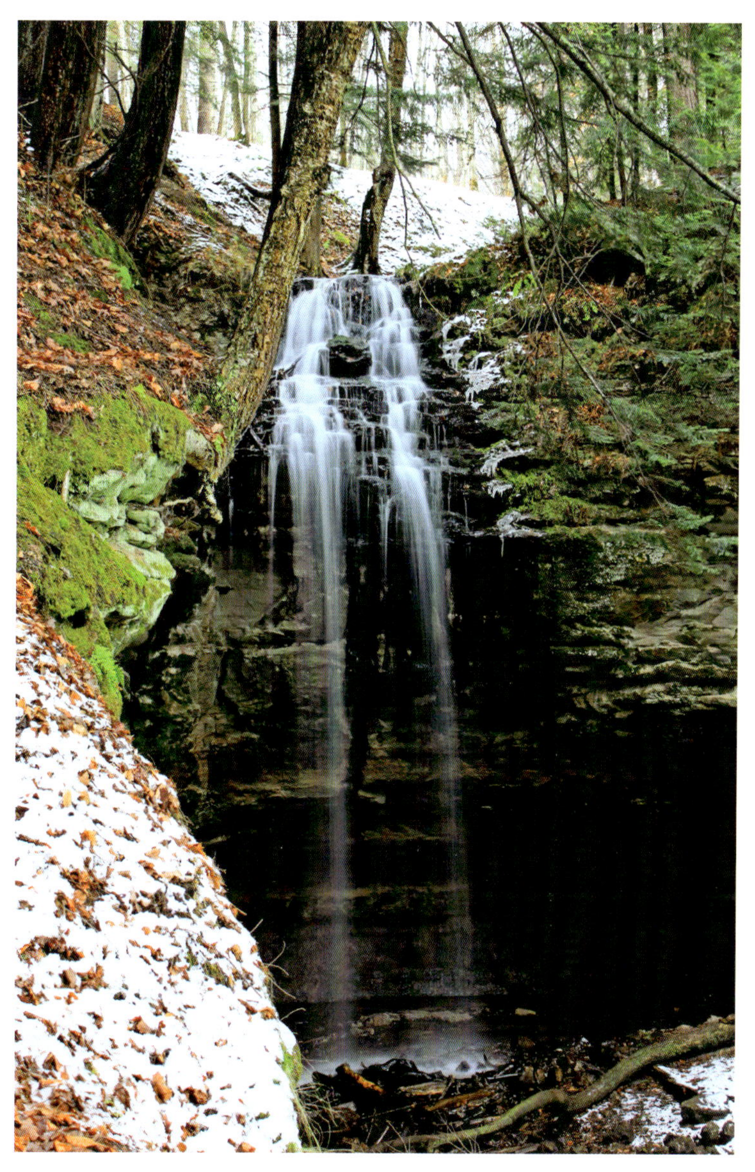

First Snow:
Olson Memorial Falls

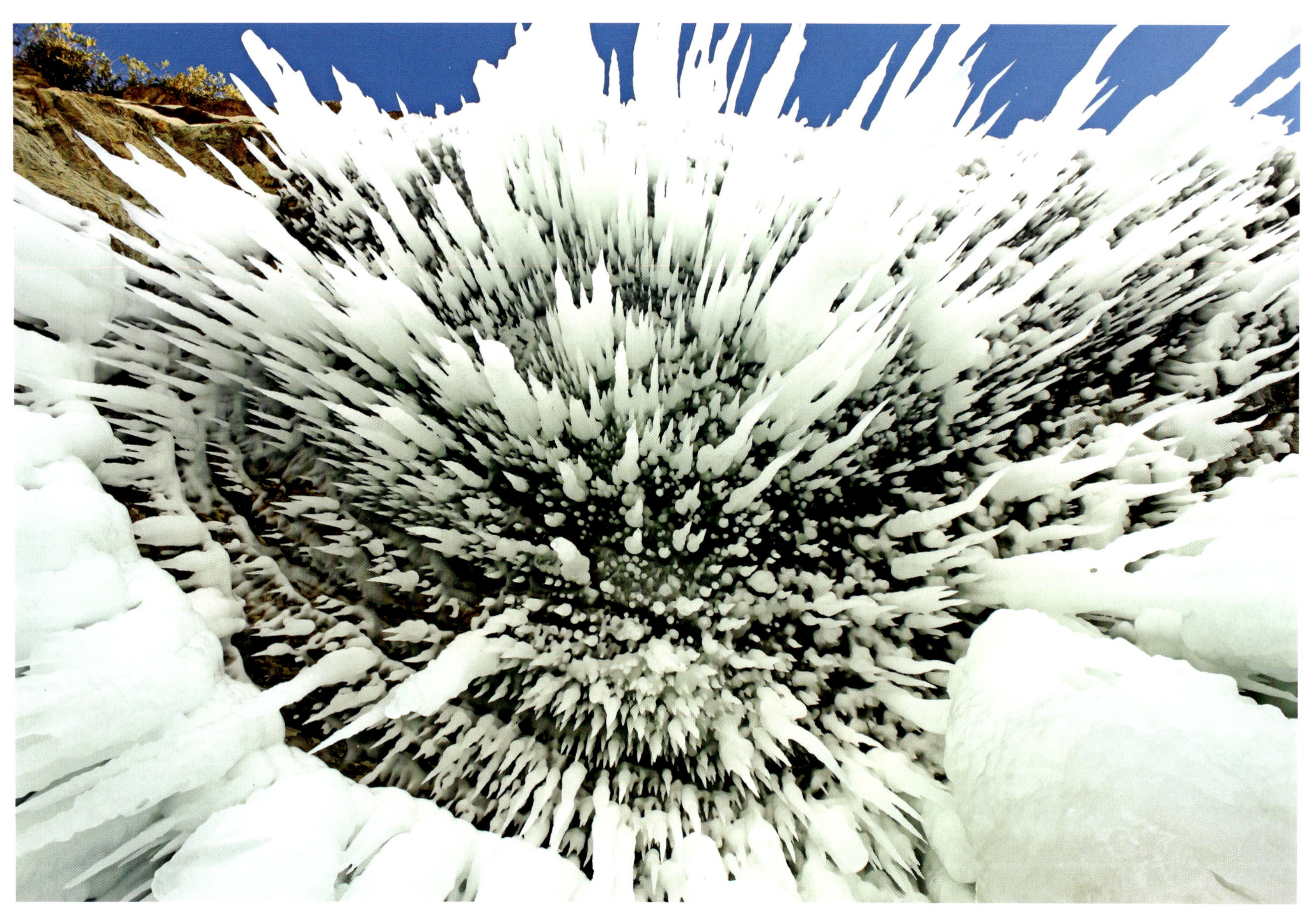

Cold Steel

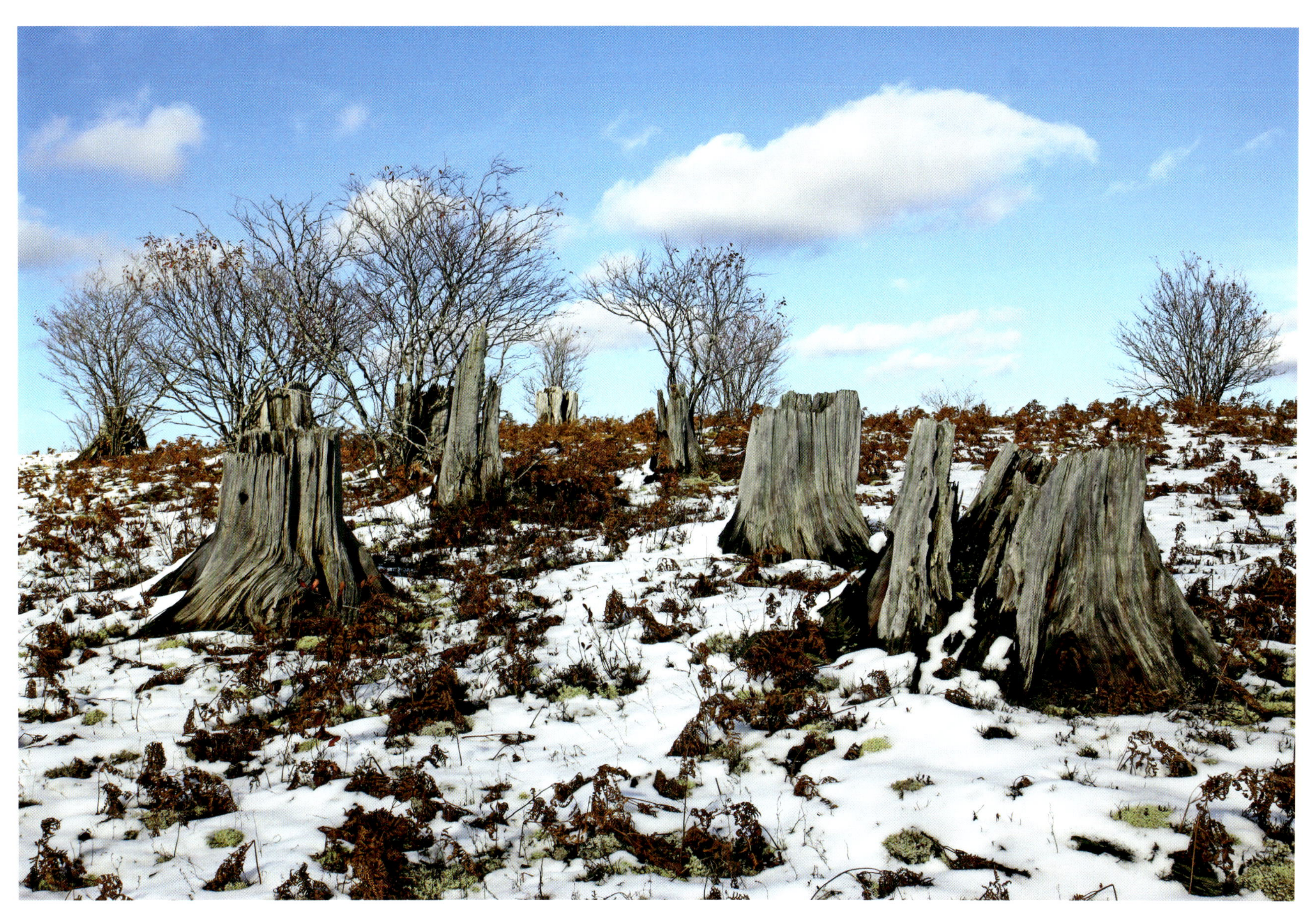

Generation Gap

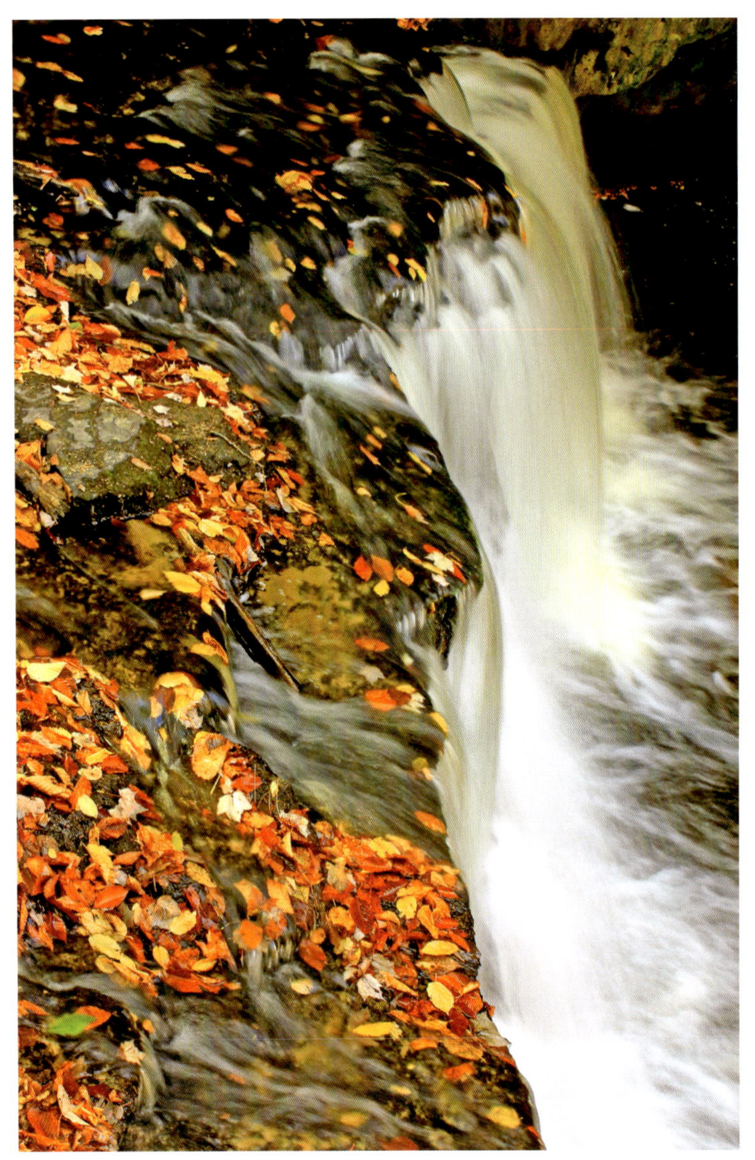

Fall Confetti:
Mosquito Falls

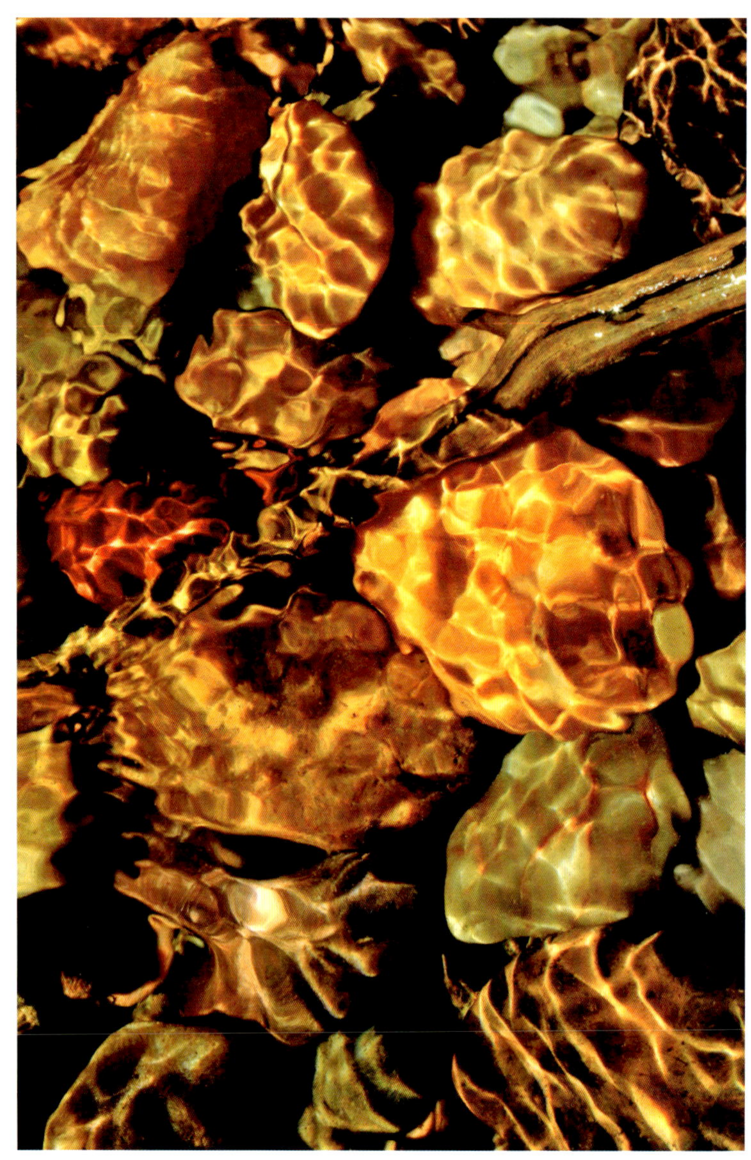

Sticks and Stones

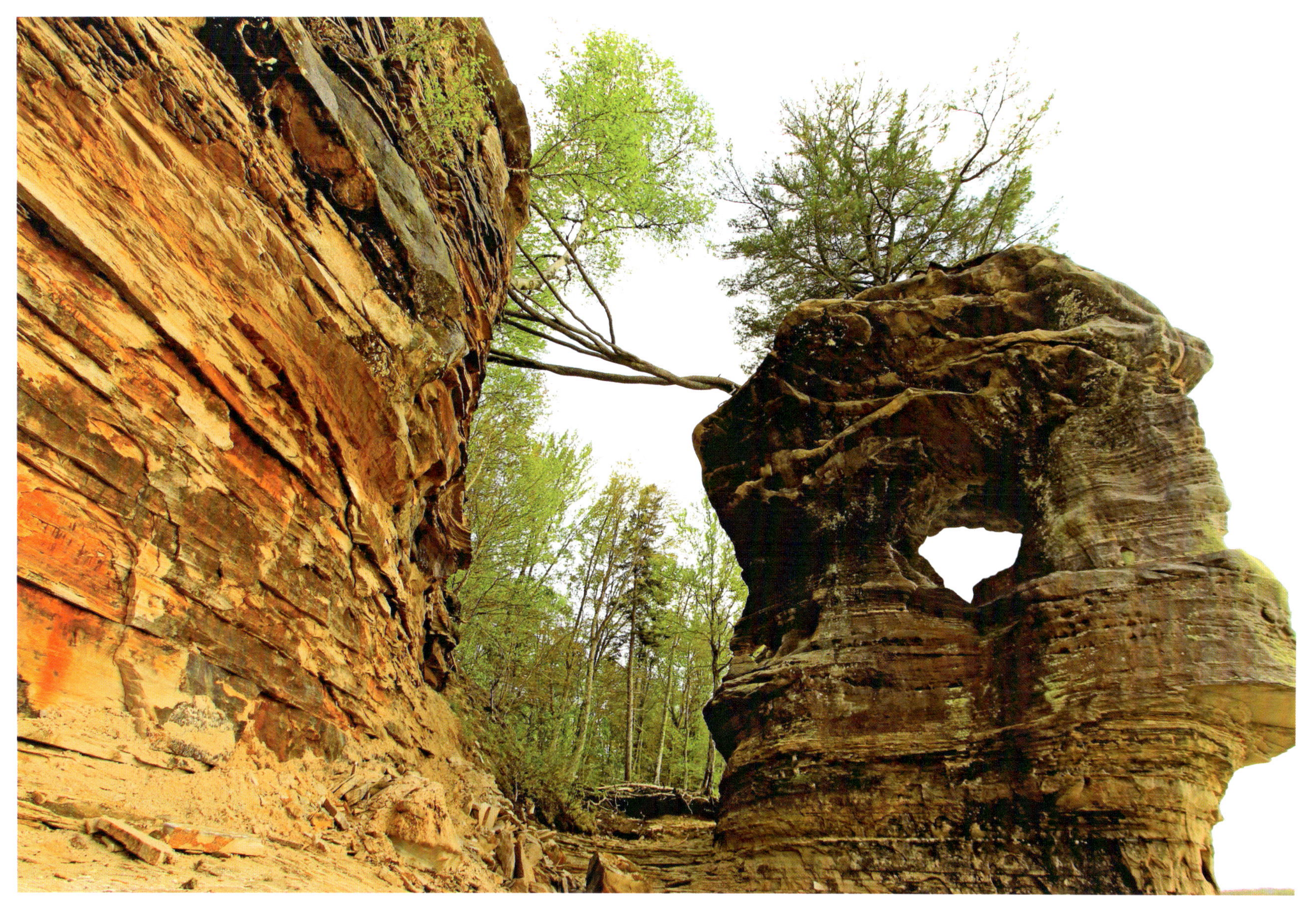

Life Line: Chapel Rock

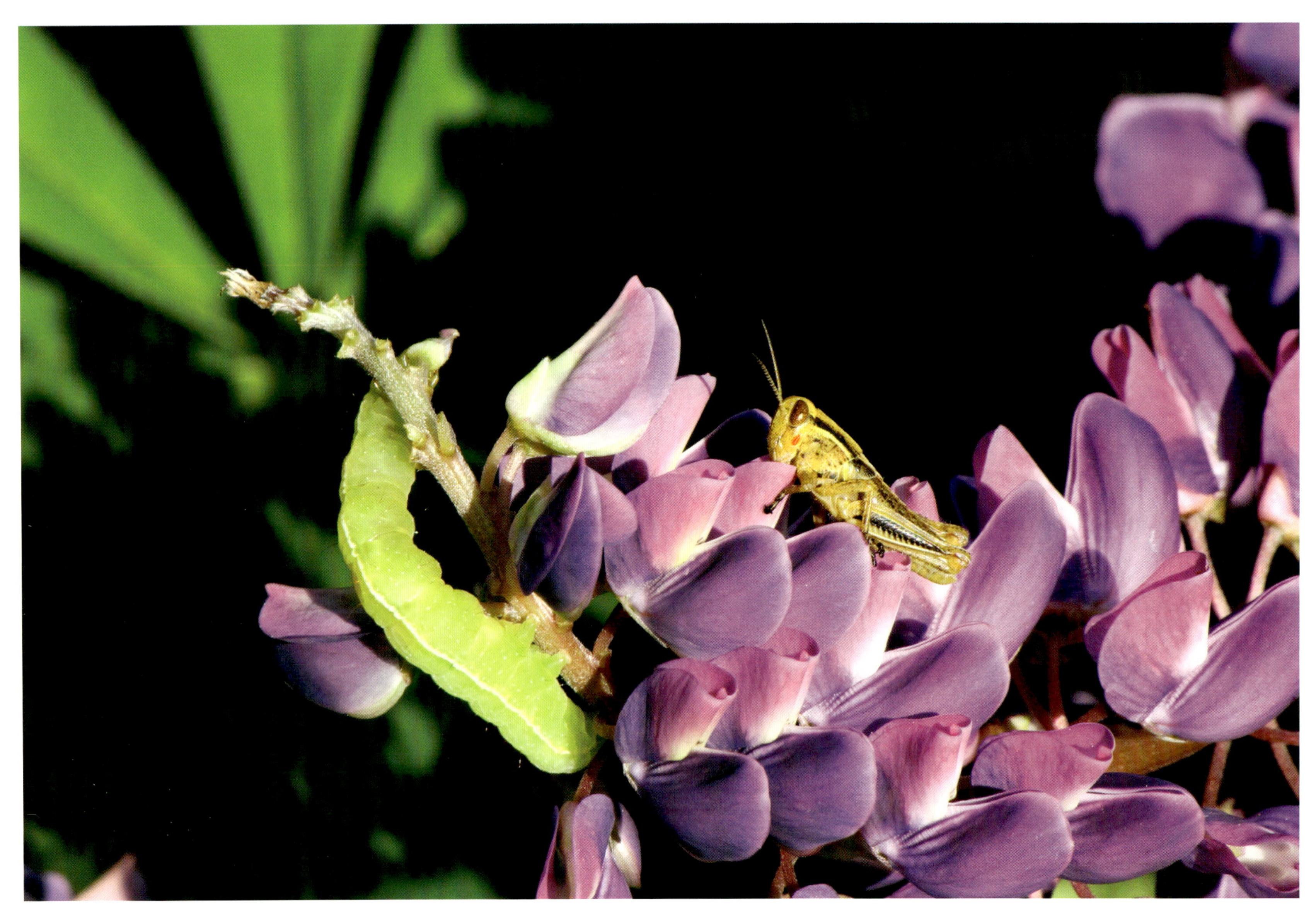

Having a Friend for Lunch: Lupine

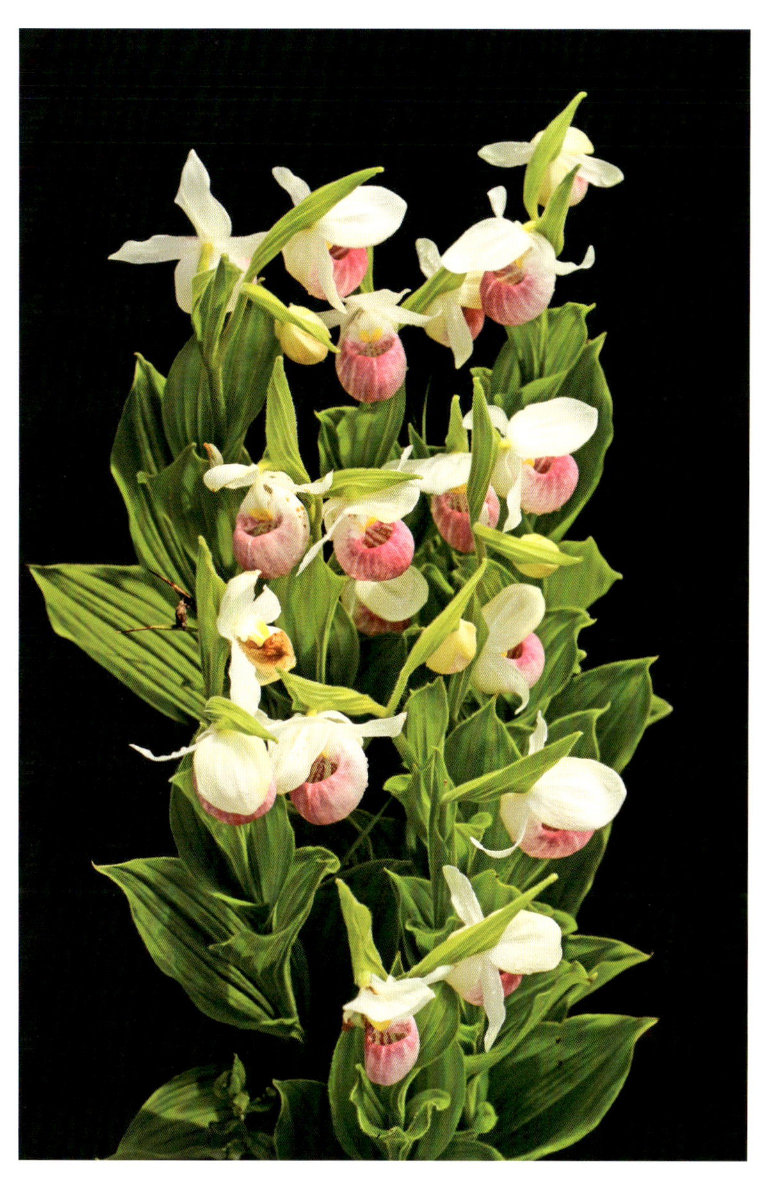

Showy Lady Slippers

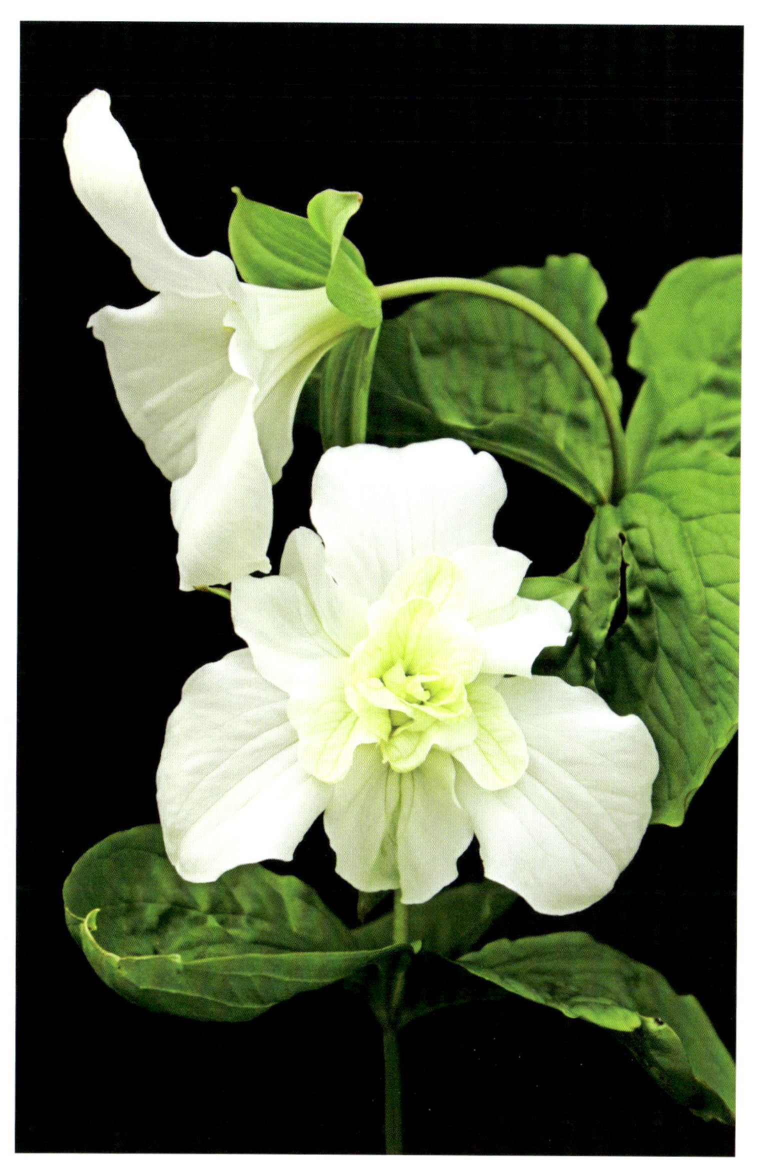

Double Trillium

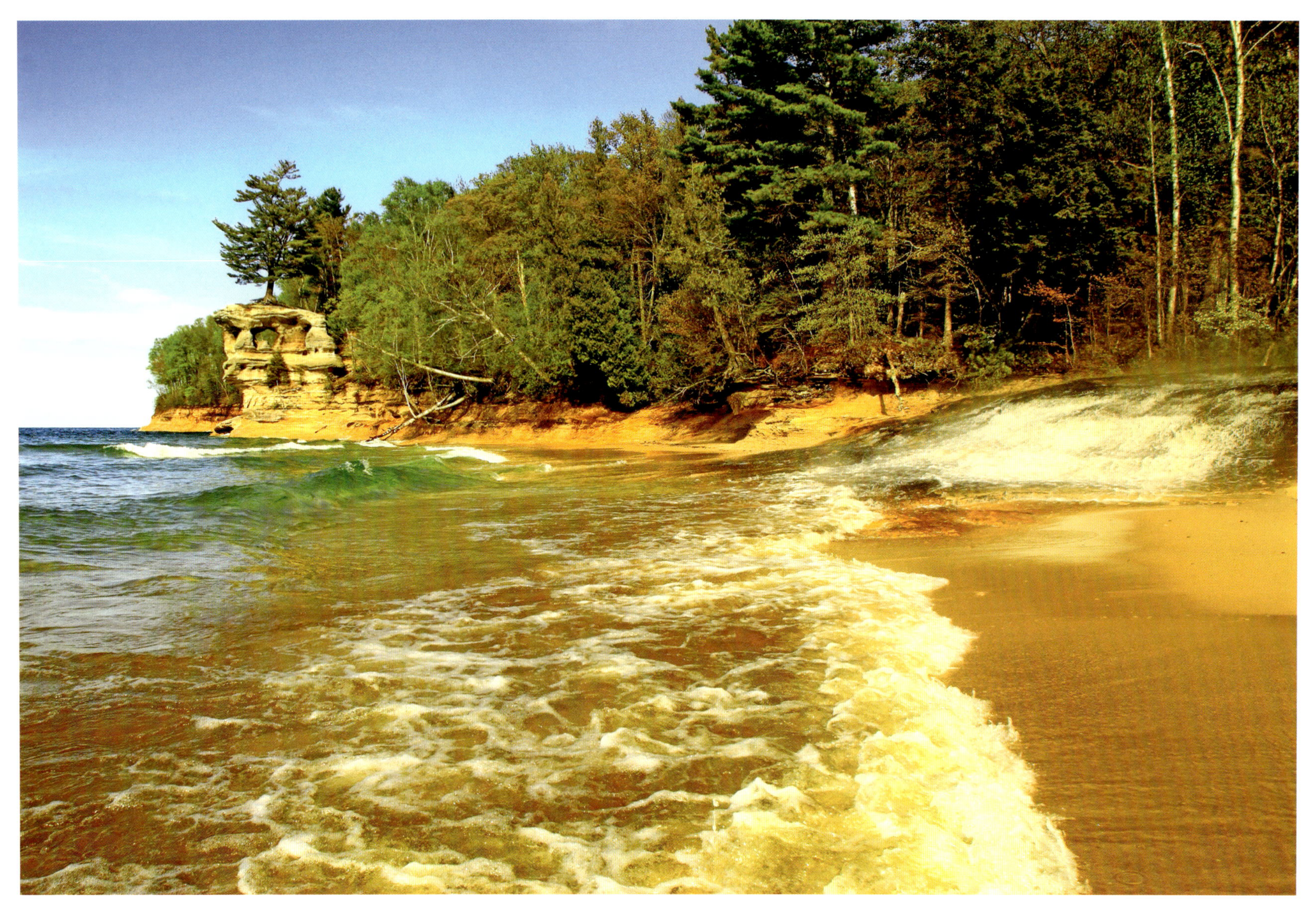

Watercolors: Chapel Beach

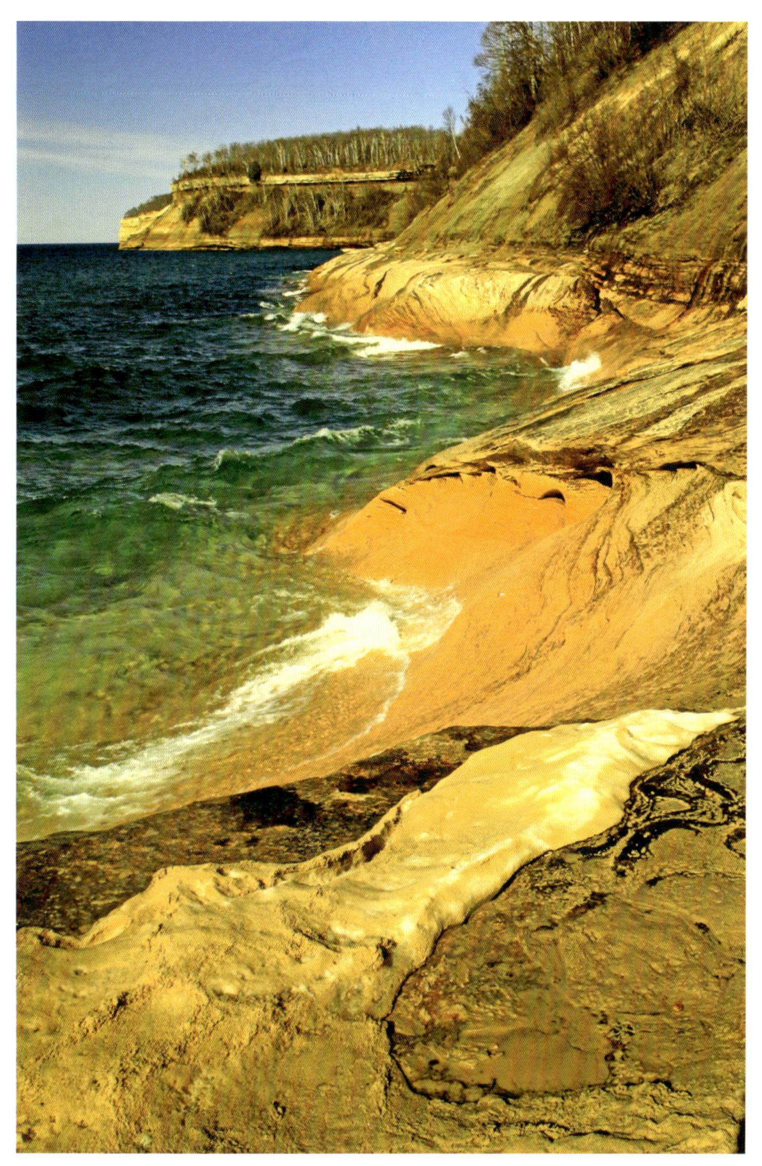

Melting Pot

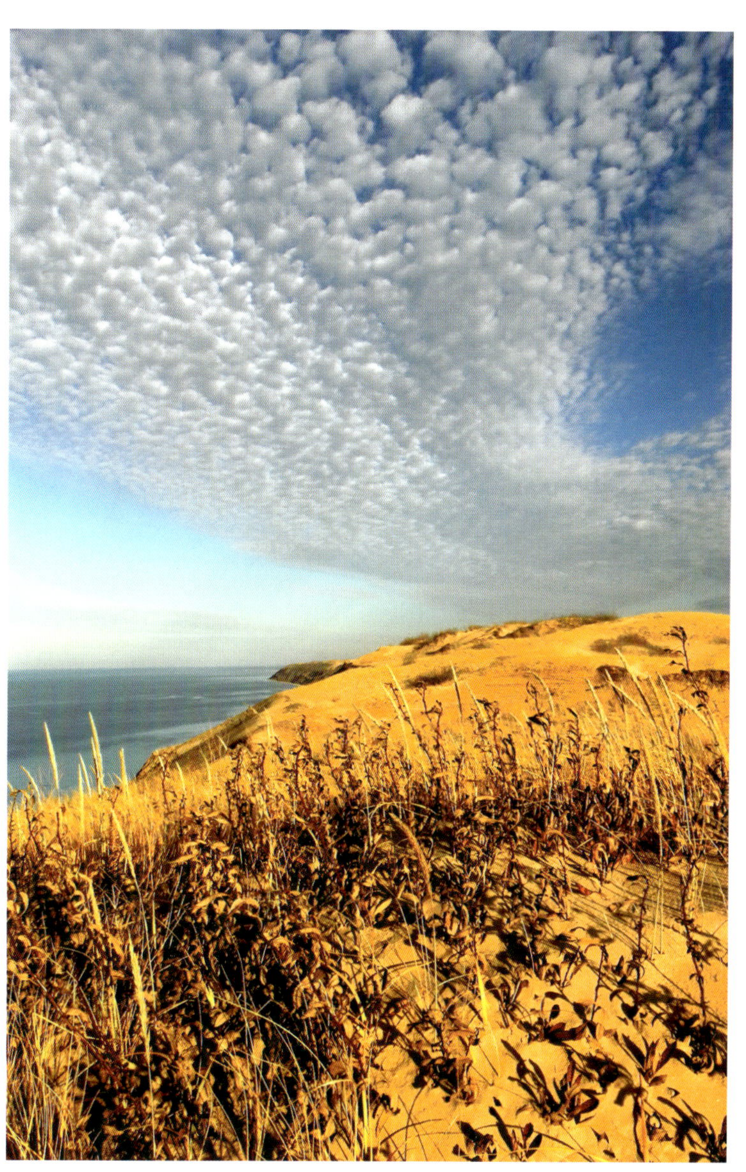

Head in the Clouds:
Grand Sable Dunes

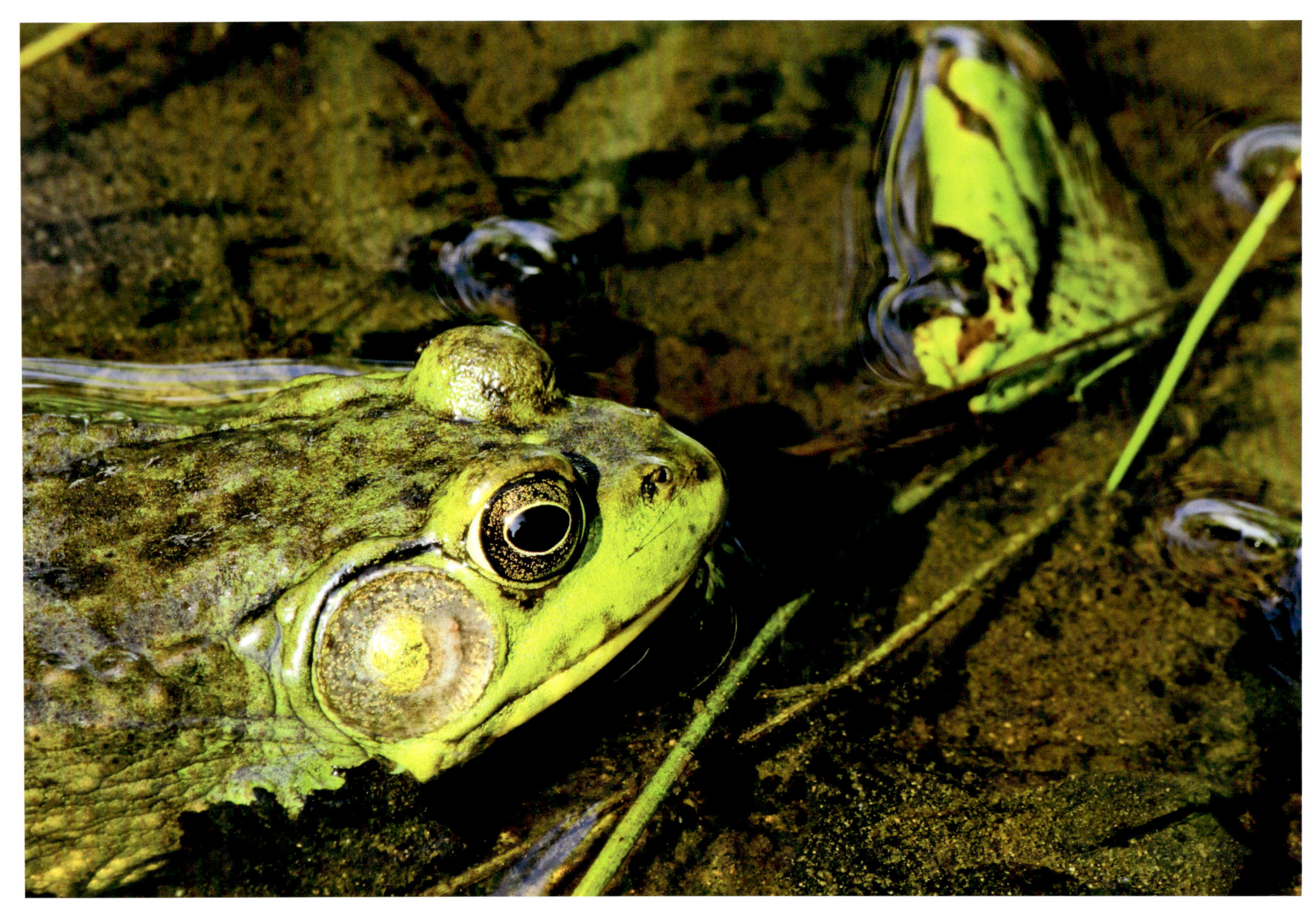

Looking for Love in all the Wrong Places

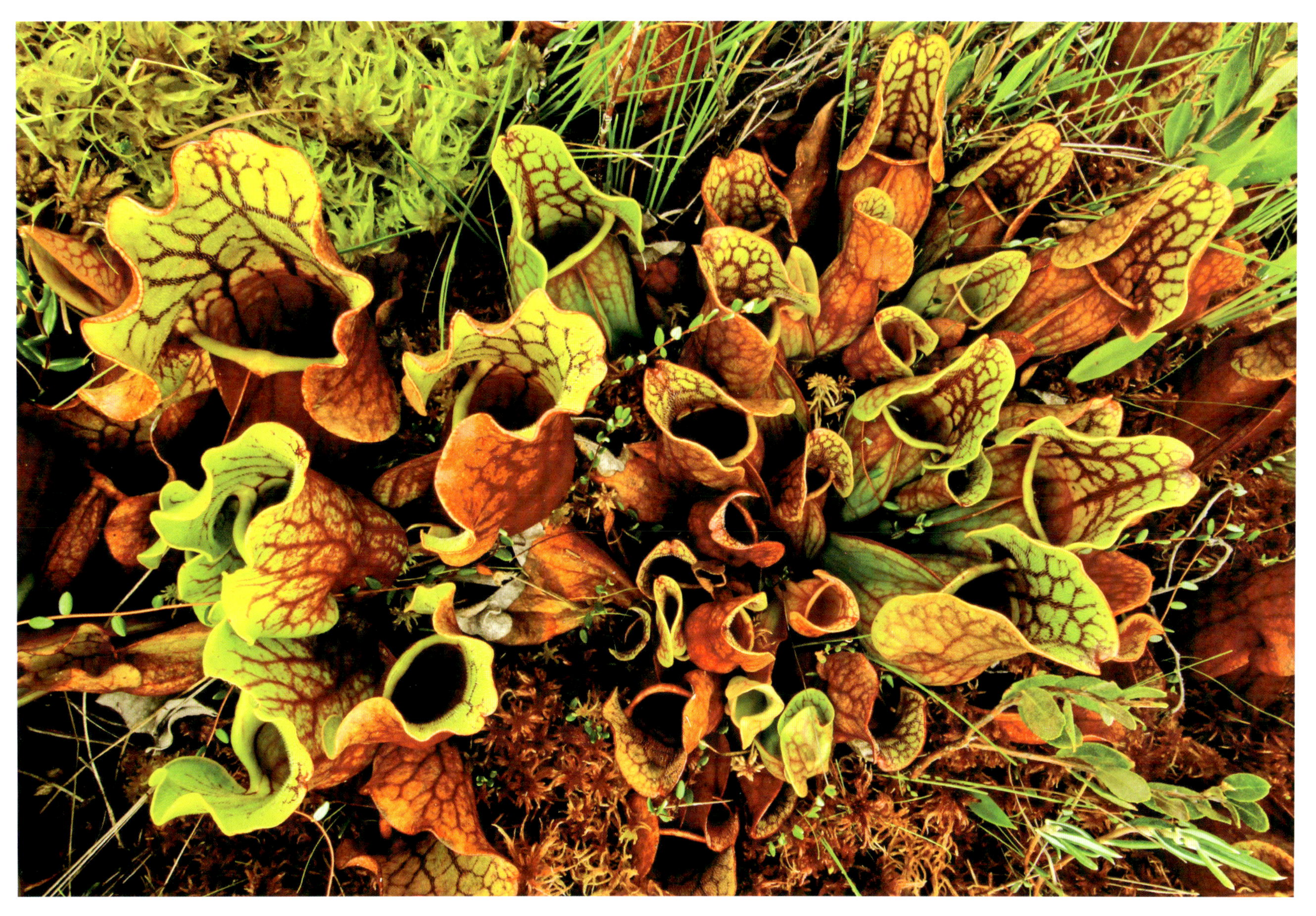

Carnivore Carnival

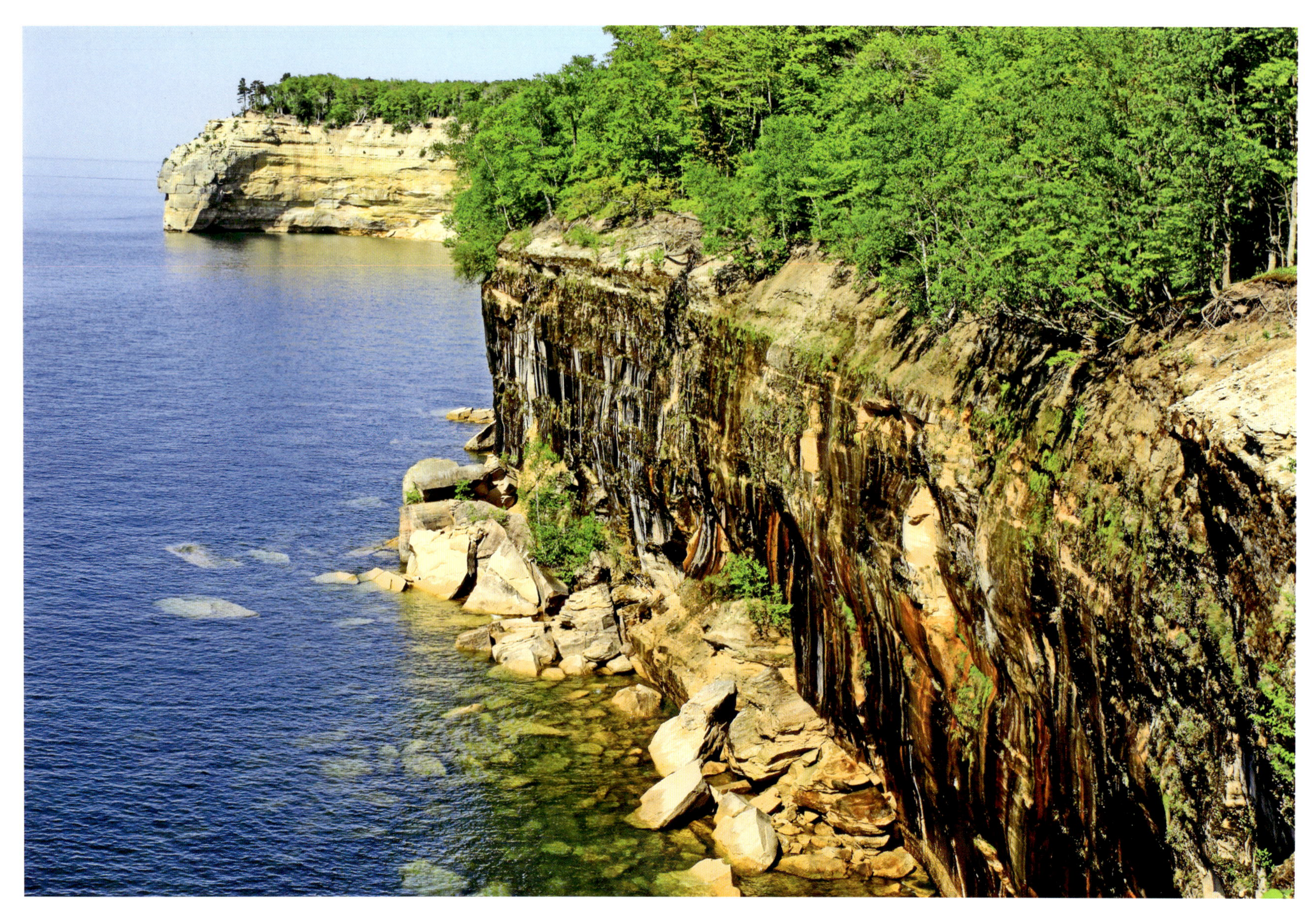

Nothing but Blue Skies

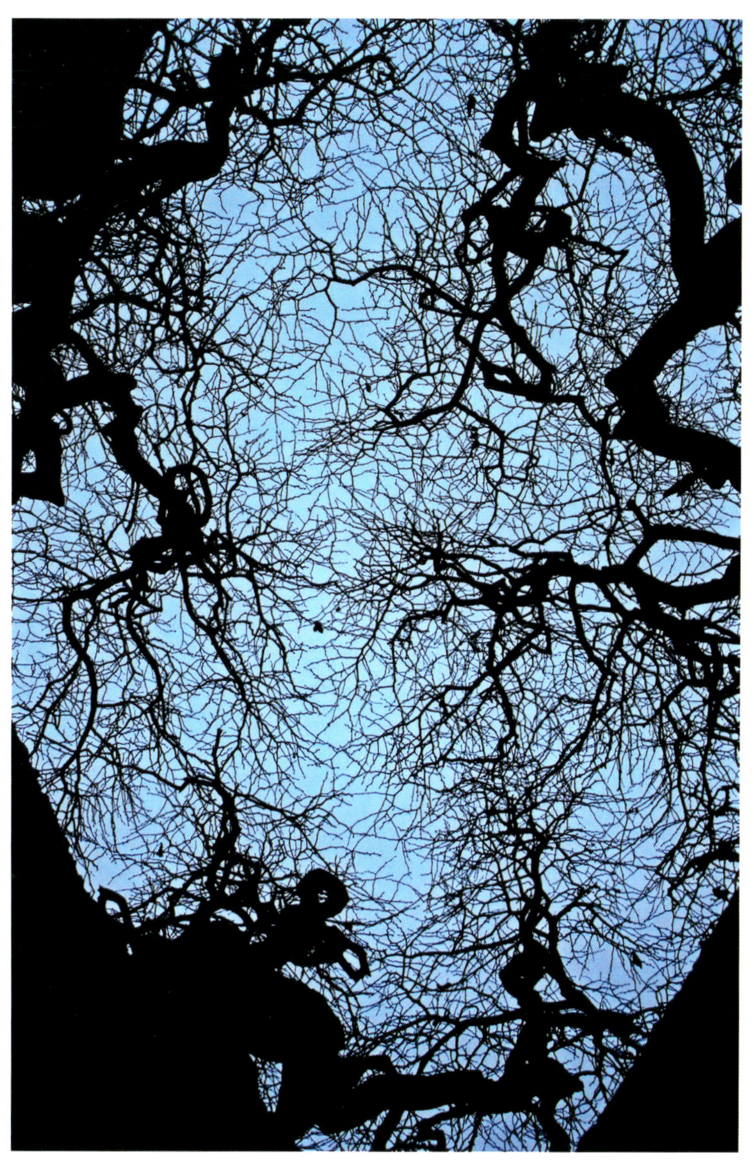

Enchanted Forest

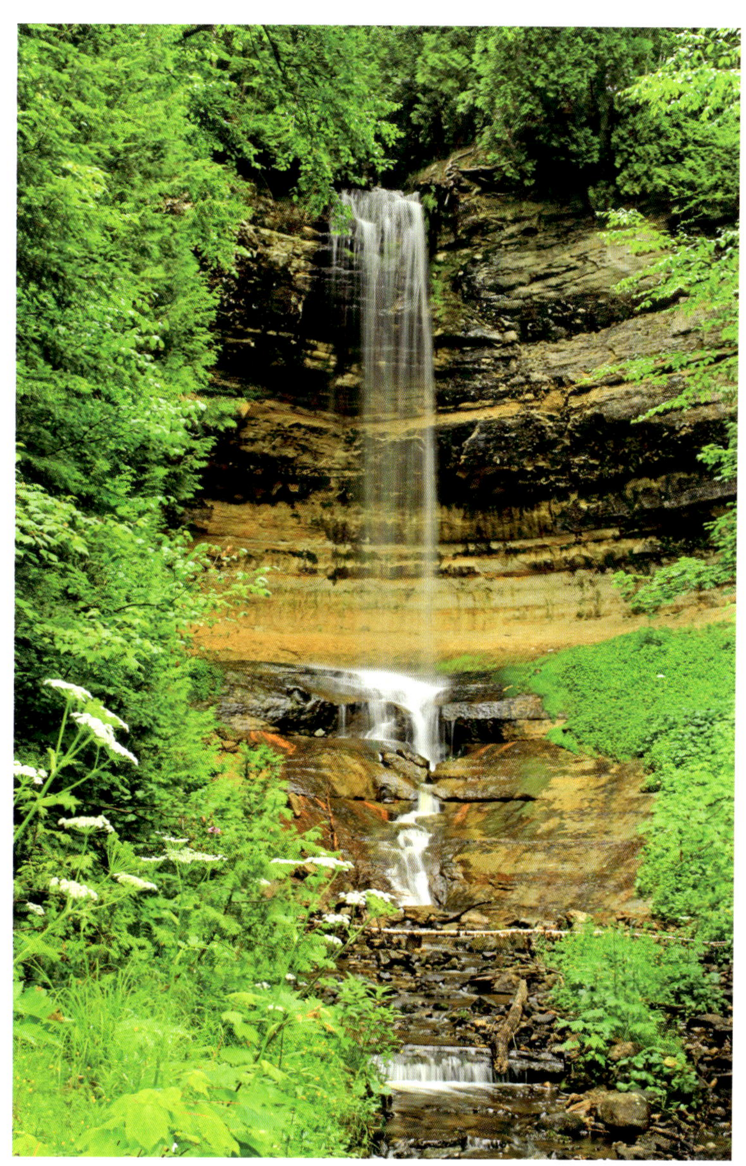

50 Shades of Green:
Munising Falls

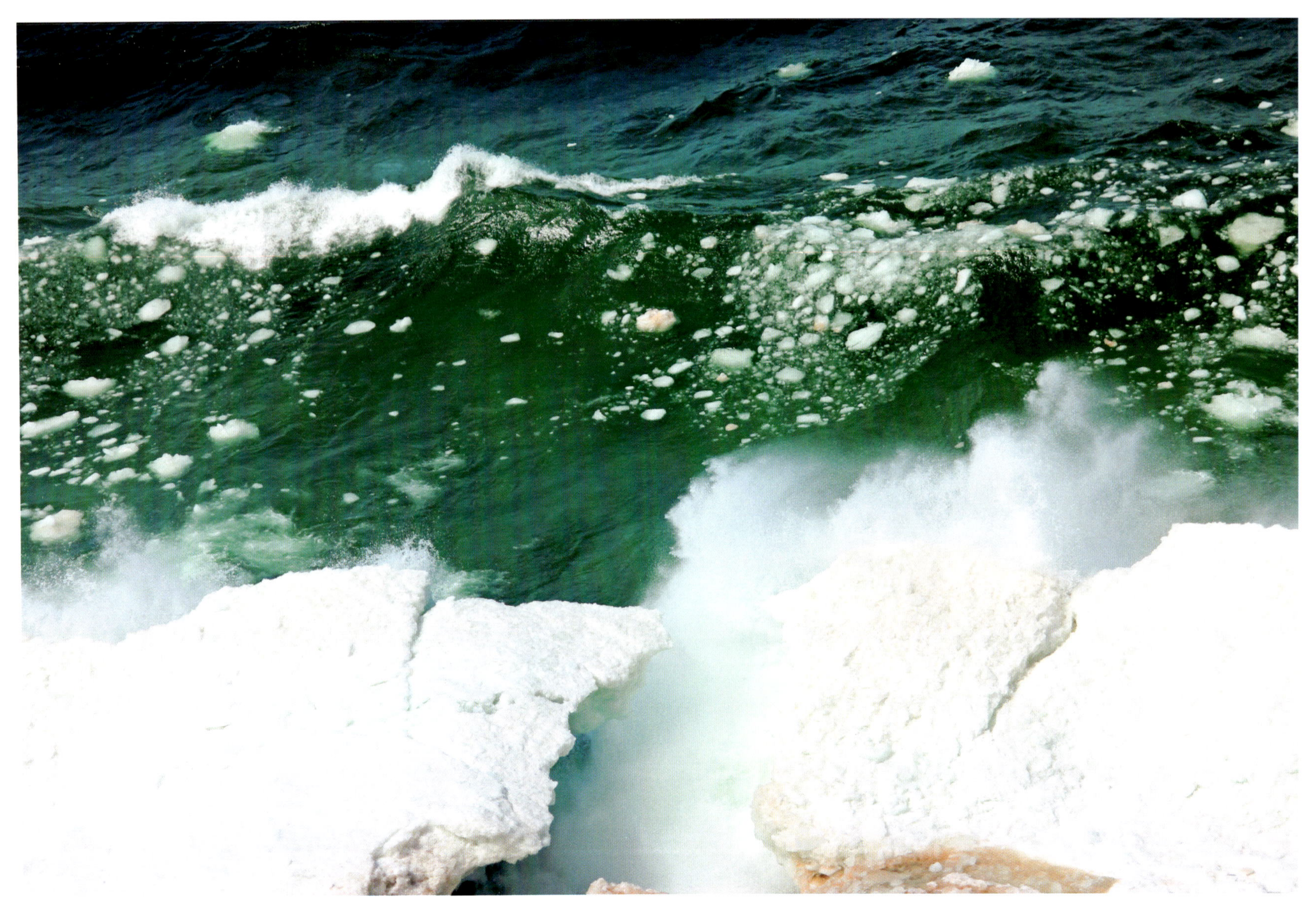

Wintergreen

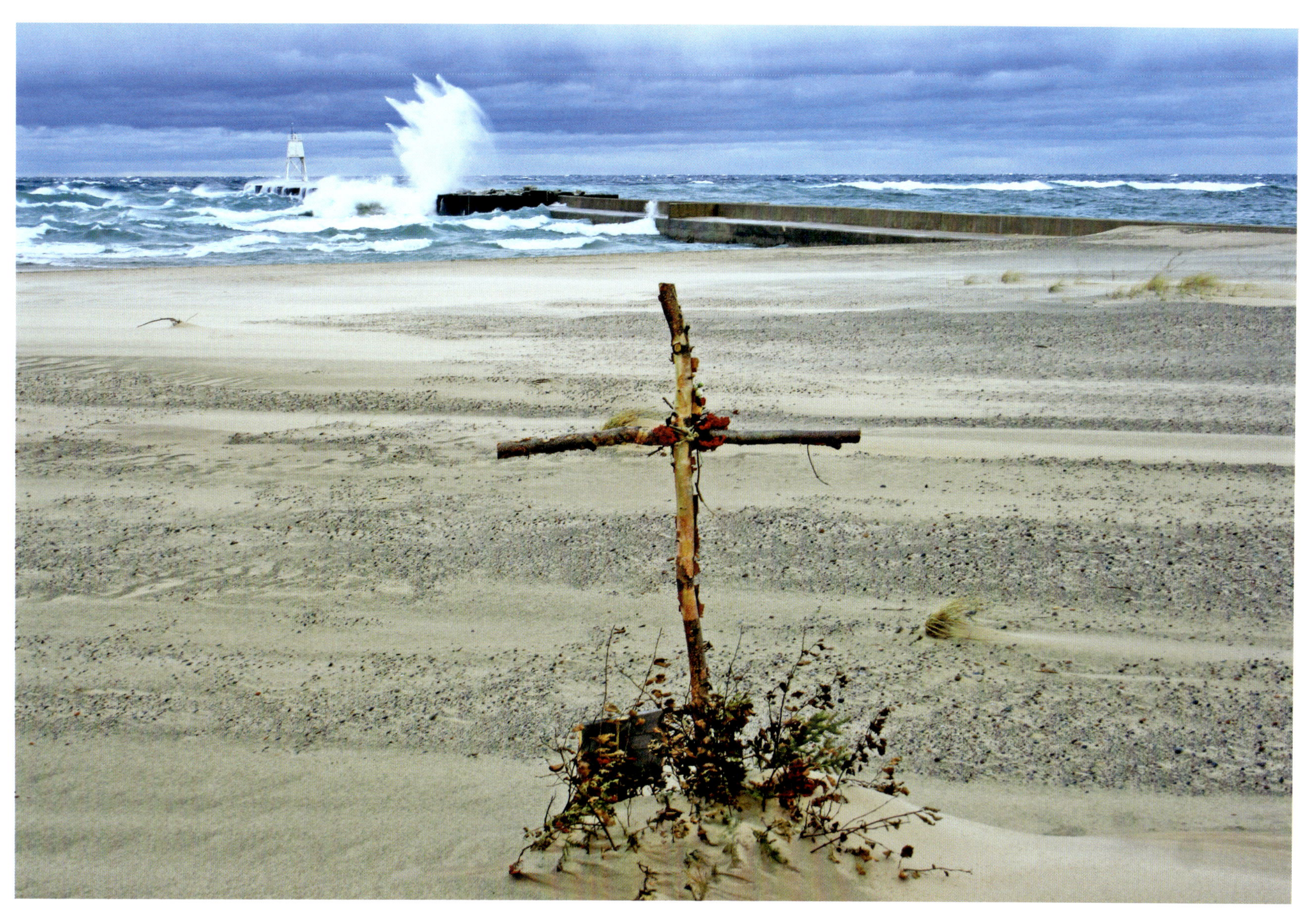

Paying Respect

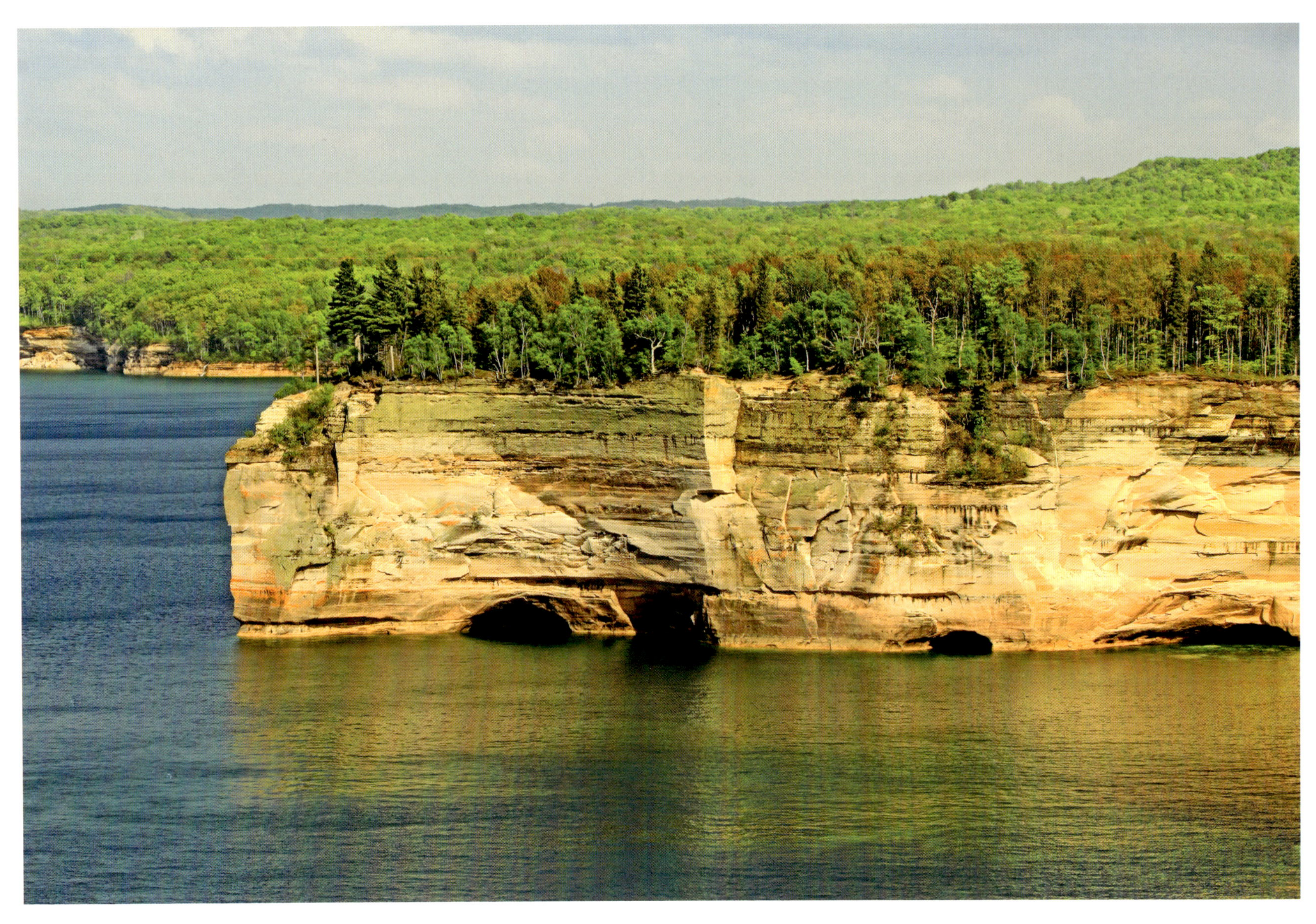

A Bright Sun Shiny Day